Abstinence Cinema

Abstinence Cinema

Virginity and the Rhetoric of Sexual Purity in Contemporary Film

CASEY RYAN KELLY

RUTGERS UNIVERSITY PRESS

NEW BRUNSWICK, NEW JERSEY, AND LONDON

LIBRARY OF CONGRESS CATALOGING-IN-PUBLICATION DATA

Kelly, Casey Ryan, 1979–
    Abstinence cinema : virginity and the rhetoric of sexual purity in contemporary film / Casey Ryan Kelly.
        pages cm
    Includes bibliographical references and index.
    ISBN 978–0–8135–7511–7 (hardcover : alk. paper)—ISBN 978–0–8135–7510–0 (pbk. : alk. paper)—ISBN 978–0–8135–7512–4 (e-book (epub))—ISBN 978–0–8135–7513–1 (e-book (web pdf))
    1. Virginity in motion pictures. 2. Sex in motion pictures. I. Title.
    PN1995.9.V55K45 2016
    791.43'6538—dc23
    2015024451

A British Cataloging-in-Publication record for this book is available from the British Library.

Visit our website: http://rutgerspress.rutgers.edu

Manufactured in the United States of America

For Diane and Marvin Kelly

CONTENTS

ACKNOWLEDGMENTS

Books are never written alone. This book was made possible by generous support from Butler University, including internal grants from the Butler Awards Committee; the Gender, Women's, and Sexuality Studies Program; the College of Communication; and the Department of Critical Communication and Media Studies. I am especially grateful for the generous editorial assistance provided by John Mugge in the Office of the Provost and the staff support provided by Melissa Friedman of the College of Communication. The hard work of my research assistant, Alexandra Pierce, was also instrumental in the timely completion of this manuscript. I am also indebted to my department and colleagues across Butler University for their support and encouragement throughout the completion of this project. Finally, I am appreciative for the feedback I received from the students of my course "Virginity and Sexual Politics of Film," a group of extraordinary students who allowed me to use our conversations and lectures as a sounding board for the ideas developed in this book.

Beyond my home institution, I am thankful for the support of Rutgers University Press. There are not enough ways to thank Lisa Boyajian and Rutgers for their enthusiastic support of this book. Lisa and Rutgers made the publication process enjoyable, and their stewardship of this project was absolutely essential to the quality of my work. I would also like to thank the anonymous reviewers for their hard work, helpful commentary, and dedication to making this a successful manuscript.

It is hard to estimate how many people contributed to my conceptualization of this project. Many people directly helped develop this project through reading, commentary, and conversation. I would like to thank the members of my department: Kristen Swenson, Ann Savage, Allison Harthcock, Kristen Hoerl, and Chris Gilbert. Countless conversations also contributed to this book, including dialogue with Ageeth Sluis, Vivian Deno, Terry Carney, Chad Bauman, Kate Seigfried, Leslie Hahner, Scott Varda, Claire Sisco King, Ashley Mack, Jonathan Rossing, Bryan McCann, and certainly many others. I would also like to thank the colleagues and mentors who contributed to this project—perhaps without knowing it—by providing support and encouragement throughout my career.

These individuals include Angela Aguayo, Daniel Brouwer, Dana Cloud, Bonnie Dow, Rosa Eberly, Jason Edward Black, Danielle Endres, Lisa Foster, Ronald Greene, Heather Hayes, Justin Killian, Charles Morris III, Ryan Neville-Shepard, Meredith Neville-Shepard, Kent Ono, Catherine Palczewski, Jessica Prody, Mark Radamacher, Michelle Rodino-Colochino, Rae Lynn Schwartz-Dupre, Mary Triece, Kirt Wilson, Mary Vavrus, and Anjali Vats.

I would like to especially thank Matthew May and Michael Lee for their love, camaraderie, and support over the past decade. In the same regard, my parents, Diane and Marvin Kelly, deserve a special acknowledgment for their support throughout my life and career. Finally, I thank my spouse and colleague, Kristen Hoerl, for her unwavering love and encouragement. Her influence is in everything I do, scholarly or otherwise. This book could not have been written without her and I am incredibly lucky to have such a gifted and supportive partner. This book is the product of a large and diverse social support network, both personal and professional, for which I will be forever grateful.

Parts of chapter 4 were previously published as "Feminine Purity and Masculine Revenge-Seeking in *Taken* (2008)," *Feminist Media Studies* 14, no. 3 (2014): 403–418.

Abstinence Cinema

Introduction

The Cinema of Abstinence

At the beginning of the 2000s, the election of President George W. Bush appeared to validate the cultural agenda of an evangelical Christian movement concerned with promulgating heterosexuality, traditional family values, and abstinence until marriage.[1] The new administration's focus on premarital sexual abstinence as the solution to nearly every social problem—from teenage pregnancy to violent crime—rendered sexuality the one aspect of personal life not subject to the free-market ideology of privatization.[2] Emboldened by having one of their own in the White House, members of the abstinence until marriage movement called for a renewed commitment to protecting children and the heterosexual nuclear family from assaults by sexual dissidents.[3] One of its icons was the image of the vulnerable young girl whose protection from adult sexual desires justified extreme adjustments to public policy. From secondary education to social service administration, fundamentalist Christian leaders advocated abstinence until marriage as an emergency response to a growing sexual panic about America's youth and the family.

These nervous energies reverberated across American culture. Take, for instance, Catherine Hardwicke's *Thirteen* (2003), a film that both reflected and amplified the same sexual anxieties abstinence advocates cultivated, drawing attention to the new social dangers and moral ambiguities of girls on the cusp of adolescence. *Thirteen* directed public attention to the precarious (if not perilous) state of the nation's pubescent daughters. The film embodied the anxieties of a culture addled by the moral imperatives of abstinence and marked a reactionary vacillation in cinematic vision(s) of virginity. Melanie Freeland (Holly Hunter) is a divorced single mother struggling to raise her thirteen-year-old daughter Tracy (Evan Rachel Wood) and her brother Mason (Brady Corbet). Tracy drifts from being a modest honor roll student to an out-of-control teenager who, lacking parental guidance, succumbs to the influence of peer pressure and begins engaging in petty crime, drug use, sex, and self-abuse. Melanie struggles to reclaim her daughter from the influence of Tracy's friend Evie (Nikki Reed), whose seductive and deviant behavior warps Tracy's moral judgment. The traumas of divorce and the lack of fatherly influence seem to sabotage Melanie's efforts to regain control of her daughter, even as Tracy resolves to once again be a "good girl." Symbolizing the pernicious and seemingly inescapable cycle of self-abuse brought on by teen sex and drug use, the film concludes with Tracy alone on a merry-go-round, screaming. The film's ending offers a foreboding projection of Tracy's future: with her innocence lost and her mother helpless, there seems to be little chance of her stepping off the carousel to make a fresh start.[4]

While it is clear that the film was not constructed as an evangelical morality tale, its narrative maps seamlessly over what Mas'ud Zavarzadeh calls a cultural "grid of intelligibility" in which the emerging political ideology of the moment promulgated alarmism over the fate of the nation's daughters.[5] *Thirteen* resonated with neoconservative cultural discourses that decried the crisis of single motherhood, the scourge of teenage pregnancy, and the collapse of traditional family values. The vulnerable thirteen-year-old girl in a state of crisis was the tragic counterpoint to the relatively well-adjusted adolescents with bright futures who had appeared just a few years earlier in the film *American Pie.*

The 1999 release of Paul Weitz's *American Pie* narrated a new and relatively progressive tale of virginity loss in which suburban youth discover the unknown and mystifying nuances of intimacy, pleasure, and relationships. The film is noteworthy for its avoidance of stigma and shame, acceptance of female sexual agency, and acknowledgment that virginity is but one developmental aspect of personal intimacy. In the film, four high school friends—Jim (Jason Biggs), "Oz" (Chris Klein), Kevin (Thomas Ian Nichols), and "Finch" (Eddie Kay Thomas)—make a pact to lose their virginity by prom night. Throughout the group's raunchy adventures, each character is forced to revise his initial perspective of virginity loss in ways that displace its significance in the coming-of-age narrative. After a series of embarrassing sexual mishaps, Jim ultimately evades the spirit of the wager by inviting a seemingly naive band geek to prom who is, in fact, quite comfortable with her sexuality. After prom, Jim is delighted by the prospect that he had been used for sex and that his female partner was both gratified and casual. Oz and his love interest Heather discover that emotional fulfillment can accompany physical intimacy, Kevin and longtime girlfriend Vicky come away from virginity loss with few regrets about the fact that they will part ways as they set out for college, and Finch sleeps with one of his compatriot's mothers (Mrs. Stiffler).

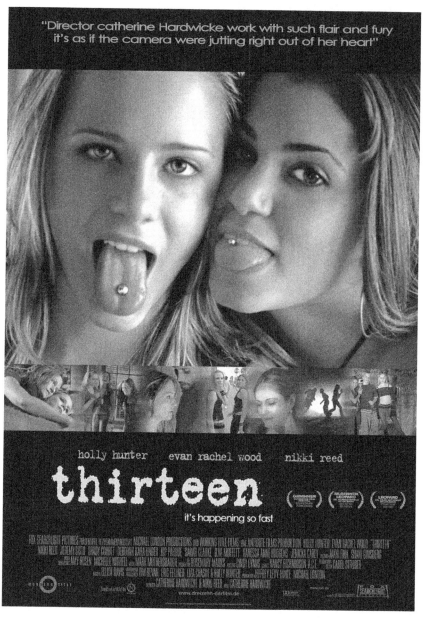

FIGURE 1. The "out of control" girls of *Thirteen*. DVD. Directed by Catherine Hardwicke. Los Angeles, CA: Fox Searchlight.

FIGURE 2. Poster for *American Pie*. DVD. Directed by Paul Weitz and Chris Weitz. Universal City, CA: University Pictures Home Entertainment, 1999.

While the film revolved around the sexual inexperience of young men, *American Pie* untethered virginity loss from the moral turpitude and tragic consequences depicted in *Thirteen*. Instead, the film foregrounded both the challenge and pleasure of exploring the complexities of intimacy. What emerges as most important in the film are a clearer understanding of sexuality, partner selection, and the role of sex in relationship development. Though not without its failings, the film closed a decade of relatively silence on virginity with some promise that popular cinema might continue to invite spectators to consider less repressive and threatening narratives of virginity loss than those depicted in previous decades.

Of course the films do not directly speak to one another. Yet juxtaposing these texts for a momentary comparison illustrates how cinematic tales of virginity bespeak the ideological struggles that are active in society at a particular moment in time. In the short time between *American Pie* and *Thirteen*, the tale of virginity loss depicted in popular entertainment was augmented by the material and rhetorical reorientation of social policy toward abstinence until marriage. The sexual politics of the Bush administration reignited the panic over teenage sexuality in order to present abstinence as the only safe and moral choice for youth.[6] Whereas films in the 1990s were relatively silent on the subject of virginity, *Thirteen* introduced a decade of cinema preoccupied with its causes and consequences.[7] From within a cinematic milieu of sexual ambivalence and projected fears emerges a portrait of virginity so fraught with risks and dangers that abstinence until marriage becomes the only empowering, or even the only, viable option.

The panic-stricken representations of sexualized out-of-control teens that appear in films such as *Thirteen* illustrate the central argument I advance in this book: popular cinema contributes to the ideological salience of a growing neoconservative movement that seeks to reestablish abstinence until marriage as a social and political imperative. While evangelical Christians often decry the sexual permissiveness of Hollywood, filmmakers' recent preoccupation with both the dangers of sex out of wedlock and the virtues of virginity in a sex-saturated culture establishes an ideological outpost for sexual conservatism within the terrain of popular culture. Historical surveys of sex in Hollywood films demonstrate not only that depictions change as sexual attitudes and behaviors change within the wider culture but also that cinema is itself a site of ideological contestation, a kind of cultural proxy war over what kind of sexual morality should govern public and private life.[8] In this book, I examine how the abstinence until marriage movement has augmented and realigned the cultural narrative of virginity by attending to the valorization of virginity and lifestyle abstinence in contemporary American films.

Throughout this book, I use the term *abstinence cinema* to bracket and conceptualize an emerging constellation of disparate film texts from 2000 to the present that collectively and in their own way articulate the meaning of virginity, youth sexuality, ideal femininity, father-daughter relationships, hegemonic masculinity, and the family within the symbolic and discursive repertoire of the abstinence movement. The cinema of abstinence is composed of films that represent virginity and sexual purity in ways that prioritize both the utopian and dystopian visions of pro-abstinence discourse. These films are evidence of how cultural articulations of virginity are heavily invested in maintaining both feminine purity and hegemonic masculinity.

For instance, the immensely popular five-film *Twilight* saga emphasizes the mortal dangers of sex out of wedlock and offers a family-values portrait of abstinence as the pathway to virtue, romance, fulfillment, and feminine empowerment. *The 40-Year-Old Virgin* domesticates the post-sexual-revolution man-boy by reacquainting him with the virtues of monogamy and late-in-life abstinence. Steve Carell's portrayal of Andy, a midlife virgin who mistakes his fear of women for respect, redefines abstinence as a healthy and stabilizing alternative to a culture of narcissism and casual sex. In the horror and action adventure genre, films such as the *The Possession* and *Taken* both traffic in motifs of lost fatherhood, blaming the corruption of young girls on the collapse of the traditional nuclear family. Allegorically, these features capitalize on public anxiety about the precarious state of the nation's innocent virginal daughters. The raunchy teen comedy genre (*Easy A* and *Superbad*) supplants virginity loss with unconventional yet clean teenage romances. Meanwhile, the many lurid spoofs of these films exploit the culture's burgeoning moral panic about virginity and abstinence. While sex remains prominent in Hollywood film and television, this selection of films demonstrates that in the early twenty-first century, the concept of abstinence until marriage is pushing back against the liberalization of sexual attitudes. One of the remarkable things about this body of films is the persuasiveness of the abstinence message as it makes its way across the genres.

In this book I analyze these films because each text refracts a disparate yet fundamental aspect of contemporary abstinence culture. Each film provides audiences with the discursive resources to make sense of abstinence until marriage as a viable political ideal.[9] This project examines films as social texts that attempt to negotiate and fix the meaning of virginity. The perplexing valorization of abstinence as a valuable commodity, a pathway to emotional fulfillment, a mechanism for bodily autonomy and protection, and the key to greater ultimate sexual fulfillment by virtue of delayed gratification implies that representational defenses of the ideological mission of advocates of virginity in fact exist in the midst of what they argue is a permissive sexual culture. Thus, in this book I explore how the rhetoric of the contemporary abstinence until marriage movement migrates from the public to the popular. Through an examination of texts that refract different elements of abstinence discourse, I show how virginity is transformed into not only a necessary and revolutionary ideal but also a progressive and feminist one. I am concerned with how films construct a cultural environment that brings popular culture into close contact with conservative sexual ideals and with the disturbing consequences of pro-abstinence rhetoric in a cinematic form.

In the remainder of this introduction, I present four basic claims that inform and frame the analysis of the films examined throughout this book. First, I chronicle the rise of the abstinence-until-marriage movement, attending to the extent of its proponents' social influence and the key aspects of their rhetoric and world view. Second, I examine how Hollywood portrayals of virginity and lifestyle abstinence have changed over time and how their representation in contemporary film attests to the cultural force of the abstinence movement. Third, I explain the ideological work of pro-virginity discourse in film as a force that absorbs and counteracts the goals of feminism and sexual liberation. Finally, I explain how a critical rhetorical approach to film illuminates the processes by which the political struggles of the virginity movement within contemporary American culture make their way onto the big screen and into the popular imagination.

The Rise of Abstinence Culture

Abstinence until marriage is a defining feature of fundamentalist Christian sexual morality. The Christian Bible includes dozens of passages that identify premarital sex as a sin, including 1 Thessalonians 4:3–8, which reads, "this is the will of God . . . that ye abstain from fornication: that every one of you should know how to possess his vessel in sanctification and honor; Not in lust of concupiscence, even as the Gentiles which know not God."[10] In fundamentalist Christian doctrine, abstinence is not only protection against carnal sin but preparation for heterosexual marriage and ultimately for procreation. Focus on the Family explains it this way: "As Christians, the concept of reserving sex for marriage is a part of God's original plan. In fact, it was an integral product of creation. Indeed, during creation, the gift of sex was among those things God declared to be 'very good.' In the beginning, God created man and woman, ordained marriage and gave sex, both as a gift and a responsibility, to mankind."[11] However, some Christian denominations have differing views on the importance of virginity before marriage. For instance, though the Episcopal Church and the United Church of Christ promote abstinence, they also support comprehensive sex education, birth control, and family planning.[12] However, "born-again" Christian faiths and some conservative sects of Catholicism unequivocally reject all versions of nonmarital sexuality. Although the significance of abstinence until marriage exists along a continuum within Christian faiths, the concept structures Christian beliefs about morality, marriage, childrearing, and traditional family values.

While Christians have purportedly practiced abstinence until marriage for centuries, the rise of the Moral Majority movement in the early 1980s is credited with bringing a biblical understanding of sexuality into the American public sphere. In a groundbreaking violation of the Baptist church's longtime separation of religion and politics, Rev. Jerry Falwell founded the Moral Majority as a national organization designed to mobilize evangelical voters and lobby for the implementation of Christian principles in public policy.[13] Janice Irvine argues that the Moral Majority's pro-family rhetoric and strong condemnation of comprehensive sex education persuaded sympathetic Republicans to make abstinence-only curricula and marriage training central components of their policy agenda.[14] Falwell's influence with evangelical publics gave his organization tremendous power to shape social policy, and his routine admonishments of America as a nation in moral decay energized newly minted "family values" politicians in Congress and the Reagan administration. In 1981, Congress passed the Adolescent Family Life Act (AFLA) to promote "chastity and self discipline" and "family centered" approaches to sex education through faith-based organizations.[15] The passage of the AFLA marked the transformation of abstinence until marriage from a solely Christian doctrine to a public policy response to the putative moral decline precipitated by the liberalization of sexual attitudes during the 1960s and 1970s.

The emergence of abstinence until marriage as the centerpiece of the New Right beginning in the mid-1980s can be explained in part by the movement's disdain for feminism and the "sexual revolution." Ruth Rosen notes that the conservative movement blamed feminists (and gays and lesbians) for introducing hedonistic values and decadence into American culture. She notes that for the New Right, "an independent woman was by definition, a selfish, self-absorbed creature who threatened the nation's 'traditional values.'"[16] Conservatives identified access to legal abortions (culminating in the 1973 *Roe v. Wade* decision of the U.S. Supreme Court) and the pill as evidence that the movement for women's liberation had both threatened the family and endorsed promiscuity without consequences. The Moral Majority and the New Right promoted abstinence as part of a nostalgic project that expressed longing for patriarchal family structures, male breadwinners, and traditional sex and gender roles.[17]

Social conservatives used the liberalization of sexual attitudes since the 1950s to argue that a return to the traditional family should be a national imperative.[18] Since the mid-twentieth century, the publication of studies such as Alfred Kinsey's *Sexual Behavior in the Human Male* (1948) and *Sexual Behavior in the Human Female* (1953), followed by William H. Masters and Virginia E. Johnson's *Human Sexual Responses* (1966) and *Human Sexual Inadequacy* (1970), cultivated public awareness about human sexuality that went well beyond acts of procreation. Repeated studies of American sexual attitudes and behaviors revealed attitudes toward dating, casual intimacy, and premarital sex that were more permissive than was once believed. By the early 1980s, only 33 to 37 percent of Americans believed that premarital sex was always wrong.[19]

Since the passage of the AFLA, more than $1.5 billion in federal grants has been committed to abstinence-only education and faith-based abstinence initiatives.[20] Over the past thirty-four years, abstinence programs have proven impervious to changes in administration and social attitudes. With support from the Clinton administration, Congress passed the Personal Responsibility and Work Opportunity Reconciliation Act (PRWOA; 1996), which vastly increased funding for AFLA programs and established a steady stream of appropriations that continued into the next administration.[21] Replacing federal welfare programs with Temporary Assistance for Needy Families (TANF), the PRWOA mandated marriage education and abstinence training for poor women receiving public assistance.[22] In addition to the $250 million that states received to support abstinence-only education, states that reduced the number of out-of-wedlock births were awarded federal "legitimacy bonuses" totaling $100 million.[23] In 2001, President George W. Bush established additional revenue streams for abstinence programs through the Community-Based Abstinence Education initiative, which authorized the Department of Health and Human Services to award grants to develop abstinence curricula, bypassing state-level control of funding decisions.[24] The Bush administration's Healthy Marriage Initiative provided an additional $500 million for marriage training and incentive programs, including a public media campaign to promote marriage and abstinence.[25] Bush also made abstinence education and marriage promotion one of the centerpieces of his HIV/AIDS prevention campaign in Africa.

In 2010, despite President Barack Obama's purported efforts to undo the expansion of abstinence-only programs, congressional Republicans reintroduced abstinence-only education through an amendment to the Patient Protection and Affordable Care Act, which was funded at $50 million a year through 2014.[26] While President Obama has expressed opposition to abstinence education, organizations such as the Family Research Council that explicitly proselytize for abstinence in their promotional materials continue to receive millions of dollars in grants through TANF, Medicaid, and ongoing "healthy marriage" programs. Andy Kopsa's exposé of abstinence programs found that "an entire federally funded evangelical economy took root during the Bush years, and under Obama it continues to thrive."[27]

As opposed to comprehensive sex education, abstinence curricula promote virginity as the only safe method of contraception. Abstinence programs disparage condoms and other methods of birth control, rely heavily on appeals to fear and shame, and in some cases proselytize about sex out of wedlock as a sin. A comprehensive congressional study of abstinence programs that Representative Henry Waxman released in 2004 also found that curricula routinely contained medically inaccurate information, explicitly proselytized, and advanced discriminatory gender stereotypes.[28] For instance, the report found that the WAIT training program (Why Am I Tempted?, a curriculum from the Center for Relationship Education that has received numerous federal grants) erroneously asserted that HIV/AIDS is spread through casual contact with tears and sweat.

Despite the billions of dollars spent, there is no evidence that abstinence education and training work. A 2009 study published in *Pediatrics* found that virginity pledgers were no less likely to engage in premarital sex than non-pledgers. In fact, 82 percent of pledgers actually denied that they had even taken the pledge. Pledgers were less likely to use contraception in their sexual debut, a fact attributable to the stigma surrounding condoms and birth control in abstinence-only education.[29] Two other studies in the *Journal of Adolescent Health* reported that abstinent teenagers were also more likely to engage in genital play and oral and anal sex.[30]

Notwithstanding the mounting evidence of its inefficacies and dangers, advocates continue to tout abstinence-only as the solution to everything from poverty and teenage pregnancy to unemployment and violence.[31] This thirty-four-year sustained public policy effort to promote abstinence has also had a profound effect on American culture. Over the past decade, the number of organizations advocating virginity and sexual purity has proliferated; they include True Love Waits, Lifeway Ministries, Silver Ring Thing, Independent Women's Forum, Concerned Women for America, National Abstinence Clearinghouse, National Abstinence Education Association, Focus on the Family, and the Family Research Council. True Love Waits and Silver Ring Thing claim to have secured abstinence pledges from approximately 2.5 million teenagers.[32] Silver Ring Thing even takes its initiatives beyond the church and classroom by sponsoring abstinence-themed Christian rock festivals that culminate in young concertgoers signing virginity oaths and wearing "purity rings" to demonstrate publicly their adherence to lifestyle abstinence.[33] Tapping into a growing evangelical consumer market, abstinence organizations and ministries have created a cottage industry of virginity gear that includes apparel, books, jewelry, and other accessories with slogans such as "virgins are hot," "virgins rock," and "don't drink and park . . . accidents cause kids."[34] Abstinence organizations also help put on nearly 4,000 annual "purity balls," father-daughter dances where young girls make public pledges to their fathers to remain chaste until marriage.[35] Meanwhile, the parenting, teenage literature, self-help, and faith and spirituality sections of bookstores include hundreds of popular and best-selling titles valorizing virginity, courtship, and traditional marriage.[36]

Sexual purity has even grown more permissible among entertainment celebrities in the United States, propelled by spokespersons such as Miley Cyrus, Julianne Hough, Selena Gomez, Bristol Palin, Jessica Simpson, Jordin Sparks, Britney Spears, the Jonas Brothers, and Tim Tebow, all of whom at one point publicly pledged to remain "pure" until marriage.[37] In addition to film, television is now replete with valorizing depictions of abstinence. MTV now produces two programs—*Virgin Territory* and *The Virgin Diaries*—that chronicle the lives of individuals and couples who took abstinence pledges. Meanwhile, the CW's *Jane the Virgin* depicts a pious but beleaguered virgin whose moral convictions are tested by a sex-saturated culture. NBC's *Baby Borrowers* takes a slightly different approach by adopting a "scared straight" reality format that puts teenagers through tests that reveal the costs and dangers of sex and pregnancy. From print and celebrity culture to film and television, abstinence has become a part of mainstream popular culture.

Sex and Abstinence on the Big Screen

As the abstinence movement has had a profound impact on the cultural narratives of virginity loss, representations of abstinence have evolved to reflect more conservative social attitudes toward sexuality. Tamar Jeffers McDonald argues that virginity may seem like an "old fashioned object" to appear in contemporary cinema, yet it is "one of perpetual currency within popular culture and the various cinemas that serve it."[38] And though the abstinence movement often reviles Hollywood for contributing to a sex-saturated culture, many new cinematic representations of virginity are consistent with a conservative ideology of sexuality, gender, and intimacy.[39] Narratives of virginity preserved and virginity lost are refashioned to fit different time periods but frequently remain tethered to a deep root of American puritanism in which the loss of sexual purity is precipitated by moral, physical, and social crisis.[40] While each moral panic over sexuality is historically specific, the desire to control women's bodies remains constant.

Catherine Driscoll explains that despite its historical ebbs and flows, virginity is a recurring element of film because "it intersects historically specific and highly gendered experiences of adolescence with the political opposition between tradition and change."[41] Put differently, representations of virginity consistently renegotiate the status of adolescence with the sexual politics of a particular cultural moment. In fact, some of the earliest popular films in the 1910s sensationalized the threat of foreign vice trusts that purportedly sought to abduct innocent, virginal white girls and sell them into sex slavery. White slave films such as *Traffic in Souls* (1913) and *Is Any Girl Safe?* (1916) were a warning to the nation to protect the purity of its white daughters.[42] Even D. W. Griffith's

The Birth of a Nation (1915) reminded popular audiences of the supposedly insatiable sexual desires of black men and valorized the Ku Klux Klan as it defended the sexual purity of white women against the U.S. South's mythic black rapist. Although virginity is not mentioned in these films, they illustrate how from its inception cinema has been enlisted to elevate the protection of women's physical and moral integrity to a national imperative.

During the reign of the Motion Picture Production Code (1930–1968), Hollywood mandated that teenage sex and virginity loss happen off screen. To the extent that it was inferred or obliquely represented, the Production Code mandated that teenage sexuality be linked to tragic consequences. For instance, *The Moon Is Blue* (1953), a comedy in which a virginal actress (Patty O'Neill) spurns the sexual advances of two interested bachelors, was rejected by censors for depicting "an unacceptably light attitude towards seduction, illicit sex, chastity, and virginity."[43] Even though the film does not imply that sexual intimacy out of wedlock took place and concludes with a marriage proposal at the top of the Empire State Building, the Production Code judged any lighthearted references to virginity to be too salacious for the big screen. Timothy Shary points out that during this period, discreet references to virginity loss were accompanied by extreme consequences, including physical, moral, and emotional danger.[44] To overtly represent virginity was to evoke a taboo that could not be named, although depictions of the severe consequences of its loss were allowed.

Many films of the late 1960s were more consumed by the politics of the era than by virginity and teen sexuality, and 1970s films dealing with virginity loss were "few and inconsequential."[45] It was not until the 1980s that films such as *Little Darlings* (1980), *Fast Times at Ridgemont High* (1982), *The Breakfast Club* (1985), *Weird Science* (1985), and *Dirty Dancing* (1987) included explicit and in some cases nuanced discussions of virginity, sexuality, reproduction, and abortion vis-à-vis young adults. The early part of the decade also included a wave of lighthearted teen sex-quest films involving pacts, wagers, and alliances to shake off the stigma of virginity. Films such as *Meatballs* (1979), *The Last American Virgin* (1982), *Goin' All the Way* (1982), *Losin' It* (1982), *Porky's* (1982), and *The Sure Thing* (1985) appeared before public awareness that HIV/AIDS was a heterosexual public health crisis. As a result of AIDS and rising teen pregnancy rates, there was a significant decline in teen sex-quest films after 1986.[46] While Shary is less sanguine about the sexual optimism of early 1980s sex-quest films, other scholars such as Lisa Dresner argue that in this brief moment—between the 1970s rhetoric of sexual liberation and Reagan-era "just say no" abstinence campaigns—teen films venerated and empowered the decisions girls made about sex without overtly exploiting them.[47] These films contrast with features such as *Risky Business* (1983), in which the virginity loss of Joel (Tom Cruise) to a young prostitute named Lana (Rebecca DeMornay) spawns a joint financial venture to market the experience to others for profit. But overall, the decade closed with somber silence about the topic of virginity and teen sexuality.

In contrast, the 1990s vacillated between the reactionary film *Kids* (1996), featuring drug-addled and AIDS-infected "virgin surgeons" who deflowered naive young girls, and the sex-positive *American Pie* (1999), in which both adolescent boys and girls thoughtfully negotiate not just virginity but also romantic relationships and intimacy. Although there was a patchwork of subplots related to virginity in films such as *Boyz n the Hood* (1992), *Scream* (1996), *Titanic* (1997), and *Cruel Intentions* (1999), most teen films of the decade include characters who are already sexually active before the start of the film or simply do not foreground virginity in the narrative. Hollywood did not revisit virginity until the 2000s; this time with a host of films that overinflate the personal and social value of remaining chaste, imploring audiences to think more carefully about the potentially dangerous repercussions of sexual activity. The anti-sex conservatism of the early 2000s continues to stifle the national conversation about sexuality, creating a welcoming environment in which audiences can become reacquainted with the virtues of abstinence.

Abstinence in a Postfeminist Age

Starting in the late 1980s and early 1990s, conservatives began to augment their response to feminism and the sexual revolution by incorporating postfeminist rhetorics of choice and empowerment while discarding the movement's sexual politics. As Bonnie Dow writes, "The problem of the nuclear family (e.g. the isolation of women, the gender-based division of labor, domestic violence, marital rape, lack of control over reproduction) that are central to radical feminists' understanding of 'woman' as a social category or sex class does not figure in postfeminist discourse."[48] As exemplified by Marilyn Quayle's infamous 1992 address to the Republican National Convention, conservatives argued that not all women desired the feminist movement's version of liberation and that the family could still provide greater fulfillment than professional success.[49] This conservative version of feminism reconciled women's professional goals with hegemonic masculinity, calling for men to maintain their traditional roles as husbands, fathers, and family breadwinners.

This historical development of postfeminist culture explains how it is that the conservative portrayals of sexuality I analyze in this book can so easily be folded into films with feminist overtures. Consider, for instance, how the contemporary abstinence movement has both successfully cultivated public anxieties about youth sexuality while selling abstinence as an enactment of personal empowerment. The movement's ability to cultivate active participation among

American youth suggests that beyond the fear appeals and proselytizing there is now something edgy and emboldening about virginity. There is, of course, a significant difference between abstinence rhetoric that comes from a teen sex icon and such rhetoric that comes from an octogenarian male pastor. The popular success of abstinence outside public policy can be explained in part by the movement's appropriation of contemporary feminism. Christine Gardner argues that abstinence supporters "are recasting an essentially feminist argument of 'my body, my choice' and persuading teenagers that they are choice-making individuals who can control their bodies and wait for sex."[50] Indeed, as one abstinence advocate suggests, "purity is nothing if not feminist," pointing out that "it is far more dignifying for a woman to have control over her own body than to give in to exploitive demands by men."[51]

This nominal embrace of feminism is an example of the abstinence movement's co-optative response to progressive challenges. As Yvonne Tasker and Diane Negra suggest, the term "backlash" is an insufficient signifier for the conservative cultural response to women's liberation and the sexual revolution. The term cannot fully describe how from the 1980s onward, neoconservatives domesticated, mainstreamed, and co-opted feminism as a defense of their principles. The abstinence movement's appropriation of "my body, my choice" exemplifies how the key terms feminist activists used in relation to legal abortion and access to contraception have been stripped from their context and redirected to support the idea that virginity and biblical marriage can be counted among a number of empowering and fulfilling lifestyle choices for women.

Thus, abstinence cinema represents the historical convergence of conservative sexual ideologies and contemporary postfeminist culture. Postfeminist discourses routinely celebrate women's liberation while insisting that the feminist political activism that made it possible is anachronistic.[52] Pointing to gains in areas such as education, employment, and politics, highlighting the myriad career and lifestyle choices available to women today, postfeminists insist that feminism has outlived its social utility. As the beneficiaries of past feminist struggles, women practice feminism in its current form not through collective political action but by making individual choices. As Elspeth Probyn argues, postfeminist culture elevated women's choice as the prevailing enactment of contemporary feminism.[53] In this way, Sarah Projansky adds, "postfeminism absorbs and transforms aspects of feminism in ways that, at minimum, dissociate feminist concepts from political and social activism."[54] This decontextualized and depoliticized notion of feminist agency is ultimately illusory because women can still be admonished for making the wrong choice when faced with dilemmas involving career and motherhood. Conversely, women who refuse to support or live by feminist principles can be acknowledged as "empowered" merely for their capacity to make that decision.[55]

The construction of abstinence as a sex-positive feminist ideal attests to what Angela McRobbie calls postfeminism's "double entanglement," the coexistence of neoconservative and antifeminist values with "the process of liberalization in regard to choice and diversity in domestic, sexual, and kinship relations."[56] In other words, because postfeminist discourse disarticulates the feminist rhetoric of choice from its sexual politics, it permits neotraditional and antifeminist ideologies to coexist without contradiction. Feminism is recast as a consumer demand for more lifestyle options and the politics of those choices as beyond reproach. Infused with the economic logic of consumerism, feminism becomes at once everything and nothing. In this cultural environment, former vice-presidential candidate Sarah Palin can both support rolling back women's reproductive rights and be labeled by the media as a feminist icon.[57] Women who opt for traditional motherhood can be framed as the embodiment of Betty Friedan's political ideals.[58] And advertisements for everything from padded bras and thongs to Virginia Slims and Kentucky Fried Chicken valorize women's consumer power as testament to how far women have come since the 1950s.[59]

The films I examine in this book are by-products of the historical development of postfeminist culture. In film's focus on young women's virginity, sexual abstinence, traditional motherhood, and biblical marriage are part of the rich mosaic of lifestyle choices available to women. Aligning themselves with postfeminist ideals, abstinence advocates have repackaged their beliefs to fit what Probyn calls the "new traditionalism," a cultural rediscovery of the supposedly immutable truths concerning women, work, and the family. In this mode, feminism is translated into a personal expression of bodily will, the kind of individualistic imperative that is at the heart of late capitalism. Like the ideology of individualism, abstinence (post)feminism reminds women that wrong choices do in fact exist. That is to say that there are appropriate ways to harness one's bodily autonomy. Deviations from what is supposedly natural are fraught with personal failure and physical harm (guilt, shame, disease, pregnancy, God's disapproval).

Postfeminist culture also reshaped the cultural narrative of male sexuality and virginity loss. While appeals to men's essential nature as fathers, husbands, and breadwinners was a large part of the conservative response to the sexual politics of second-wave feminism, the more accommodationist male stance was to take the edge off hegemonic masculinity by incorporating some feminine sensibilities (i.e., the male who was in touch with his "feminine side") and invest their energies in figuring out "what women want." In this way, abstinence for men is an opportunity get to know what interests women without the complications of a physical relationship and, at the same time, contain the threat of women with a more empowered and active sense of sexual agency. Male abstinence is also a postfeminist ideal in the sense that it still promises sexual ecstasy for men, but within the confines of neotraditional marriage. It accommodates feminists' demands for greater relational equality without challenging the institutions that inspire the movement's emphasis on sexual politics. In the films I examine in this book, abstinence enables men to curtail the feminist threat to hegemonic masculinity through accommodation and incorporation. For instance, the sensitive beta male of *The 40-Year-Old Virgin* responds to a perplexing world of female sexual agency by getting reacquainted traditional romance through late-in-life chastity. This decision is also framed by the rhetoric of choice: men and women are liberated from the vicissitudes of desire by choosing the old traditionalism.

Depoliticizing Girlhood

Abstinence advocates argue that purity is an idealized lifestyle ethic that extends well beyond an individual's sexual choices. Achieving a state of purity requires that an individual also abstain from music, entertainment, food, clothing, books, social activities, or any other physical or mental activity that might lead to impure or lustful thoughts. Even when individuals lose their physical virginity within Christian marriage, they remain pure by abstaining from lustful thoughts and behaviors that pollute the mind and body. In abstinence discourse, the period before adulthood is represented as particularly perilous. Yet it is also constructed as a time of innocence before children are confronted with the harsh realities and perverse desires of adulthood. Remaining pure is a way for an individual to extend the innocence and naiveté of adolescence into adult life. Particularly for young girls, it is imperative to "be un-adults—young, naïve, and impressionable."[60] In abstinence culture, the ideal mind and body of the individual (particularly a young girl) is a tabula rasa, a blank slate that remains unsullied by adult choices.

Abstinence cinema idolizes a pre-political subjectivity that is untarnished by seemingly perverse expressions of sexual identities and the "adultness" that constitutes public life, from the recognition of sexual identities as political projects to the more mundane adult behaviors such as drinking, entertainment, and nightlife. Abstinence films construct the morally virtuous subject as a childlike individual who willfully remains untouched by the forbidden knowledge, experiences, and desires of an adult public culture. Insulation of the self and protection of others offer a fantasy of total purification, or redemption from the tragic knowledge of adulthood. The virgin, then, is both metonym and icon of a pure and virtuous society.

The fetishizing of abstinent young girls represents a divestment in feminist politics. Tasker and Negra argue that "as postfeminism has raised the premium on youthfulness, it has installed an image of feminism as 'old' (and by extension moribund)."[61] Through the depiction of the vulnerable/virginal girl who represents ideal femininity, abstinence cinema implicitly silences and negates the adult woman who embodies feminist political subjectivity. In abstinence cinema, the only choice that matters for women is whether or not they decide to remain abstinent until marriage. The feminist notion of choice is dissociated from the reproductive politics of the older generation and rearticulated to encompass, if not privilege, prefeminist ideals. Of course, the smart and empowering decision is to choose extended adolescence, which holds the promise of perpetual insulation from "adult" desires. By implication, girls lose the moral attributes of innocence and naiveté that make them socially valuable when they exercise the agency and autonomy bequeathed to them by their feminist predecessors. The lesson offered is that good girls know that their place is not in the tarnished world of public life.

The postfeminist rejection of political activism is also extrapolated to an overarching privatized model of citizenship. According to Frances Gateward and Murray Pomerance, popular culture portrays young girls as "values in themselves, to be appropriated and colonized at any expense of spirit and some considerable expense of capital."[62] Lauren Berlant's concept of "infantile citizenship" is instructive in terms of how the little girl, or in this case the virgin, is used to construct ideal notions of political subjectivity.[63] The child is idealized in U.S. public culture because s/he is "not yet bruised by history: not yet caught up in the processes of secularization and sexualization; not yet caught in the confusing and exciting identity exchanges made possible by mass consumption and ethnic, racial, and sexual mixing; not yet tainted by money or war."[64] It is in the name of the anonymous innocent child that adult policymakers "write laws, make culture, administer resources, control things."[65] It is imperative, then, that depictions of adult desires be removed from the public sphere and that sexual intimacies be relegated to private life or legislated out of existence.

Abstinence advocates believe that ideal citizens choose purity in both public and private life. In abstinence culture, the personal sphere of domesticity offers refuge from the perverse desires and available temptations of the public. At the same time, education, public policy, and popular culture all must be evacuated of references to sexuality outside of marriage. In this vision of civic life, adult citizens are subjected to the same norms of appropriateness as children in public conversations about sexuality and sexual identities. Moreover, if civic life refuses to conform to the norms of abstinence culture, the only alternative is withdrawal (for instance, homeschooling or stay-at-home motherhood). In recent films, the sexually pure or abstinent individual offers lessons in both proper personal intimacy and civic participation that attest to the moral virtue of privatization. There is moral value in remaining sheltered from the public expression of sexual identity and the amoral character of public life.

For instance, in the *Twilight* saga, Bella chooses an immortal life of perpetual adolescence in marriage with Edward at the expense of her adult ambitions, including an education, a career, community life, and growing old. Also consider the privatization of sexual identities represented in *The 40-Year-Old Virgin*. While his friends and co-workers are perfectly comfortable expressing their sexual perversions in public, Andy finds it disrespectful and inappropriate to be open about private intimacy. Andy offers a pathway to born-again virginity, or the possibility of living pure even after a public life of sexual immorality. He is a morally virtuous model of masculinity not only because he remains abstinent until marriage but also because he is a gentleman who keeps his sexual desires private. An even more reactionary stance is adopted in the film *Taken*, a film in which "good girls" must realize the sexual dangers of public life or forgo male protection. This film even features punishment by sexual violation for girls who challenge the privatized model of feminine subjectivity. In their own ways, the other films analyzed in this book contribute to an image of public life as either perverse or dangerous and the private sphere as a place of purity and protection.

Abstinence and the Rhetoric of Film

In this book I adopt a critical rhetorical approach that views films as social texts that negotiate the status of virginity in American culture. Broadly speaking, by "rhetoric" I mean the use of language and symbolic action to foster audience identification, explain social phenomena, manage social conflicts, and construct meaning.[66] Abstinence films are part of a cultural mosaic composed of disparate rhetoric that attempts to define and elicit audience identification with popular cultural ideals. In my analysis, I do not make conjectures about how audiences actually interpret films. I am primarily interested in how films invite identification with and naturalize specific social ideals. As Kristy Maddux argues, "a close reading of the text reframes the question of audience effects, asking . . . what discursive resources each text makes available to its audience members."[67] Thus, in this book I examine films as part—but not the totality of—the cultural discourses that participate in a renewed moral panic about sexuality.

A rhetorical approach to film elaborates how discourses in public culture come to be represented as reasonable commitments when they are transcoded into a popular form.[68] Cinematic rhetoric describes how films mobilize language, symbols, and imagery to construct, make sense of, and cultivate identification with some significant aspect of social existence.[69] Films are one of many significant cultural texts that provide a way of seeing, or a lens that helps spectators make sense of their social realities. The films I study in this book are rhetorical in the sense that they are a species of symbolic action with distinct conventions and techniques that instruct, orient, and direct audiences about the proper expression of sexuality and the cultural imperatives of sexual abstinence.[70] This approach connects symbolic action in film with the discourse and context of contemporary public culture in order to show how rhetorics of abstinence circulate in a variety of social texts. According to David Blakesly, such an approach illustrates how films "serve ideological functions in the broader culture (as critique, as hegemonic force, as symptomatic) that can be analyzed as having a rhetorical function, especially to the extent that rhetoric serves as the means of initiating cultural critique and stabilizing cultural pieties."[71]

A rhetorical approach also explains why particular cinematic representations invite audience identification with the sexual ideologies that are active in society. This inflection of rhetoric also displaces a focus on the aesthetic elements (as either elements of persuasive communication or as techniques of signification within a unique and self-contained text) with a focus on films as social texts that symbolize and are responsive to their context. As Barry Brummett writes, rhetoric in popular culture "is the function of managing meaning within social arrangements and it is thus a dimension of the countless acts and objects comprising a cultural environment."[72] Approached as a species of symbolic action, the rhetoric of film is less about film aesthetics and form than it is about how a film "makes sense" in a particular cultural context through a combination of plot, narrative causality, dialogue, characterization, and mise-en-scène.

In addition, films make implicit conjectures about the position of the audience in social hierarchies, the relative value of social institutions, and appropriate behaviors and social roles. Of course, rhetorical arguments look different when they are projected on screen. For instance, arguments about the meaning of virginity undergo a process of translation as they are converted from assumptions, beliefs, and discursive propositions into a visual and symbolic representation of virginity. Michael Ryan and Douglas Kellner argue that in transferring culture struggles from one discursive field to another, cinematic texts become "the site of a contest of representations over what social reality will be perceived as being and indeed will be."[73] This process of "transcoding" from one discursive field to another reflects an inevitable and subtle migration of a culture's anxieties, struggles, preoccupations, and predilections between public and popular texts.[74] As attitudes toward political institutions and social behaviors change over time, films both record and participate in the symbolic process of transformation. Thus, as the abstinence movement rose to prominence, struggles over the meaning of virginity were encoded in the contested terrain of cinema.

Transcoding describes the process by which specific fragments of discourses are embedded in media texts.

The implication of this approach to film is that critical analyses must map cinematic discourses over existing sociopolitical conflicts. This approach "involves a dialectic of text and context, using texts to read social realities and events, and using social and historical context to help situate and interpret key films."[75] Transcoding implies the presence of hegemonic struggle whereby popular culture becomes a site of a larger ideological contestation over sexuality.[76] Films are implicated in the process of hegemonic contestation because they reify abstract political ideals with intuitive narratives and concrete representation techniques. Even when content is fantastical or dystopian, cinematic verisimilitude attempts to elicit popular adherence to the ideals and values encoded in narrative. Thus, the archive for abstinence cinema consists not only of films that articulate the contemporary meaning of virginity but also the discourses of the abstinence movement, whose preferred vision of virginity can be seen when refracted through the cultural context that shaped each film's production.

Of course, symbolic action does not constitute the totality of our social reality, and tangible material forces are real and constrain social action. But it is also the case that social texts play a substantive role in shaping how we make sense of and act upon material reality. Indeed, the contemporary cinematic landscape reflects both the hegemony of abstinence culture and the gaps and fissures in the dominant ideology. Mary Ellen Brown's notion of "leaky hegemony" captures the fact that the dominant ideology is never totalizing or complete. She contends that "although hegemony is very powerful, there are always alternative politics or counterhegemonic consciousnesses struggling for recognition and thus for economic and political power."[77] While the struggle at this point is asymmetrical, abstinence cinema will continue to be challenged by public and popular dissatisfaction. Re-narrating the cultural tale of virginity in cinema will not only reflect resistance to abstinence culture but will enlist one of culture's most powerful media in the struggle for new representations and social configuration. Among the pertinent questions are these: Have the political discourses of the abstinence movement effectively saturated the most watched and revered forms of popular entertainment? How does Hollywood constrain and enable the cultural narrative of virginity loss? Will the cinematic narrative change as resistance to abstinence culture continues to coalesce? Contemporary struggles related to the concepts of abstinence, female empowerment, and sexual liberation can be understood through the tale of virginity narrated through the medium of contemporary film.

Preview of the Book

In this book I analyze a number of films across a wide spectrum of film genres throughout the 2000s: teen melodrama, romance, comedy, horror, action-adventure, and suspense thriller. In some cases virginity is the explicit subject matter of the film and in others purity and teen sexuality are in the subtext. The films I selected evince a recurring intertextual and patterned response to virginity and gesture toward a broader set of assumptions about youth sexuality in our time. Each chapter analyzes a different theme of abstinence discourse as it is refracted through a particular film or set of films. Chapter 1, "Melodrama and Postfeminist Abstinence," offers an exploration of the construction of abstinence in the *Twilight* saga (2008–2012). The billion-dollar franchise (*Twilight, New Moon, Eclipse, Breaking Dawn,* and *Breaking Dawn 2*) fuses the latent sexual anxiety of teenage melodrama with vampire mythology. This chapter explores the postfeminist dynamics of abstinence discourse, or how abstinence, neotraditional romance, and family values are sold as feminist empowerment. Adapted from the best-selling book series by Stephenie Meyer, *Twilight* depicts the torrid love affair between Bella and Edward and the complications of human-vampire romance. From courtship to eventual marriage, Bella and Edward are forced to make strenuous but seemingly noble efforts to control their physical desires. Bella must restrain her premarital sexual urges while Edward must control his thirst for human blood. I frame the *Twilight* saga as a rhetoric of new traditionalism in which chastity is sexy, heterosexual marriage is liberation, and feminism is a relic of the past. In these films, vampires—ancient yet sophisticated—are the hip guardians of a romantic world before the sexual revolution, women's rights, and gay liberation, extolling the pleasures rather than the horrors of sexual oppression/repression. The films' protagonist Bella embodies the virtues of contemporary "virgin chic": an attractive, hip, independent, rebellious daughter of feminism who also recognizes the necessity of controlling her sexual desires and personal ambitions. Demure, family-oriented, and infantile, Bella is suspended in a dependent and pre-political state of perpetual adolescence as she is inducted into the vampiric family.

Chapter 2, "Man-Boys and Born-Again Virgins," investigates the sexual travails of the contemporary cinematic man-boy and the joy of "born-again" virginity in Judd Apatow's *The 40-Year-Old Virgin* (2005). As a result of many sexual experiences gone wrong, Andy (Steve Carell) finds himself a middle-aged virgin. His stunted sexual and emotional development have led him to adolescent interests, including video games and collecting comic books and action figures. The revelation of his virginity to his co-workers initiates many episodes of forced comedic self-improvement and casual dating that ends in disaster. Ultimately, his traditional courtship of Trish (Catherine Keener) results in a series of wholesome dating rituals (picnics, bike rides) that show abstinence to be a pleasurable alternative to the revolting world of casual sex. Trish and her daughter Maria help Andy grow up, and Trish is given an opportunity to reclaim her virginity by being chaste until remarriage. The film ends with Andy and Trish consummating the marriage, followed by the entire cast of the film performing a rendition of "The Age of Aquarius" from the musical *Hair.* However, the "age of Aquarius" symbolizes for Andy the kind of great sex that rewards abstinence until marriage and directly challenges the 1960s sexual revolution. This chapter focuses on the elements of abstinence discourse that blame the collapse of family values and breadwinner masculinity on the liberalization of sexual attitudes since the 1950s. I examine how *The 40-Year-Old Virgin* advances the abstinence movement's diagnosis of what is wrong with contemporary gender roles and prescribes "born-again" virginity as the key to social stability.

Chapter 3, "Monstrous Girls and Absentee Fathers," examines our "collective nightmares" and "projected fears" about young women's sexuality that unfold in recent horror films featuring preteen girls in the grip of demonic possession. This chapter analyzes *The Possession* (2012) as a projection of the abstinence movement's worst nightmares about the disintegration of father-daughter relationships. Much like the discourses of the abstinence movement, possession films depict the nuclear family in crisis and the perils of fatherless households for young girls. The similarity between the rhetoric of demonic possession and the ritualistic imperatives of abstinence discourses demonstrate how horror films resonate with neoconservative anxieties about young women's sexuality. This chapter illustrates how possession films legitimize purity culture's fear that without patriarchal protection, burgeoning womanhood might precipitate a crisis in masculinity and the traditional nuclear family.

Chapter 4, "Abstinence, the Global Sex Industry, and Racial Violence" examines how contemporary action-adventure films use the concept of feminine purity to justify racialized masculine violence. This chapter looks primarily at the film *Taken* (2008), which depicts the murderous rampage of an ex-CIA agent seeking to recover his teenage daughter from foreign sex traffickers. *Taken* articulates a demand for a white male protector to serve as both guardian and avenger of white women's "purity" against the purportedly violent and sexual impulses of dark-skinned men. A neocolonial narrative retold through film, *Taken* infers that the protection of white feminine purity legitimates both male conquest abroad and overbearing protection of young women at home. I show how films about defending the innocence of young white women reinvent the mythic dark-skinned rapist to reestablish the necessity of male protection rackets. This chapter explores how abstinence discourse relies on a public panic over the sexual threat to young women's bodies.

Chapter 5, "Sexploitation in Abstinence Satires," explores the meaning of virginity as articulated in the 2000s revival of the teen sex adventure and its low-budget knock-offs. This chapter looks at what I call "virginsploitation" films, including exploitative Hollywood features such as *Superbad* (2007) and *Easy A* (2010), which I contrast with a shadow low-budget industry that spoofs cinematic anxieties about virginity in films such as *American Virgin* (2000; 2009), *I Am Virgin* (2010), and *18-Year-Old Virgin* (2012). The contemporary Hollywood teen film sets the stage for an ambivalent form of sexploitation that illustrates the presence of cultural anxieties that make virginity and abstinence exploitable concepts. This chapter examines the notion of virginity as a commodity or a gift with exchange value in a sexual and cinematic economy. Both the cleaned-up teen sex comedy and its spoofs capitalize on the abstinence movement's image of virtuous virgins beleaguered by a sex-saturated culture.

In the conclusion, I argue that despite its growing prevalence in film, abstinence until marriage is a contested ideal that is subject to revision and transformation. In addition to examining the implications of abstinence cinema, I examine a series of feature films that reflect feminist and other counter-hegemonic responses to the abstinence movement's vision of sexuality, girlhood, and the family. This brief analysis covers films such as *The Virginity Hit* (2010), *Teeth* (2007), *The To-Do List* (2012), *Whip It!* (2009), and *How to Lose Your Virginity* (2013). These films register alternative rhetorics of female sexuality and empowerment that, while not a panacea, might help craft a new cultural narrative of virginity and coming of age.

Overall, the films I examine in this book provide a disempowering model of young femininity. They reduce the individual morality of adolescents to whether or not they have sex before marriage. They lack nuanced father-daughter relationships, images of young women as physically and emotionally empowered, and representations of a spectrum of intimacies. Collectively, they build a case for overbearing protection of young women and for extending adolescence well into adulthood. These films sell audience members the new traditionalism, inviting them to believe that chastity and sexual repression are the newest form of personal empowerment. I suggest that alternative models of youth sexuality and feminine power exist in a variety of independently produced films that point to possible representational strategies that resist, or at least augment, the abstinence movement's colonization of popular culture.

1

Melodrama and Postfeminist Abstinence

The *Twilight* Saga (2008–2012)

In *Our Vampires, Ourselves*, Nina Auerbach writes that "every age embraces the vampire it needs."[1] In other words, vampires are protean figures who—from Gothic literature to contemporary film and television—are continually remolded to reflect the fears and desires of a particular age. Banished from the daytime, forced to sleep in coffins and subsist on human blood in relative exile, the Gothic vampire symbolized a range of dark desires associated with social exclusion and sexual deviance. Most notably, the vampire's penetrating fangs and hypnotic charisma were masked articulations of sexual transgressions and taboo desires that could not be named in the context of nineteenth-century public morality.[2] Eugenia DeLamotte argues that the implicit sexual terror of vampirism was "the threat of physical violation—a transgression against the body, the last barrier protecting the self from the other."[3] If vampirism in the Victorian era reflected the historical period's latent curiosity about illicit sexual desires, then what do the newly beautified, Americanized, and wholesome vampires of the *Twilight* films say of sexuality in contemporary American culture?

Forced to embody both traditional morality and contemporary sex appeal, the makeover of the cinematic vampire in the *Twilight* films exemplifies and attempts to resolve the ongoing tension between the prurient interests of popular culture and conservative nostalgia for traditional Victorian morality. In this chapter, I contend that the wholesome update of the vampire reflects the growing influence of conservative voices that have adjusted their strategy for recruiting youth to present chastity as sexy, ritual courtship as hip, and chivalry and purity as romantic. Moreover, abstinence proponents assert that young women's pursuit of "Prince Charming" and a fairy-tale marriage are more fulfilling than dating and a career.[4] As a bellwether of sexual attitudes, the popular mainstreaming of socially conservative vampires marks the abstinence movement's efforts to domesticate illicit sexuality by making what was old new again. This new conservative vampire registers the abstinence movement's appropriation of postfeminist ideals to rebrand attachments to Victorian morality as the new sexual revolution.

Through an examination of the neotraditional vampires of the *Twilight* films, this chapter uncovers the tropes that have helped abstinence advocates rebrand chastity and ritual courtship as chic, edgy, and even "cool." The films enact a postfeminist melodrama in which the pursuit of feminine purity is the only safe and morally virtuous pathway to personal empowerment.

Grossing over $3.3 billion to date, the *Twilight* saga is the most successful series of vampire films and one of the most successful movie franchises in the history of Hollywood.[5] The films were adapted from Stephenie Meyer's successful young-adult books of the same name, which have sold one hundred and sixteen million copies worldwide as of 2015 and have been translated into more than thirty different languages.[6] Meyer's novels and their film adaptations— *Twilight* (2008), *New Moon* (2009), *Eclipse* (2010), *Breaking Dawn 1* (2011), and *Breaking Dawn 2* (2012)—are part of a broader cultural revitalization of the vampire that unburdens the supernatural creature of its once hideous and malevolent past. In company with Charlaine Harris's *Southern Vampire Mysteries* and its adaptation in the HBO series *True Blood* (2008–2014), the twenty-first-century vampire has gone mainstream. In part, the popularity of *Twilight* rests with a refurbished vampire who ditched the cape and the crypt for luxury cars, fit physiques, and contemporary couture. The new vampire is sexy and fashionable and even desires genuine romantic relationships with humans. Although they retain their dangerous edge, the vampires of *Twilight* are wholesome and beautiful companions of humankind that are no longer constrained by their affliction.

The *Twilight* saga chronicles the torrid romance of seventeen-year-old Isabella (Bella) Swan (Kristen Stewart) and 109-year-old Edward Cullen (Robert Pattinson), a vampire masquerading as a high school student in the small town of Forks, Washington. The films depict the travails of their courtship, with special emphasis on Edward's attempts to control his thirst and protect Bella's life and virtue from both human and supernatural forces. Their interspecies romance is made possible only by the mutual repression of their desires: Edward's thirst for human blood and Bella's desire for sexual intimacy. Like most literary vampires, Edward is physically powerful and controlling. While these attributes typically render vampires terrifying, in *Twilight* they are employed to make what is otherwise a very traditional courtship ritual seem dangerous but exhilarating.

Twilight presents a dramatic shift in the vampire narrative, one that is perhaps well suited for a sexually regressive political landscape. *It* shares more in common with Victorian novels such as *Wuthering Heights*, *Jane Eyre*, and *Pride and Prejudice* than it does with Bram Stoker's *Dracula* (1897) or Anne Rice's *Interview with the Vampire* (1976). In the *Twilight* saga, the members of the Cullen vampire family drive expensive cars and live in a luxurious home.[7] The Cullens are beautiful, popular, and perpetually young. And while these new vampires retain much of their physical prowess and supernatural power, they control their thirst by feeding only on animals. Instead of fearing the daytime, the Cullens seem to revel in it, and their skin shines like diamonds in the sunlight. Indeed, the only thing "old" about the new vampire is their morality. Sexy as he may be, Edward is a Victorian gentleman who believes in monogamy, true love, and sexual abstinence until marriage. As audiences learn through his courtship of Bella, the new vampire is the hip, youthful custodian of a much older and traditional sexual morality. *Twilight*, then, transforms vampirism from an exploration of dark and illicit desires to a celebration of sexual repression and heterosexual romance. If the vampire is indeed a malleable figure who symbolizes the state of a culture's sexual politics, *Twilight*'s new vampire marks a transition from sexual liberation to liberation from sexuality. Given the series' immense popularity and zealous fandom, the *Twilight* saga is an ideal set of cinematic texts through which to explore the revival of the old traditionalism (sexual abstinence, traditional motherhood, male chivalry) at work in new forms that embody both sex appeal and a youth sensibility of "cool."

A critical analysis of the *Twilight* films illustrates that the mystery and sex appeal of the new vampire thinly veil a nostalgic fantasy of a world sanitized of illicit sexual desire and stabilized by heterosexual marriage, chivalry, and the traditional nuclear family. As a postfeminist melodrama, the series illustrates the odd confluence of abstinence culture (symbolized by the Cullen family) and postfeminist conceptions of female empowerment (represented by the illusory set of choices available to Bella). Although *Twilight* depicts a moderately empowered female protagonist who is vested with decision-making power, Bella is presented with dilemmas in which the only reasonable or desirable alternative is to embrace the inevitability of patriarchy or participate in her own subjugation. Whereas sexual abstinence and traditional marriage offer romance, true love, family, economic mobility, protection against illicit desires, and perpetual youth, feminism is portrayed as moribund. Put differently, sex outside marriage, careerism, independence, and personal autonomy are all associated with atrophy, death, and dystopianism. At the same time, the film's conflation of choice with empowerment elevates Bella's embrace of purity and traditionalism to a more successful and fulfilling model of feminist politics.

Thus far, many feminist scholars and popular critics have focused on the *Twilight* saga's religiously conservative undertones and implicit valorization of abstinence until marriage. I agree with many of these assessments. However, the films' abstinence rhetoric is at its core a rejection of the structure and norms of contemporary society itself, particularly for women. Bella's romantic union with the Cullen family symbolizes a utopian fantasy that lurks within abstinence culture, wherein a retreat to the traditional family offers a remedy for a human society that is dangerous, sinful, and ultimately disappointing. In this world, abstinence until marriage is preparation for a domestic life in which women's sexual desires and personal autonomy are confined within the structure of the neotraditional family. In the *Twilight* saga, vampires no longer represent illicit sexual desire but instead offer a reprieve from a society polluted by desire and destabilized by feminism. Bella's retreat from public life is well compensated: a romantic world filled with enchantment, beautiful ageless bodies, conspicuous consumption, unbound economic mobility, and of course familial immortality. Sexual abstinence in the *Twilight* films becomes sutured to a much larger political vision: returning to a nostalgic world before feminism, sexual liberation, and secularism disturbed the once-rigid boundaries between the public and domestic spheres. The *Twilight* saga is so significant because the films' utopian vision constitutes the symbolic markers of sex appeal and female empowerment that it ultimately undermines. Pro-abstinence messages in the *Twilight* saga leave audiences with an illusory choice between a public and autonomous life that ends in death and a barricaded world of romance and perpetual adolescence.

The Structure of the *Twilight* Universe

The *Twilight* saga consists of five adapted screenplays written by television producer Melissa Rosenberg in consultation with the series' original novelist, Stephenie Meyer. Much like other serial adaptations such as the *Harry Potter* and *Hunger Games* series, financial incentives to continue the lucrative franchise resulted in a turnover of directors, who included Catherine Hardwick (*Twilight*), Chris Weitz (*New Moon*), David Slade (*Eclipse*), and Bill Condon (*Breaking Dawn 1* and *2*).[8] While there are many minor differences between the novels and films, the fundamental narrative remains intact.[9]

Ultimately, the narrative follows a traditional heterosexual romance that proceeds from friendship and courtship through engagement, marriage, and reproduction. But Bella and Edward's relationship produces two significant tensions that drive the narrative forward. First, Bella's essential human traits are a constant liability to both herself and the Cullen family. For vampires, Bella is an inexplicably unique specimen. Unlike other humans, Bella's blood is intoxicating. Thus, bringing her into contact with other, less refined vampires is a unique risk to her safety and to the Cullen family. While the easy solution would be to "turn" Bella, Edward finds the corruption of her soul and virtue to be a selfish and unacceptable outcome. As a Victorian gentleman, Edward engages in constant self-loathing and expresses ambivalence concerning his feelings for Bella. He suggests that the only way he can protect Bella is to be with her, yet he finds himself to be a constant danger to her moral and physical well-being. At some moments he is compassionate and loving, while at others he is manipulative, distant, and even abusive. Convinced that he is a danger to Bella, Edward and his family temporarily relocate to Volterra, Italy, where Edward can watch Bella from a distance. Their relationship is overwrought with references to Shakespeare's *Romeo and Juliet* and motifs of "star-crossed lovers," including (failed) suicide attempts by both Edward and Bella upon hearing false reports of each other's death.

Once Edward resolves to return to Forks and continue his courtship of Bella, the two reach a grand bargain in which Edward will "turn" Bella and consummate their relationship if she agrees to marry him. Bella consents, but only if she can experience sexual intimacy after their marriage but before her transformation. Despite the supposed physiological impossibilities, Bella's human traits betrays her yet again when she becomes pregnant with Edward's child during their honeymoon. Edward is forced to transform Bella during childbirth to save her from the parasitic vampire-child inside her womb. Although Bella survives childbirth, the half-human, half-vampire child amplifies the tensions between humans and the vampire orthodoxy. For the vampire monarchy in Volterra, vampire children are an abomination because they cannot control their thirst and are incapable of camouflaging their vampiric existence from humans. Although Bella invites dangerous if not mortal conflict between the Cullens and the vampire authority, her daughter is born with the supernatural power to foster insight, perspective, and peaceful unity among the individuals she touches. The child's residual human traits and supernatural power help avert a final apocalyptic battle between the Cullens and their allies and the Volterra monarchy.

Second, Bella and Edward's romance exacerbates (but ultimately resolves) long-standing tensions between supernatural forces. Forks is the site of a tenuous truce between the Cullens and the Quileute Indian tribe, a pack of shape-shifting werewolves who have a historic hatred of vampires. Jacob Black (Taylor Lautner), a Quileute member, jeopardizes this tacit peace by pursuing a romantic relationship with Bella. Although Bella eventually chooses Edward, throughout the first four films she is torn between a mortal life with a warm-blooded wolf and an undead but immortal existence with a cold-blooded vampire. Edward and Jacob struggle not only for Bella's love but also for the right to protect her from malevolent vampires. The birth of Bella's daughter, however, resolves the tensions between the Cullens and the Quileutes by creating a shared interest in the child's salvation. Jacob "imprints" on Bella's daughter, which he describes as an involuntary form of coupling whereby wolves commit themselves to another in either a romantic or familial sense. Reflecting the "true love waits" trope, imprinting requires that Jacob delay consummating their romantic courtship until Nessie is ready for marriage. Thus, Bella's child not only gives Bella strength and purpose but also guarantees a consolatory romantic relationship for Jacob while bringing peace to the supernatural world.

The *Twilight* Phenomenon

Since the early success of German expressionist films such as *Nosferatu* (1922) and *Vampyr* (1932), Hollywood productions such as *Dracula* (1931) and *Mark of the Vampire* (1935), and the formulaic horrors created by Hammer Film Productions such as *The Horror of Dracula* (1958), vampires have evolved into iconic cinematic monsters.[10] Many scholars of horror films note that because vampires tend to embody threatening and taboo desires, they are always in transition.[11] In other words, vampires evolve to reflect transformations in political and cultural attitudes toward gender and sexuality. By and large, celluloid vampires have maintained their Gothic transgressiveness throughout popular films such as *Martin* (1978), *Nosferatu the Vampyr* (1979), *Fright Night* (1985), *Once Bitten* (1985), *Vamp* (1986), *Near Dark* (1987), *The Lost Boys* (1987), *Bram Stoker's Dracula* (1992), *Interview with the Vampire* (1994), *Blade* (1998), *Shadow of the Vampire* (2000), *Queen of the Damned* (2002), *Let the Right One In* (2008), and *Abraham Lincoln: Vampire Hunter* (2012) and in television series such as *Dark Shadows* (1966–1971) and *Buffy the Vampire Slayer* (1997–2003).

The *Twilight* saga is remarkable for its transformation of vampires from what Auerbach calls the "hideous invaders of the normal" to icons of the conservative institutions and ideologies they once menaced.[12] William Day explains that this reversion is made possible by subtle changes in the vampire narrative over the past thirty years from revulsion to exhilarating fascination. He writes, "The central event in vampire stories over the last thirty years is the vampire's transformation from monster or object of covert fascination into a protagonist embodying our utopian aspirations to freedom, self-acceptance, self-expression, and community outside the restrictions and limitations of conventional middle-class American society."[13] Although they remained terrifying outsiders, post-sexual-revolution vampires began to offer audiences liberation from their repressed desires. This growing sense of audience identification with vampire protagonists also made it possible for the pendulum to swing in the other direction. As vampires lost their status as transgressive and irredeemable outsiders, they became easier to enlist in the project of propping up mainstream hegemonic institutions. As a result, the *Twilight* films have been able to successfully appropriate the vampire's occult power for a family-friendly audience in search of traditional romance.[14]

Despite deviating from its Gothic roots, the vampire genre, now in a newly wholesome and conservative guise, has never been more popular. In addition to breaking box office records, the *Twilight* saga has cultivated an extensive and devoted fan base. The film's producers maintain an active relationship with a fan community that includes 1.43 million Twitter followers and forty-five million Facebook followers.[15] The opening of each film was preceded by legions of young fans camping in tents for midnight screenings and special DVD releases available at Borders, Walmart, and Toys "R" Us.[16] But the popularity of the *Twilight* saga goes well beyond young adults. As of June 2015, TwilightMoms.com boasted over 49,000 Twitter followers.[17] In fact, 40 percent of fans, or self-proclaimed "Twi-hards," are over the age of twenty.[18] The fan experience for *Twilight* even extends to fan conventions (TwiCon); fan fiction; homemade music; *Twilight*-themed ocean cruises; tours of Forks, Washington; spinoff novels such as *Twilight in Volterra* and *Twilight in Forks*; and even *Twilight*-themed erotica.[19] At the same time, the vehemence of the pushback against the series almost matches the intensity of the self-described Twi-hards. In addition to countless anti-*Twilight* blogs, websites, and Tumblr pages, the saga is panned in parody films such as *Vampires Suck* (2010) and *Breaking Wind* (2012). In 2013, *Breaking Dawn 2* won seven Razzies, including one for worst picture.[20] In addition to garnering generally poor reviews, the films have been criticized by popular columnists for everything from glorifying abstinence to making abusive relationships sexy and exhilarating.[21]

Despite the recent scholarly attention to *Twilight*, Stephenie Meyer disavows any symbolic or politically salient messages in her work. She explains, "I never meant for [Bella's] fictional choices to be a model for anyone else's real life choices. She is a character in a story, nothing more or less. On top of that, this is not even realistic fiction, it's a fantasy with vampires and werewolves, so one *couldn't* even make her exact choices."[22] Despite Meyer's best efforts to depoliticize the series, popular culture inevitably draws from other discursive fields to make its messages salient to audiences. While it is easy to dismiss the *Twilight* saga as low-culture popular entertainment for young adults, it is significantly more productive to analyze and explain how its message makes sense of our social context. A wave of other scholarly books—most of which deal most directly with the novels—indicates that it is a mistake to ignore how the saga's message affects youth culture, particularly that of girls.[23] Popular novels and films seldom feature a young and empowered female protagonist. As Natalie Wilson notes in *Seduced by Twilight*, the novels are innovative in that they represent an active and enjoyable female sexuality.[24] Consistently, the scholarly defense for studying *Twilight* is that girl culture is too often cast aside as a series of frivolous and apolitical texts. For instance, Melissa A. Click, Jennifer Stevens Aubrey, and Elizabeth Behm-Morawitz argue for a fan-based perspective that views girls as active or resistant readers of the series. Working from Angela McRobbie and Jenny Garber's landmark essay "Girls and Subculture" and Janice

Radway's *Reading the Romance*, they argue that in order to evaluate the *Twilight* films scholars must listen to the narratives of girls themselves and how they use the films' messages for their own empowerment.[25]

My analysis in no way denies that fans adopt oppositional readings of popular texts or repurpose oppressive messages. I also do not want to suggest that the films are designed to dupe naive young girls. *Twilight* fans are capable of identifying with Bella as a model even as they might acknowledge the coexistence of other disempowering representations of women. Instead of making conjectures about the audience, my analysis is concerned with the kinds of discursive resources or models of sexuality the *Twilight* films make available to audience members. A critical analysis of the films as cultural texts reveals aspects of the *Twilight* films that might otherwise be overlooked, including representations that illustrate the influences of abstinence messages on popular culture writ large.

A Bad Romance; or, Of Lions and Lambs

The *Twilight* saga draws liberally from the conventions of cinematic melodrama.[26] In classical melodrama, the protagonist's struggles are dramatized by introducing romantic pathos, domestic turbulence, sentimentality, and moral polarization between forces of good and evil, heroes and villains.[27] In melodramas that adopt a feminine point of view, female protagonists grapple with forces of fate or the seemingly immutable structures of society, vacillating between "empowerment and imperilment."[28] Although Laura Mulvey suggests that melodrama deviates from the male gaze of classical cinema by offering the possibility of female sexual agency, many feminist film theorists posit that melodramas too frequently offer an essentialized version of traditional femininity as a curative for hegemonic masculinity.[29] Consider how in a film such as *Beauty and the Beast* (1991), Belle offers herself to the Beast in exchange for her father's release. Her feminine affect and ethic of care not only save her father but coax out an enchanted prince from the Beast's violent and aggressive exterior. As Pam Cook suggests, the female protagonist of the "women's picture" can only mediate but never destroy or remake society.[30] Such a protagonist is confronted by society when she deviates from fate or gender and class expectations. In short, her agency is still circumscribed by societal constructs.

In this regard, *Twilight* not only remakes the vampire but recasts the genre's female lead as a melodramatic heroine who, like her predecessors, must grapple with the inevitability of sacrifice, the tragedy of affliction (in this case, vampirism), and choice among competing suitors (Edward or Jacob). The film's heightened emotionality and moral polarity ultimately translate Bella's expressions of agency into a stifling search for "true love," a struggle beset by the forces of good and evil. And like Belle of *Beauty and the Beast*, Bella must assume great personal risk to tame the beast and redeem her prince. The films' sentimentality and emphasis on self-sacrifice in the pursuit of love suggest that women cannot "have it all," so to speak. In other words, expressing intimate desire and harboring personal ambitions are incommensurate with "true love" and appropriate social roles for women.

Drawing from melodramatic convention, the *Twilight* saga also constructs sexual intimacy outside marriage as dangerous—if not deadly—and the heterosexual courtship ritual as necessarily fraught with repression, pain, and sacrifice. As Wilson observes of the novels, the relationship between danger and "true romance" encourages audiences to pursue tumultuous relationships that might result in their own subjugation.[31] By associating desire with mental and physical anguish, the films normalize pain and even masochism as a necessary feature of romantic relationships. The treacherous nature of Bella and Edward's romance suggests that even when they are painful, self-restraint and abstinence until marriage are the only tried and true method for asserting control over sexual passion. And while pain is sutured to romance, it pales in comparison with the suffering that is unleashed when individuals succumb to their desires. Throughout the films, pain frequently accompanies desire as a reminder that indulgence or "losing control" ensures disorder and suffering. Thus, the films offer a confusing portrait of romance in which pain—even abuse and control—must be endured to reap the rewards of true love.

While the use of melodrama structures the films' painful portrait of "star-crossed lovers," their confusing portrait of painful desire also draws its resonance from abstinence culture. For virginity advocates, sex outside wedlock invites a host of horrific personal and social consequences. As one prominent abstinence advocate, Randy Alcorn, contends, premarital sex is a slippery slope to personal ruin. He writes, "Soon there's lust, sin, devastation, disillusionment, loss of respect, conflict, insecurity and sometimes unwanted pregnancy and sexually transmitted diseases. Many young people end up angry and bitter at themselves and others because they bought the lie, the relationship is ruined and now they are paying the price."[32] Chief among the risks to teenagers is the risk of "losing control" throughout the process of dating and courtship. For instance, the advocacy organization Love Matters warns about "intense hugging, passionate kissing and anything else that leads to lustful thoughts and behavior. Anything beyond a brief, simple kiss can quickly become dangerous."[33] Alcorn provides a more specific elaboration on how courtship quite often goes wrong: "If one of you begins to be stimulated even by an apparently innocent physical contact, then both of you should back off immediately. If you don't back off, you are choosing to stay on a canoe headed toward a waterfall. This is not just wrong, it's stupid. Those who allow their minds to dwell on what's immoral and who engage in sexual stimulation together shouldn't be surprised when they have sexual intercourse. It's simply the natural result of the choices they've made."[34] As this passage suggests, abstinence advocates believe that relationships are always at risk of peril and therefore require a stalwart commitment to purity to avoid the slippery slope to personal ruin.

In most cases, abstinence discourse blames women for provoking male sexual desires. Abstinence curricula suggest that girls can inadvertently invite dangerous and unwanted male attention, including rape. The *Sex Respect* teacher's manual warns, "Date rape is a crime that young women must be on the lookout to avoid."[35] Similarly, the *Why kNOw* sixth-grade curriculum suggests that "the young girl learning to understand her changing body often has no idea the effect it has on surrounding males. Signals she doesn't even know she is sending can cause big problems."[36] As another student workbook contends, "Girls need to be aware they may be able to tell when a kiss is leading to something else. The girl may need to put the brakes on first in order to help the boy."[37] These abstinence instruction manuals also suggest that girls are socialized to pressure men for sex despite the fact that this is not a part of their physical/emotional hard wiring. Their job, then, is to control the escalation of physical intimacy or invite tragic consequences. Abstinence advocates construct testosterone as a hormone that is difficult to control and that women must be careful not to provoke their male partners. They must help them control their desires through modesty and rigid self-restraint.

The *Twilight* films capture this attitude toward sex and relationships by constructing a portrait of young romance imperiled by the characters' destructive impulses of desire. In short, true love requires one to endure pain and put oneself in situations where physical intimacy risks personal annihilation. *Twilight* begins with a scene depicting a deer being chased through the woods by an unseen but dangerous entity. In a voiceover, Bella explains: "I've never given much thought to how I would die. But dying in the place of someone I love seems like a good way to go. So I can't regret the decision to leave home." This introduction suggests that Bella, symbolized by the innocent fawn, will have to put herself at risk of injury and death if she wants to find true love. Her innocence and purity will attract and render her vulnerable to the threatening masculinized forces of the supernatural world. As they come from different worlds, the nearly insurmountable obstacles to Bella and Edward's relationship require both to be willing to put their lives in jeopardy to be with one another.

Bella's decision to pursue a relationship with Edward requires her to consciously sacrifice her friendships with Jessica and Jacob and inevitably to jettison her mortal family and plans for the future. As early as the first film, the all-consuming and perhaps self-destructive nature of their relationship becomes clear. At the outset of their courtship, Bella emphatically states, "I was unconditionally and irrevocably in love with him." Amplified by Kristen Stewart's aloof and deadpan delivery, Bella's detachment from all social rituals and personal aspirations of young adults suggests that Edward is her only life interest. Until she becomes a vampire, Bella's love for Edward is her defining human trait. As a result, Bella becomes depressed and quasi-suicidal during their separation in *New Moon*. This film includes a lengthy montage scene of Bella staring blankly out her bedroom window as months pass by, followed by scenes of Bella's recurring night terrors. Trying frantically to reach Edward, Bella sends torrid e-mails to his stepsister Alice, one of which concludes, "The pain is the only reminder that he was real, that you all were." When Bella becomes aware that Edward may be watching her from a distance, she begins engaging in risky and adrenaline-charged activities to hear his voice in her head or even to provoke him to return to Forks. In fact, the apparent reason that she rekindles her friendship with Jacob is so that she can repair old motorcycles, only to drive them recklessly. Bella even plunges off a cliff into the ocean, only to be saved by Jacob from certain death. As evidenced by Bella's self-destructive tendencies, the films equate desire with suffering and frame pain and self-risk as expressions of love. Perhaps more troubling for young women is the idea that true love should be prioritized over all other personal ambitions, even at the risk of their emotional and physical well-being. In the *Twilight* saga, a life without a man is ostensibly meaningless and love is only true if it is worth dying for. As Bella characterizes her commitment to Edward in *Breaking Dawn 2*, "this means more than my life. That's how much I love you."

In the *Twilight* saga, the agony of true love is overshadowed by the extreme risks of losing control. Edward's struggles with physical intimacy suggest that his rational and moral capacities are easily overwhelmed by more primitive and animalistic desires. Like the warning from True Love Waits, even innocuous activities such as touching and kissing might lead to the worst imaginable consequences. For instance, Edward describes Bella's blood as his "own personal brand of heroin," so powerful that any physical intimacy could activate his uncontrollable thirst. The first time they kiss alone in Bella's bedroom, Edward is reluctantly compelled to pull himself away and the two are forced to translate their mutual physical desire into a night of playful conversation. At first Bella is offended that Edward is not sexually interested in her, but as Edward reminds her, "I still don't know if I can control myself." Even as their honeymoon approaches in *Breaking Dawn*, Edward wants to delay sex indefinitely—or at least until Bella is a vampire—because "it's too dangerous." In this way, the films conflate vampire "thirst" with a kind of primal male sexual desire that can be contained only by avoiding physical intimacy during courtship. Put differently, male sexual desire *is* the vampire that dwells within, and when provoked it threatens women's physical integrity and moral virtue with penetrating fangs.

For Bella, despite her active interest in sex, losing control is associated with acquiring Edward's thirst without his capacity for self-restraint. The female vampire—a being with an active thirst and a capacity to penetrate—transgresses patriarchal gender roles and represents the threat of an uncontrollable female sexuality. In becoming a vampire, Bella would transition from a relatively passive female sexuality to an active and predatory male sexuality. Whereas the primal nature of male sexuality is reified by Edward's self-description as a "sick masochistic lion," the innocent naiveté of female desire is punctuated by Bella's acknowledgment that, as a human, she is a "stupid lamb." Like the endangered fawn depicted in the series' opening, the lamb is also an icon of innocence, naiveté, and, above all, vulnerability. Bella's dangerous escalation of her physical relationship with Edward suggests that safe and morally apposite female sexuality is passive and requires appropriate male guidance. In contrast, a vampiric sexuality portends chaos and disorder. For instance, as their marriage approaches in *Breaking Dawn*, Bella is captivated by a dystopian vision of her white-themed wedding turned red. In her dream, the Volterra monarchy arrives amid dark skies, decayed flowers, and Bella and Edward standing, satiated, atop a pile of discarded bodies. At another point, Bella posits, "everyone says that once I'm changed all I'll want is to slaughter the whole town." Bella's anxious anticipation of such a radical reversal in desire and power suggests that

FIGURE 3. Bella and Edward have a night of conversation to help control their mutual desire. *Twilight*. DVD. Directed by Catherine Hardwicke. Universal City, CA: Summit Entertainment, 2013.

there is something uniquely menacing about female vampires. As Barbara Creed contends, the fanged mouth of popular culture's female vampire connects the unconscious mind of the audience with the primal uncanniness of the mythic *vagina dentata*, or a toothed vagina with the capacity to castrate men. Such a representation of female vampires "warns man about the dangers of female sexuality that is not brought under strict control and regulation."[38] An embodiment of patriarchal anxiety, Bella-as-vampire symbolizes the monstrosity of a masculinized female sexual drive that cannot be controlled by men.

Bella's active sexual urges are contained by her masochistic desire to be dominated and her submission to Edward's authority. Even though he describes himself as a masochist, Edward's violent and controlling behavior more accurately characterizes him as a sadist. He watches Bella while she sleeps, disables her truck so that she cannot see Jacob, controls who she can and cannot see, lies frequently, and makes decisions without her input. Moreover, Edward is conflicted by feelings of love and a pained desire to do harm to her. But Bella is the one in the relationship who expresses joy over being left "black and blue." Their first sexual encounters are wrought with violence, as Edward's overpowering physical strength leaves the bed in shambles and Bella covered in bruises and contusions. The presence of a soft, sentimental soundtrack belies the violent nature of their first sexual encounter and even eroticizes the violence of what is ostensibly a sadomasochistic liaison. Edward's expressions of postcoital guilt and remorse are silenced by Bella's insistence that "for a human, I don't think that it can get any better than that." Along with a romanticized portrait of Edward's manipulative behavior, Bella's enjoyment of pain during sex suggests that women derive pleasure from physical and emotional abuse. This portrayal affirms the patriarchal myth—one often relied upon by rapists and domestic abusers—that women subconsciously desire to be dominated by men. In doing so, the films discipline Bella's active and masculinized expressions of sexual desire.

Ultimately it is an idealized vision of marriage, motherhood, and the family that contains Bella's active sexuality and channels it into productive and appropriate uses. In the films, abstaining until marriage ensures that sex is safe, morally appropriate, and pleasurable. Similar to the rhetoric of abstinence advocates, great sex and a supportive family are compensation for delaying sex and choosing monogamy. This point is accentuated by the films' embrace of the myth of the perfect "first time" for women. Despite the violence of their first encounter, Bella insists that the experience could not have been any better for her, or for anyone, for that matter. Here the film resolves the problem of repressed desire by authorizing female gratification under the guidance of a protective husband. Indeed, the problem of desire gets worse after Bella's transformation, as Bella expresses an inability to process and adequately control her appetite. She tells Edward, "You really were holding back before. I'm never going to get enough of this. We never get tired, we never need to rest, or catch our breath, or eat. I mean, how are we going to stop?" Her lack of restraint retroactively legitimizes Edward's insistence upon marriage before the two unleash their repressed desires. As her husband, it is Edward's responsibility to guide and channel Bella's thirst. Bella's compensation is the kind of pleasure that is possible only if one abstains until marriage.

Bella's experience contrasts with that of Victoria, a malevolent female vampire who conspires to destroy the Cullens. Victoria uses sex and vampiric powers to seduce men and create new vampires willing to carry out her orders. Ostensibly, Victoria is a portrait of the dangers of female promiscuity. When female desire is unleashed without proper male guidance, it poses a significant danger to society. In contrast, Bella's unbridled desire is finally channeled into motherhood after she is improbably impregnated during her honeymoon. Bella's parasitic vampire child is both a "miracle" and a threat to her life. While the films accept the premise that sex can be pleasurable, audiences are reminded that its ultimate purpose is for procreation. Or, thought of in another sense, sex has painful and sometimes life-threatening consequences (even within marriage). Bella's child becomes the answer to her question "how are we going to stop?"

Controlling the Beast Within

In a reversal of the Gothic vampire narrative, the Cullens represent the films' moral compass. Their righteousness is signified by skin that shines like diamonds in sunlight and a diet that excludes the vampire's most pleasurable food source, human blood. Edward explains that a vampire's thirst cannot be indulged even in moderation because animalistic instincts will always overwhelm rational decision making. In *Twilight*, he explains, "When we taste human blood, a sort of frenzy begins, and it's almost impossible to stop." In order to reconcile their morality with their affliction, the Cullens abstain from human blood and only feed on animals. Edward explains to Bella, "I don't want to be a monster. My family, we think of ourselves as vegetarians because we only survive on the blood of animals. . . . It keeps you strong but you're never fully satisfied. It wouldn't be like drinking your blood, for instance." To protect their human-like morality, the Cullens have repressed the illicit cravings that otherwise would accompany their supernatural affliction. Their version of "vegetarianism" demonstrates that it is possible, even for vampires, to control the most powerful and instinctual desires.

The films represent all male sexual desire—human and vampire—as inherently predatory. The Cullens are exceptional not only in their ability to control their thirst but also for their adherence to traditional, Victorian sexual morality.

In contrast, the films' villains are licentious, as their lustful actions and impure thoughts reveal. This construction of male desire reflects the deep gender essentialisms of abstinence-until-marriage instruction. One abstinence curriculum textbook asserts that "for men, sexual arousal is easier, dependent on sight, and focused on genital and sexual activity as the goal. For women, sexual arousal is more difficult, dependent on words, and focused on sharing feelings. Men may use 'love' to get sex, while women use 'sex' to get 'love.'"[39] Another workbook asks, "Is it fair that guys are turned on by their senses and women by their hearts?"[40] In abstinence discourse, men have an innately powerful and difficult-to-control sex drive. Therefore, women must use their natural modesty to help men become "gentlemen" by keeping sex out of relationships. The *Heritage Keepers Student Manual* contends, "For this reason, girls have a responsibility to wear modest clothing that doesn't invite lustful thoughts." Because of their testosterone, men must acquire moral habits to control the beast within. "Real men" are, therefore, "strong, respectful, and courageous."[41]

In *Breaking Dawn 1*, Edward narrates his pathway from licentiousness to asceticism as a type of moral education. He explains to Bella that he resented the attempts of Carlisle, another Cullen family vampire, to help him control his thirst. As he recounts his early life as a vampire in rebellion, the film depicts a Gothic version of Edward in 1930s period dress, hunting and feeding on humans. Edward stalks his prey during a theatrical showing of *Frankenstein* (1931), in which the feelings of the undead creature mirror Edward's own self-loathing. The films soften the Gothic Edward by reminding the audience that he always respected women's virtue and only targeted murderers and rapists. Bella even rationalizes his actions by suggesting to Edward that "you probably saved more lives than you took." Carlisle offers Edward redemption for his sins by bringing him into the family and teaching him to live a moral life in spite of his affliction.

The story of Edward's moral development offers several lessons about the importance of asceticism, or the practices of discipline and austerity that constitute self-care and moral development. First, Edward's development required submission to a father (Carlisle). The films imply that the hierarchy and order of the male-headed household provide the type of structure and discipline required for private moral development. By contrast, the lone vampire, hunting humans in public, will indulge his monstrous instincts. In Carlisle's opulent glass home, Edward and his vampire siblings learn to control their thirst and peacefully coexist with humans. The open and transparent homestead symbolizes that these vampires have nothing to hide, unlike the Gothic vampires who lived in the shadows and slept in coffins. Second, Edward's transformation narrates a parallel transformation in the cinematic vampire. Like Edward, Hollywood's vampire has also exchanged the Gothic exploration of dark desires for moral lessons in self-control and assimilation. In the *Twilight* saga, the evolutionary path of the vampire is from savagery to civilization, providing a case study for how illicit desires can and must be conquered. The films change the vampire's lineage from the Gothic monster who once menaced social norms to that of the Victorian gentleman.

The Cullens' ancient notions of family values contrast with a human society that has lost its Victorian moorings. Edward's ability to read minds reveals that most contemporary humans harbor lustful, disgusting, and even violent thoughts. When Edward saves Bella from a gang of sexually charged boys in Port Angeles, he is distressed by a cacophony of inner monologues that reveal violent carnal desires. When the two are at dinner, Edward discloses that he feels very protective of her because he can read the lustful thoughts of those who surround her. He tells Bella that everyone in the restaurant is thinking about sex or money. In this scene, Edward's telepathic abilities present the audience with a dystopian portrait of modernity. Human obsession with sex and money bespeaks a morality crisis promulgated by unchecked capitalism's emphasis on the maximization of individual freedom and self-gratification. While the Cullens have learned to repress their desires, modern humans have abandoned their inhibitions.

Despite his telepathy, Edward is fascinated by the fact that neither he nor any other vampire can read Bella's thoughts. Part of Bella's allure is that she is a blank slate with a pure and unpolluted mind. Edward is intrigued by her purity, which he equates with the virtue of women in his youth. Indeed, this also explains why he spurns her sexual advances and denies her requests to be turned into a vampire. In *Eclipse*, Edward explains to Bella that his sexual rebuffs are for the benefit of her moral virtue. He posits, "It's just one rule I want to leave unbroken. It might be too late for my soul but it's not too late for yours. I know it's not a modern notion." Although the Cullens have adapted to centuries' worth of changes in style, dress, language, and custom, they remain conservative on issues of sexuality.[42] Because of their old age, the film is able to remake vampires into guardians of a traditional sexual morality that appears to have been discarded and is considered out of date by most humans. Perhaps the exigency of their affliction is what rendered their ancient morals a necessity, but the Cullens present a romantic portrayal of sexual repression rooted in the courtship rituals of the Victorian era. Edward explains, "I'm from a different era. Things were a lot less complicated. And if I had met you back then I would have courted you. We'd have taken chaperoned strolls, iced tea on a porch. I may have stolen a kiss or two, but only after asking your father's permission. I would have gotten down on one knee and I would have presented you with a ring."

Absent from Edward's nostalgic vision of heterosexual courtship before modern feminism are the perils of the cult of true womanhood and its consequences for young women. The "less complicated" time of which Edward speaks was also a period when many women had few if any legal protections, were denied the right to vote and participate in civic life, and were relegated to domestic labor and sexual servitude within the propertied relations of marriage. If his moral beliefs are derived from nineteenth-century bourgeois society, Edward's obsession with protecting Bella's virtue is premised on the assumption that women—domestic, pious, servile, and virtuous—must accept the protection of chivalrous men to sustain social order and stave off the perilous threat of licentiousness. Their courtship is also a moral education for Bella, as she must learn from the Cullens how to control her human desires, and later, her thirst. Rooted in a Victorian conception, their eventual marriage symbolizes the seamless passage of control over Bella's "virtue" from her father, Charlie, to Edward.

The New Feminism

Although the *Twilight* saga offers a romantic embrace of the cult of true womanhood, the films do not position traditional values as the antithesis of contemporary feminism. Instead, they reconcile prefeminist ideals with the goals and tenets of women's liberation. Indeed, many abstinence advocates argue that because the public is desensitized to sex, just saying "no" is an expression of empowerment. For instance, Janie Fredell, the founder of True Love Revolution, argues that chastity is a feminist, even "countercultural" conception because it is premised on asserting women's bodily autonomy.[43] Similarly, the *Twilight* films' emphasis on "choice" as the fundamental expression of female empowerment brands elective chastity, modesty, traditional marriage, and "opting-out" motherhood as fundamental aspects of feminist politics. This construction of female agency discards the rhetoric of choice sutured to reproductive freedom and bodily autonomy for a depoliticized notion of female agency as individuated decision making.[44] The valorization of choice makes all social arrangements that a woman could potentially opt into (or out of) beyond reproach, including the choice to endorse explicitly depoliticized or antifeminist ideals. Many critics of postfeminism have posited that choice is a bourgeois privilege that remains out of reach for most working-class women, single mothers, and people of color.[45] To the extent that choice is represented as boundless in mass media—while remaining heavily circumscribed by the material conditions of everyday life— women are often blamed for making decisions under conditions not of their own making.

The *Twilight* films' ethos of female empowerment is premised on this postfeminist politics of choice. Meyer's responses to feminist critics are particularly enlightening in terms of how the films rely on postfeminist discourse:

> In my own *opinion* (key word), the foundation of feminism is this: being able to choose. The core of anti-feminism is, conversely, telling a woman

she can't do something solely because she's a woman—taking any choice away from her specifically because of her gender. . . . One of the weird things about modern feminism is that some feminists seem to be putting their own limits on women's choices. That feels backward to me. It's as if you can't choose a family on your own terms and still be considered a strong woman. How is that empowering? Are there rules about if, when, and how we love or marry and if, when, and how we have kids? Are there jobs we can and can't have in order to be a "real" feminist? To me, those limitations seem anti-feminist in basic principle.[46]

Meyer's comments demonstrate how postfeminist discourse can be used to turn the tables on feminist critics, accusing them of trying to limit options for women. Like Meyer's comments, the films are also heavily invested in a model of empowerment that centers on Bella's decision-making capabilities. This vision of feminist politics places more emphasis on lifestyle choices than it does on political gains or positive outcomes for women. Bella is always in the midst of significant and often dangerous life dilemmas, and the source of her feminine power is derived from being in a position to choose Edward or Jacob, human or vampire, career or marriage and motherhood, mortality or perpetual youth.

But as within postfeminist culture, not all choices are equal. Given the romantic portrayal of vampire culture, the films suggest that choosing a human life without Edward would be a mistake. Bella's choice is ultimately illusory, as she must decide between a human life that is uninteresting, dangerous, and moribund and a morally superior existence of perpetual youth, romance, and family. The film's version of feminism is an inverted portrait of feminist agency in which women can freely choose the home and traditional motherhood as sole sources of fulfillment. This model of empowerment counteracts the diverse blueprints for social change that appear in the rhetoric of second-wave and third-wave feminism. That is to say, the films resist the second wave's emphasis of transforming political institutions and the third wave's emphasis on upending gender binaries and essentialism.[47]

First, the series' most empowered women are ostensibly children. In other words, they are perpetually young, sheltered, and meek, and their only real source of strength is their family. For an empowered female protagonist, Bella is remarkably soft spoken, bored, and expressive of no ambition outside a relationship with Edward or Jacob. Bella is also exceptionally shy and generally uncomfortable with her body. Her manner of dress communicates modesty, particularly compared to the attire of her female friends and the very adult clothing norms of her high school. Bella's modesty is accentuated by her disinterest in prom dresses (*Twilight*), her comedic inability to walk in high heels, and her discomfort with undressing around Edward even after their wedding (*Breaking Dawn 1*). Although the films desexualize Bella's dress and personal style, she remains at the center of a romantic competition between Forks's two most attractive and unattainable adolescent men. In fact, Bella is so desirable that Edward cannot withstand sitting next to her in classes until he is able to feed and bring his thirst under control. While her attractive friend and class valedictorian Jessica struggles to find a date for the prom, boys mysteriously swoon over the detached, quiet, and humble new girl.

The filmmakers avoid explicitly sexualizing the series' heroine, yet they nevertheless leave in place a subtext of sexual desire combined with female modesty. Throughout the first four films, Bella expresses no other personal ambition but to be in love. Aside from a half-hearted interest in attending college (*Eclipse*), Bella's only distinguishing personal trait is her attunement with Forks's supernatural forces. Taken together, her personal modesty and disinterest in college and a career make her suitable for a life of domesticity. Bella's sex appeal, then, is in her display of feminine virtue—not only her refusal to conform to modern and immodest norms of feminine dress but also her implicit repudiation of the idea that women can and should aspire to "have it all," both career and family.

It is also telling that both Edward's internal struggle and his competition with Jacob are about the preservation of Bella's physical and moral integrity. Bella is the object of male desire because her personal ambitions are infantile and virtuous; she is an ideal candidate for traditional marriage and motherhood. With no ambitions of her own, Bella is a blank slate on which Edward and Jacob can project their ideal version of domestic bliss. The films promote an image of female empowerment that is consistent with what Susan Faludi calls "cocooning," a portrayal of personal fulfillment found in "a retreat from female adulthood."[48] The films' overemphasis on choice as empowerment ignores the fact that Bella's agency is confined to a personal sphere of heterosexual romance. Bella's empowerment is always mediated through her relationships with men in pursuit of "true" love. And the films suggest that within the politics of intimacy, the meek and modest girl gets the guy.

In contrast, Bella's friend Jessica functions as the films' postfeminist foil. The films' portrayals of Jessica lend credibility to abstinence culture's caricature of frivolous dating and unfulfilling careerism.[49] She represents the supposedly naive optimism of contemporary mainstream feminism and provides a suitable contrast between the seemingly confusing world of modern dating and the simple rituals of traditional courtship. In many ways, she is also a caricature of Helen Gurley Brown's *Sex and the Single Girl*; she both models and offers advice that stresses the importance of female independence, careerism, and dating multiple partners before marriage.[50] As the school's valedictorian, Jessica is intelligent, career oriented, and relatively popular. She extols the benefits of taking personal risks, dating multiple partners, and planning for the future.

She even routinely expresses a love of shopping (*Twilight*; *Eclipse*), a hobby best enjoyed with financial independence. Bella and Jessica's relationship is first strained by Bella's agony over losing Edward (*Eclipse*) and then eventually severed when Bella decides to leave her human life behind to marry him (*Breaking Dawn 1* and *2*). Jessica's solution to Bella losing Edward is to suggest that she move on and date other boys. Of course, Bella and Jessica do not share the same assumptions about dating and relationships. Whereas Jessica prefers to find love through trial and error, Bella expresses faith in the idea of true and everlasting love. Jessica's notion of casual dating is made to appear quite shallow when contrasted with the infinite returns of marriage and true love. But regardless of whether one lifestyle is privileged, the concept that choice is empowerment makes neither alternative more or less feminist than the other.

Jessica's commencement address provides a fitting contrast between the putatively short-sighted gains of contemporary feminism and the timeless rewards of traditional womanhood. Like most commencement addresses, Jessica's speech deals directly with the unpredictability of the future and the rewards of taking risks. More than any of the other films, *Eclipse* is organized around questions of fate and free will. In this film Bella must choose between pursuing human ambitions or marrying Edward and becoming a vampire. This speech appears at a point in the film when Bella must make a final decision in order to satisfy Edward. While Jessica's response to her future is a confrontational "Who the hell knows," Bella's considers the pleasures of eternal permanency. Jessica declares: "This isn't the time to make hard-and-fast decisions. This is the time to make mistakes. Take the wrong train and get stuck somewhere. Fall in love . . . a lot. Major in philosophy because there is no way to make a career out of that. Change your mind and change it again because nothing is permanent. So make as many mistakes as you can. That way, when they ask what we want to be we won't have to guess. We'll know." If feminism is about making mistakes, experiencing pain, and embracing contingency, then by definition it cannot offer Bella a sense of stability or purpose. In fact, embracing the ethos of *Sex and the Single Girl* like Jessica will only guarantee heartache, failure, aging, and ultimately death. This portrayal of feminism aligns with postfeminist discourses that point to a happiness deficit created by the impossible demands of women's liberation.[51] With a moribund vision of human life before her, Bella's choice to marry Edward is a foregone conclusion. This is indicated by her declaration: "I want to tie myself to you as much as humanly possible" (*Eclipse*). Bella's friends—who will grow old and die—fail to understand the merits of her decision. In *Breaking Dawn 1*, they attend her wedding confused and even upset that Bella has decided to forgo college to marry Edward. Performing the role of "feminist killjoy," Jessica precedes a disingenuous wedding toast with the inference that Bella must be pregnant because "who else gets married at eighteen?"[52]

But Bella does not appear to expect her friends and family to understand her decision. After Bella and Edward say "I do," the wedding guests temporarily vanish, suggesting that the two perhaps will need only each other from then on. The prospect of immortality necessitates an eventual end to Bella's human community and her subsequent dependence on Edward. The pursuit of finite and worldly interests pales in comparison to the benefits of eternal youth, true love, and family.

The ability to make choices becomes tied to the ideal of personal empowerment because there are so many individuals in the films who are invested in the outcome of her decision or are actively trying to limit her choices. Jacob, who is in love with Bella, insists that she does not "understand all [her] options" and that she is "rushing into it" because "she doesn't know what she wants" (*Eclipse*). Bella explains to both Jacob and Edward that her decision is not about them but instead about what kind of life will allow her to maximize her personal fulfillment. She tells Edward, "This wasn't a choice between you and Jacob. It was between who I should be and who I am." She insists that "I'm not normal, I don't want to be" and that "I've never felt stronger and more real and more myself" (*Eclipse*). In other words, she is saying that through experiencing true love, she has found her primary source of empowerment. This passage also suggests that Bella's nonconformity and resistance to Jessica's version of careerism has put her on the path to self-actualization. In this way, opting out is portrayed as liberation from the putatively oppressive social norms that have made women unhappy and unfulfilled outside the home. At the same time, Esme (Carlisle's wife) performs the role of an aging second-wave sympathizer, lecturing a millennial girl about all the choices she has that were by and large denied to the older generation. Offering her own life as an object lesson, Esme's plea to Bella is to take advantage of all the choices that were made possible by a history of sacrifice. She explains to Bella that it is a mistake to choose a vampire life: "This is a life I would not have chosen for myself. I wish there was someone to vote no for me" (*New Moon*). For Esme, becoming a vampire was the unfortunate result of rape. She says, "I envy you. You have a choice; I didn't. And you're choosing wrong" (*Eclipse*). Bella's response is to reveal that she has given up all human aspirations, that "there's nothing I am going to want more than Edward" (*Eclipse*). As the films cultivate audience identification with Bella, this conversation suggests that from the perspective of some young women, the older generation's concept of liberation has not given adequate attention to issues of personal fulfillment (i.e., love, happiness, children, and family). In many ways, feminism is positioned on the opposite end of the spectrum from love and happiness. Older women (failed feminists) let dissatisfaction with their own lives ruin a younger generation's opportunities to find contentment. They stand in the way of progress toward a new vision of feminism that includes all potential political, social, and familial arrangements. Bella's defiance of Jacob, Edward, Esme, Jessica, and others amplifies the significance of making choices—regardless of outcome—in order to achieve liberation.

Breaking Dawn 2 concludes the saga with confirmation that Bella did, in fact, make the right choice. The film focuses on the birth of Bella's daughter (Renesmee or "Nessie") and Bella's adjustment to vampirism. The conception of the child precedes a near-fatal pregnancy that forces Edward to "turn" Bella to save her life. Bella and Nessie survive, offering each the opportunity to explore their mysterious new powers. For Bella, vampirism and motherhood transform her into a bold, assertive, and physically powerful woman. As Bella regains consciousness after her transformation, the audience is offered a vicarious experience of her rebirth through amplified sound, brightened colors, and magnified optic detail. She marvels at her own incredible strength, speed, and agility. Bella discovers that her power is the ability to shield her friends and family from other vampire powers. Nessie, who matures at an accelerated rate both physically and mentally, has the power to impart vision and perspective. This power cultivates unity and harmony among the vampires allied against the oppressive Volterra monarchy.

The construction of Bella and Nessie's powers confirms the ideological narrative emerging from postfeminist discourses that for women, "real" strength and empowerment come from motherhood, domesticity, and traditional family life. For instance, note how both sets of powers are defensive in nature and reflect an essentialist concept of feminine care. In its most simple form, Bella's motherhood and entrance into the vampiric family coincide with an innate ability to shield her family from harm. Mapped onto postfeminist discourses of motherhood, this depiction coheres with the assumed immutability of maternal instincts and the idea that motherhood is a natural source of female strength and empowerment. Bella's profound strength and confidence attest to both women's suitability for childrearing and the strength of familial institutions.

At the same time, Nessie's power bespeaks the sociopolitical unification function the image of a child purportedly provides. First, Bella chooses to continue her miraculous pregnancy despite the prospect that her half-human, half-vampire fetus could starve her to death. Still in disbelief about Bella's improbable pregnancy, Edward is terrified by folklore attesting to the monstrous nature of vampire children. As Bella's health deteriorates, Edward expresses anger over Bella's decision to continue the pregnancy without his input, declaring that "you decided this on your own" (*Breaking Dawn 1*). What ultimately convinces Edward that the pregnancy is worth the risk to Bella's life is his ability to communicate with the fetus in the womb. He tells Bella that the fetus "likes the sound of your voice" and "is good and pure." In *Breaking Dawn 2*, the infant is even able to describe to Bella her memories from the womb.

Ostensibly, the films offer an anti-abortion argument in defense of fetal personhood. Bella's choice to continue the pregnancy is supported by the fetus's incredible level of cognition and her capacity for thoughts, feelings, and memories. At the same time, the child is instrumental in Bella's rebirth as a vampire. The fetus's threat to Bella's life forces Edward to turn Bella into a vampire and thus create a family for perpetuity. The child both unifies the family and brings Bella newfound strength and fulfillment.

The child even resolves tensions between the Cullens and the Quileute nation. Jacob "imprints" on Nessie, ensuring an involuntary and unbreakable bond between the two of them. This obligates the Quileute to protect and defend the child against any external threats. Read as a kind of anti-abortion discourse, Breaking Dawn 1 and Breaking Dawn 2 suggest that fetuses are not just persons but also miracles that unify families and heal communities. Because of this, protecting them is worth risking the health and safety of the mother. This depiction diverges from the films' rhetoric of choice and aligns more closely with the anti-abortion slogan "it's a child, not a choice."

Here, Berlant's concept of "infantile citizenship" is particularly instructive. Public culture is saturated with images of fetuses, infants, and children in need of protection and in whose name laws and norms are passed that regulate the entire body politic. The child stands as a citizenship ideal, a subject who is innocent and remains unmolested by adult desires. Symbolically, the infant functions as a unification device that joins citizens in efforts to create a public that is protective of children and sanitized of anything that might be harmful or damaging to them. Nessie's supernatural abilities mirror the symbolic power of the child to unify the public in efforts to mandate that dangerous desires remain out of public view. The Volterra monarchy believes that vampire children are an abomination because they cannot control their thirst and lack the discretion needed to keep vampire life secret from human society. Breaking Dawn 2 chronicles the Cullens' efforts to enlist the supernatural world—wolves included—to defend the child. The Cullens' herculean endeavor to protect Nessie and the significant risks they assume when confronting the Volterra regime suggest that children are a community's raison d'être. Nessie's birth restructures the supernatural universe around the image of the innocent child in need of protection. In the name of the child, the Cullens and their allies prepare to go to war, quite possibly risking complete annihilation. The post-Volterra world would supplant adult desires, institutions, and practices with familial bonds and a sense of community structured around the image of the child. For the first time, the vampire world will consider building families of "blood"—in the sense of human reproduction—rather than families of convenience. The introduction of children and traditional motherhood helps complete the Cullens' moral and familial development.

Whither the Public Life?

The Cullens' long lifespan and Alice's psychic abilities have enabled them to accumulate a vast private fortune and live unburdened by the economic strictures of work. They drive expensive cars, wear high-end clothing, jet around the world, and live in a spectacular home that features glass walls, refined artwork, and all the outward signs of conspicuous consumption. The postmodern aesthetic of the Cullen home provides a stark contrast with Count Dracula's medieval fortification in the remote landscape of Gothic Romania. This contrast illustrates yet another significant transformation in vampire folklore that is in many ways unique to the *Twilight* films. Unlike vampires who have been damned—by both social convention and supernatural curse—to a marginal existence as social outcasts, the Cullens have attained nearly all of human society's autonomy and consumer comforts. The family's home is not Dracula's prison-tomb but instead a beautiful sanctuary where the Cullens can enjoy private luxury. Their abode even has luxuries that are unnecessary for vampires, such as a kitchen and beds, presumably to create an impression of normality. Ironically, Edward notes that the glass-walled home is actually the "one place you don't have to hide" (*Twilight*). After marriage, Edward and Bella are allowed to retreat to their own idyllic cottage, adjacent to the Cullens' home, where they can have their privacy. By the standard of the American Dream, the Cullens' lifestyle is desirable and worthy of emulation, characterized by private luxury, personal mobility, and wholesomeness. In many ways, the Cullens are the all-American family: they value the family structure, live by the standards of traditional morality, and even enjoy baseball.

The wealth and freedom of the vampire life cast doubt on the notion that living in the midst of human society is even desirable. In the *Twilight* saga, the home is a sanctuary from dangerous and sinful desires of human society. The Cullens' provisional participation in public life is designed to camouflage their affliction and support their private existence as a family. They insist on keeping their identities private, or in Edward's words, "we do not make a spectacle of ourselves" (*New Moon*). They do not express nostalgia or a yearning desire for social enfranchisement. They do not want to make their identities public, nor do they want to transform social attitudes about vampires or advocate for political ideals of greater equality and inclusivity. They have harnessed their own social exclusion to make a comfortable private life that is sheltered, moral, and timeless. The Cullens' ability to craft an idyllic home in spite of social exclusion suggests that family—rather than civil society or the individual—is the most basic building block of the polity. The unintended yet positive results of marginalization have revealed that privatization is the remedy for collective social problems. Unlike the vampires in *True Blood*, who attempt to "mainstream" by "coming out of the coffin" to live publicly visible lives that might transform the social stigma against them and contribute to the social good, the vampires of the *Twilight* saga prefer to keep their identities and interests private. At the same time, the Cullens' undeniable financial success is a panegyric to the social myths about universal upward mobility, that personal initiative and hard work, buttressed by the gendered division of labor in the home, guarantee success and fulfillment. The films project a fantasy of the total privatization of social life in which the family supports private moral development and provides social stability.

If the Cullen family represents the ideals of privatization, then Bella's choice to join the family symbolizes her rejection of a public life. As a vampire, Bella is required to sever all ties with the ephemeral community of humankind, including her friends and loved ones. At best, her attempts to maintain ties with Charlie are forced and self-defeating. But Bella's retreat from human society is ultimately compensated for with a life of unlimited mobility, privileged class status, and eternal youth. While the human world that represents the public is a place tainted by desire, the vampire life allows Bella to live without constraints, including a life of refinement, opulence, and virtue. The films offer a utopian vision of motherhood without the societal constraints of financial resources, physical labor, aging, and the so-called forced choice between career and motherhood. In the Cullen sanctuary, Bella can experience motherhood without its attendant struggles and, above all, without competition from other potential sources of fulfillment.

The films' representation of domestic bliss resolves many of the criticisms that can be leveled against a young woman who chooses to marry so young. This is significant in light of the fact that early marriage has recently been added to the abstinence movement's agenda. Advocates argue that early marriage clarifies that the goal of abstinence is to produce stable families and honor God's will.[53] Some defenders of the practice contend that the typical problems with early marriage are actually the result of financial difficulties, immaturity, and mismatched relationships. Early marriage not only decreases the length of the postponement of the initiation of sexual relations and sexual fulfillment, it also jumpstarts the process of building Christian family structures. In this context, what is remarkable about the *Twilight* films is that they make early marriage appear both feasible and desirable. For Bella and Edward, finances will never be a concern. Edward's old age and Bella's old soul resolve any concerns that the couple is not mature enough for marriage. Most of all, the construction of Edward and Bella as soul mates would suggest that their marriage is not one of convenience or an arrangement designed to satiate their physical desires. Without specific scriptural references, their union provides an exemplary model for the early-marriage platform. The films' heavy emphasis on marriage and family stability is a fitting complement to the related imperative of remaining pure.

Finally, Bella and Edward's idyllic marriage and domestic life buy into the abstinence movement's "Prince Charming" effect. According to books such as *Before You Meet Prince Charming*, *Raising Maidens of Virtue*, and *The Princess and the Kiss*, girls must remain sexually pure if they want to eventually marry a prince.[54] Abstinence literature promises young girls romantic fairy-tale weddings followed by a life of luxury in the care of a rich and handsome man. Beverly LaHaye argues that nothing could be more natural: "Girls are romantic. From early childhood, their fantasies are of Prince Charming, not sex. Ask a five-year-old girl playing with her dolls what she wants to be when she grows up and she will probably say, 'a mommy.' She automatically thinks of family and childhood. Ask a five-year-old boy, and his answer will almost never be 'a father.' He thinks in vocational terms of being a fireman, a policeman or a ball player."[55] This literature suggests that the desire for a royal wedding followed by domestic cocooning is hardwired into women's nature. However, this goal is attainable only if girls save their virginity as a gift for their husbands on their wedding night. Edward and Bella's fairy-tale wedding and domestic comforts sustain this Prince Charming mythology. Edward, the mysterious but alluring gentleman, sweeps Bella off her feet to an eternal life of domestic bliss that is unburdened by financial constraints. Bella's self-restraint before marriage and her retreat from a public existence after marriage is well compensated by the care and protection of her mythical prince. As with purity literature, the *Twilight* films invite young women to set aside their aspirations and physical desires for the fantasy of Prince Charming.

Savagery and Civilization

The notion of "true womanhood" has always been accompanied by an idealized construction of white masculinity that is demonstratively chivalrous, protective, and ruggedly individualistic. For purity advocates, too, "real men" are "strong, respectful, and courageous."[56] According to one abstinence textbook, simply stated, "a man protects."[57] Similarly, mannerly and ascetic self-restraint was a defining feature of Victorian manhood. However, masculine violence was appropriate if society deemed it to be vital to the defense of feminine virtue. In the name of "saving women," white men have excused innumerable acts of barbarism and conquest, including the lynching of African American men, massacres of Native Americans, and global military interventions.[58] White masculine violence in defense of women is often predicated on the myth of a hypersexualized Other with diminished mental capacities and an innate inability to exercise moral and physical self-restraint. The clash between the civilized white male and the dark-skinned savage also provides a point of contrast that illustrates the incommensurability of Western and non-Western values, the presumed triumph of the former over the latter. Although this construction of hegemonic masculinity necessitates curtailing women's autonomy in the name of protection, it is often shrouded in decontextualized appeals to Western feminism in order to "save brown women from brown men."[59]

Throughout the *Twilight* saga, Edward invokes the threat of dark masculinity as an excuse for violence and control. Implicitly, the competition between Edward and Jacob is a racialized conflict between a civilized Euro-American sense of manliness and primitive indigenous masculinity. The films enact a neocolonial drama in which a mythic white hero is summoned to protect women's virtue against the marauding sexuality of a dark-skinned Other.[60] After a violent competition for Bella, Edward subdues Jacob and neutralizes the threat the Quileute wolves pose to his family. Jacob's inevitable acquiescence to Edward (for the sake of mother and child) symbolizes the putative choice of indigenous men in a colonized world: assimilate or go extinct. Edward symbolizes the colonizing force of Western civilization, inexorably conquering the supposedly inferior indigenous peoples in its path. Even the provisional treaty between vampires and wolves, which protects the Quileute territory from vampire incursions, is ostensibly discarded in Bella's defense. This colonial subtext is thinly veiled: Edward is a refined Victorian gentlemen and Jacob is an indigenous male, capable of taking animal form, living among a tribal society more closely connected to the land.[61] Whereas stylish dress and shining white skin characterize the Cullens, wolves are frequently represented by their muscular physiques and animalistic instincts. For instance, Jacob and his pack are frequently depicted shirtless in primitive wilderness, where they engage in competitive displays of physical prowess, primal athleticism, and hulking physiques. Their savage masculinity is also symbolized by their rage—manifest in frequent transformations to animal form—and their "heat," an exceptional kind of hot-bloodedness connected to their animal identities. The films overemphasize the wolves' brooding masculinity by almost exclusively representing them as pubescent young men with a musty and repellant odor. While the Cullens are clean and refined, the Quileute are wild, dirty, and full of rage. As Jacob says in *Breaking Dawn 2*, "it's a wolf thing."

The distinction between civilized vampires and savage wolves is also reflected in their disparate political and social structures. The films conflate antiquated European governance structures with civilization and Native American forms of social organization with pack-animal behavior. The vampire world is governed by a medieval-style European monarchy, complete with royalty, nobility, feudal patronage, and territorial vassals across the world that

FIGURE 4. The Quileute pack members display their physical prowess. *The Twilight Saga: New Moon.* DVD. Directed by Chris Weitz. Universal City, CA: Summit Entertainment, 2013.

ostensibly sustain a global empire. In contrast, wolves maintain a loose tribal structure in which alpha males and elders are at the top of the hierarchy. In contrast to Euro-American courtship rituals, romantic coupling in Quileute life is based on an animalistic instinct that compels individuals to "imprint" on one another and thus bond to one another for life. By portraying Native Americans as shape-shifting wolves governed by primal impulses, the films suggest that tribal life and governance structures mirror the social organization of pack animals. The Quileute people are constructed as "noble savages," enviable for their wisdom and connection to the land yet deplorable for their attachment to a barbaric way of life that remains trapped in a distant and irretrievable past. Thus, the films replicate the binary distinction between nature and culture that Patricia Hill Collins has argued is at the heart of American racism and colonialism: culture arises from humankind's ability to subjugate nature and indigenous people (who are indistinct from nature) must be conquered or assimilated.[62] The Western nature/culture binary archetype codes nature as feminine, waiting to be subdued by masculine forces and cultivated as private property;[63] hence the colonialist construction of the Native American lands of North America as "virgin," "pristine," "untouched," "pure," "open," and "vacant."[64] The Quileute land and way of life are governed by the kinds of primitive instincts of an inferior masculinity that humans and vampires subdued or abandoned to develop more advanced ways of life.[65]

The confluence of racial ideology and hegemonic masculinity excuses Edward's sadism. Furthermore, the films' preoccupation with Bella's choice between two romantic relationships overlooks the masculine violence perpetrated in her name. Edward's violence is directed not only at Jacob but also at a number of other licentious vampires who share a thirst for Bella's intoxicating blood. The films cultivate a sense of constant danger from predatory men and invite audiences to sympathize with Edward's compulsive need to protect Bella. This ever-present threat of savage masculinity to Bella's purity warrants Edward's violent and manipulative impulses and even codes his actions as valiant and romantic. Of course, Bella's purity is the pretext for a male "protection racket" that offers her safety and security from "bad men" at the cost of her freedom and autonomy.[66] Bella's purity, symbolized by the strange potency of her blood, unwittingly invites sexual aggression and violence from bad vampires (James, Laurent, and Victoria) when she moves without the protection of Edward. Thus, the films appeal to a neocolonial notion of manhood to save women from both savage men and themselves.

The Joys of Repression

The refurbished vampires of the *Twilight* saga are dreadfully banal. Their normality would not be noteworthy if it were not for their allegiance to a utopian vision of a moral order before the sexual revolution challenged repression on a cultural scale and before feminism made the personal political. Why is this the vampire we need? Mary Hallab suggests that perhaps part of the answer is that American culture no longer needs the vampire to unburden it from repression.[67] Part of her rationale is that American culture is "oversexed," that the ubiquitous hypersexualization promoted by advertising and celebrity culture, the frank sex talk of lifestyle magazines, the paternity crisis depicted on self-help television, among other examples, have rendered sexuality commonplace in public culture. As a malleable symbol with sexual connotations, could it be that the vampire of an oversexed culture is a mysterious outsider only if she or he promotes abstinence and the traditional family?

Part of the answer is less about the "oversexing" of American culture than it is about the depoliticization of sex and sexuality that has accompanied postfeminist culture. As Ariel Levy argues, sexual issues in public discourse have been untethered from feminist reproductive politics so that participating in *Girls Gone Wild* videos and other aspects of what she calls "raunch culture" fall under the banner of "my body, my choice."[68] What makes this all the more confusing is that the abstinence movement has also appropriated postfeminist discourses to argue that choosing virginity until marriage is a statement of bodily autonomy, or true feminism. Either way, the politics of sexuality and sexual identities are redacted from public discussion about sex acts.[69] The problem is not oversexing per se but rather that oversexing is mistaken for sexual liberation. Oversexing becomes the reason for the creation of a new vampire who is sexy without being sexual. The *Twilight* saga's vampire is a perfect synthesis of two disparate and contradictory public attitudes about sex that culminates in a perplexing adage that "chastity is sexy."[70] The Cullens—attractive but wholesome—symbolize how repressed sexual desire can be redirected and assimilated into a nostalgic vision of family values. The *Twilight* saga does not repudiate sex but instead reconciles sexual desire with traditional morality. It is a message attuned to young girls immersed in abstinence education: sexual pleasure is dangerous unless it is expressed within the confines of a monogamous heterosexual marriage. In other words, "it" is worth the wait.

Finally, the freedom and fulfillment experienced by the new vampire reflect a profound cynicism about living a public life. The curse of the Gothic vampire was that she or he was banished from society, forced to live for eternity as an outcast. Although they were mysterious and powerful, vampires' ostracism from normal human society presumably constituted an existence that no one would choose to have. The desirability of modern vampire life is attuned to the ongoing privatization of citizenship, or the relocation of civic duties and public goods to the individual and the family.[71] The Cullens display a home life that is the sole source of personal fulfillment and social support, particularly for women. The advantage of a vampire life is that it is free from the demands of civic responsibility and the material constraints of labor. They project a fantasy of total privatization. For women, this necessitates readjusting their definition of success and personal satisfaction to revolve around being a wife and mother.

This message is not much different from religious discourses that call on women not to attend college so they can train for domesticity. In 2013, Fix the Family, a Catholic-centered advocacy organization that promulgates traditional family values, posted a controversial article in which the group provided "6 (+2) reasons to NOT send your daughter to college."[72] The premise was not all that different from the reasons Bella chose a vampire life with Edward: the world outside the home is dangerous and sinful, girls in contemporary society cannot learn how to be good wives and mothers, careerism is unfulfilling, and girls should not have anything to prove to the world. Bella's adventures flesh out the notion that "cocooning" can be a source of female empowerment. Retreating to the newly refurbished vampire life makes the pain and suffering of sex, dating, and careerism obsolete.

2

Man-Boys and Born-Again Virgins

The 40-Year-Old Virgin (2005)

Late at night after work, four men sit around a poker table drinking beer and swapping stories of sexual conquest and raunchy adventures. The group goads Andy, a self-professed "gentleman" who does not "kiss and tell," to share "the nastiest shit you've ever done." As he struggles to contrive a story perverse enough to satisfy his friends—at one point comparing a woman's breast to a "bag of sand"—the group realizes that this "gentleman's" fledgling and defensive attempts to project his sexual prowess are the result of his sexual inexperience. An anomaly among contemporary bachelors, Andy is a virgin at age forty. His late-in-life chastity is neither elective nor pious; it is the outcome of a defeatist malaise that set in following a series of traumatic emasculations during his youth at the hands of sexually empowered women. For Andy, the instability of courtship norms, the dissolution of traditional gender roles, and the hypersexualization of his social world have made sex a source of neurosis and confusion. Unlike his male co-workers who seek fulfillment through serial dating, Andy still lives in a world where he spends his leisure time with video games, comic books, and action figures. The vicissitudes of sexual desire prompted Andy to retreat to a preadolescent world where women remain a mysterious Other and physical urges are displaced by childlike pleasures. With his shameful secret now public, Andy is left with no choice but to be inducted into the culture of dating—with his co-workers as guides—if he is to recover his enfeebled manhood and find his proper place in the heterosexual order.

The 40-Year-Old Virgin (directed by Judd Apatow) is a 2005 romantic comedy that depicts the travails of Andy (Steve Carell) in his efforts to overcome his fear of intimacy and enter the ranks of adulthood. Andy is aided by three sexually experienced but ultimately dysfunctional male co-workers who provide him with dating advice, sex tips, and male camaraderie as he navigates the per-plexing terrain of contemporary dating and explores the supposedly enigmatic desires of the modern woman. The incongruence of a forty-year-old man with boyish sexual inexperience produces a series of awkward comedic tensions that are amplified by the failures of his friends' conflicting and often-disastrous dating advice. Andy's sexual woes are resolved through an uncomfortable but wholesome courtship with Trish (Catherine Keener), who helps Andy transcend his adolescent lifestyle. While he struggles with how he will reveal his secret to her, Trish's insistence on holding off a physical relationship provides spec-tators with a contrasting take on chastity in which abstinence until marriage provides a pathway to personal vitality and social stability late in life, even after decades of failure. In the end, the film resolves the male characters' sexual mal-adjustments with a return to traditional coupling, monogamy, marriage, and family. After Andy consummates his marriage to Trish and experiences sexual ecstasy for the first time, the cast—newly coupled and fulfilled—performs a ren-dition of the song "Age of Aquarius" from the 1960s countercultural musical *Hair*. Andy's secret provides an occasion for introducing the neurotic man-boy to the deep fulfillment of ritual courtship.

Instead of repudiating abstinence, *The 40-Year-Old Virgin* offers it as a potential remedy for the confusing sexual norms of a culture destabilized by the presence of active female desire and fluid gender roles. The film expresses supreme dissatisfaction with the culture of casual dating and invites audi-ences to consider if there is not an alternative that is less confusing and more wholesome. Thus, in its indictment of dating and its valorization of a sexually moral protagonist, *The 40-Year-Old Virgin* refashions abstinence messages to address grown adults. Increasingly, abstinence advocates have been pursuing new ways to extend the concept of purity beyond populations of teenagers and young adults. One motivating factor for this strategic adjustment is that new studies show that 80 percent of evangelical Christians aged 18 to 29 report that they have engaged in premarital sex.[1] Since Christians (and non-Christians) are dating, delaying marriage, and even having premarital sex, the abstinence movement not only stresses the benefits of later-in-life virginity but has also capitalized on the concept of "born-again" or "secondary" virginity.[2] Ostensibly, secondary virgins recommit to chastity after engaging in premarital sex so that they can attain a fresh start in pursuit of marriage. Laura Carpenter notes that both secular and Christian communities introduced the concept of second-ary virginity following "the late-1960s shift toward more permissive standards of virginity."[3] Secondary virginity is a personal makeover that promises redemp-tion and satisfaction for individuals who may have faltered in their efforts to remain pure.[4] The concept reminds adults that purity is a lifelong pursuit for both men and women. Displaying the benefits of late-in-life and secondary virginity, *The 40-Year-Old Virgin* addresses how individuals can remake their sex lives despite their past failures.

The 40-Year-Old Virgin represents how abstinence can be marketed to adults, especially men. The overarching message is that secondary virginity can remake adult men beleaguered by the confusing norms of a sex-saturated culture. Whether characters are chaste or sexually promiscuous, the film suggests that all the characters' maladjustments and childish immaturities are a result of a post–sexual revolution ethos in which men's traditional courtship rituals have been supplanted with a more active and autonomous female sexuality. Like similar romantic comedies, the film's irreverence and gross-out humor draw attention away from the text's more conservative elements, namely its efforts to tame female sexual agency, eschew queer and homosocial desire, and instruct audiences in the benefits of monogamy, neotraditional romance, and late-in-life virginity. This chapter explores how the cinematic portrayal of secondary virginity in the romantic comedy genre promises to turn comically enfeebled man-boys into wholesome breadwinning men. Secondary virginity offers a new portrait of romance in which abstinence can instill weak men and overly empowered women with the forgotten family values of 1950s America.

The Post–Sex Revolution Man-Boy

With the help of co-writer Steve Carell, *The 40-Year-Old Virgin* translated Judd Apatow's comically dysfunctional beta male from his earlier television endeavors in *Freaks and Geeks* (1999–2000) and *Undeclared* (2001–2003) into what has become a cinematic subgenre of flawed men in maladjusted romance. As director, writer, and producer, Apatow displays a lead male who is typically either suspended in a state of adolescence[5] or alienated from conventional forms of hegemonic masculinity.[6] Exemplified in *The 40-Year-Old Virgin*, Apatow's version of the romantic comedy invites audiences to experience the humorous difficulties of love, sex, and relationships from the perspective of the self-conscious melodramatic male. This particularly dysfunctional man-boy provides a stark contrast to the neurotic confidence man in need of object lessons in "what women want."[7] While physically an adult, the melodramatic man-boy is emotionally underdeveloped, behaviorally immature, and riddled with the self-doubt of adolescence.

Since 2000, the man-boy has been sufficiently present in cinema for scholars to observe this character's contribution to the species of the "neotraditional" romantic comedy, an ironic and self-consciously styled satirization of the "chick flick" designed to reach male audiences.[8] With the man-boy at its epicenter, the neotraditional romantic comedy disabuses audiences of the myths of true love and creates space for men to express their anxieties about sex, dating, and the precariousness of homosocial bonds. But despite their confessions of masculine ineptitude, these films recuperate a mythos of manhood that takes into account this comically stunted and newly feminized male. Film scholars have invented a number of neologisms for this recent elaboration of the genre, including "bromance,"[9] "homme coms,"[10] "dude films,"[11] and "animal comedies."[12] While Jeffers McDonald argues that this take on the romantic comedy "seems more numerous than influential," the film's critical acclaim and popular reception—along with Apatow's continued successful elaboration of this character type—suggest that this version of masculinity resonates in the present social context of sex, love, and relationships.[13]

The 40-Year-Old Virgin explicitly takes up the question of how four adult men can be so emotionally and sexually dysfunctional after so many years of asking the question "what do women want?" *The 40-Year-Old Virgin* brings the man-boy into focus by giving attention to the root causes of his malaise and the kind of solutions that might bring him back into the masculine fold. The film suggests that both casual sex and abstinence are flip sides of the same coin, that the fluidity of gender roles and courtship norms have enfeebled the contemporary male, and that they are looking for love in all the wrong places. In fact, popular critics received the film as an indictment of the oversexing of the contemporary male that was endearing for its displacement of casual sex with the pleasures and stability of romantic coupling. One reviewer wrote, "Sex has become so desacralized, it seems hard to believe that anyone, especially an apparently healthy man living in the age of Madonna and Maxim, Pamela and Paris, has managed to avoid getting some with someone, somewhere, at some point."[14] Michael O'Sullivan observed that the "movie's real accomplishment, particularly in this indulgence-saturated society, is in its depiction of celibacy."[15] Many of the reviews noted that Andy is in some ways more functional and well adjusted than his co-workers. For instance, David Denby noted that Andy's friends are "even more screwed up in their relations with women than he is, and delusional as well."[16]

While the film exploits the gross-out humor of casual sex and adolescent behavior, it concludes with the man-boy abandoning the world of juvenile pleasures for the kind of fulfillment derived from traditional coupling, a staple of the "chick flick" romantic comedy.[17] The recuperation of masculinity through the abject male body in contemporary cinema presents the juxtaposition of the sensitive male and revolting humor in neotraditional romantic comedies (scatological jokes, ejaculate, and other playful depictions of bodily fluids).[18] Claire Sisco King notes how depictions of abject masculinity—the revolting and wounded male body—disavow without fundamentally displacing or interrogating white hegemonic masculinity. She writes that "masculinity is itself an abject 'body' whose perpetuation and expansion depend upon its ability to open up, double itself, and transgress its own boundaries in a process I name 'abject hegemony.'"[19] While other scholars have illustrated that white masculinity is perpetuated through the absorption of Otherness (i.e., femininity, blackness),[20] King's analysis makes sense of the sentimental beta male's perplexing high stature as a new form of hegemonic masculinity. In other words, his insecurities and revolting torments enable hegemonic white masculinity to "remain amalgamated and diffuse."[21] The sensitive man-boy demonstrates not the failure but the elusiveness of hegemonic masculinity in the face of threats and challenges.

Though suddenly ubiquitous in cinema, the man-boy was decades in the making. His assimilation into the romantic comedy is responsive, if not reactionary, to the gender reversals brought about by feminism and the sexual revolution. Thus, as John Albert suggests, the "bromance" presents "an internal struggle of the male characters with their understandings of their identities and roles as men."[22] The ambivalence of the neotraditional romantic comedy enables such films to accommodate two opposing forces: men's need for gender security and an evolving articulation of masculinity tied to play and leisure. These films acknowledge the complicated nature of romance and the pleasure and potential fulfillment of sex and dating for both men and women. They often begin with a demystified depiction of men that disavows the stoic post–World War II portrait of breadwinner masculinity and replaces it with a male who is deeply flawed but nonetheless endearing because of his postfeminist sensitivity and playful anxiety about sex, gender, and heterosexuality. However, such films also channel these anxieties into the old fantasy of heterosexual monogamy and, quite often, marriage and family.

The 40-Year-Old Virgin's iteration of the man-boy places his roots in the modality of masculinity that took hold as both a reaction to and accommodation of feminism and the sexual revolution. It is a flawed character type that calls for some concept, such as secondhand virginity, to save him. Michael Kimmel notes that in the 1960s, the "masculine mystique" was exposed as a source of discontent, strain, and conflict.[23] James Gilbert adds that beginning in the previous decade, there was a growing sense that the cult of manliness was quite literally killing men.[24] Long hours at work, limited leisure time, and lack of self-care associated with breadwinner masculinity had produced not only widespread alienation but also poor health and shorter life-spans. While mens' suffering was by no means commensurate with that of women, many men expressed enthusiasm for a revision of manliness that had been forged through trials of manliness such as hard work, self-denial, and virility. The adult trappings of work and family life had left little room for the productive play and self-actualization that for many characterized male youth.

One response to this crisis in masculinity was the 1960s "playboy" promulgated by bachelor evangelist Hugh Hefner, which repackaged traditional manhood as sophistication, leisure, and self-interest.[25] The "playboy" male found satisfaction beyond marriage and the family with interests in fine wine, cuisine, art, sports, and culture. Since developing sophisticated interests and leisure activities was sutured to an ethic of play and self-gratification, virility and sexual conquest were ultimately central features of the playboy lifestyle. Of course, this new sophisticated bachelor would require a population of unattached and sexually available young women. Therefore, the playboy found promise in select feminist and countercultural discourses that indicted marriage and monogamy and called for women's sexual independence. As many feminist scholars have argued, sexual liberation ostensibly only augmented the sexual practices of women, since many men had been engaging in casual sex and adultery for some time.[26]

The newly liberated male interpreted the counterculture as an accompaniment to an "alternative male ethic" in which play, pleasure, and sex were all available on demand for men.[27] The sexual revolution, feminism, and the advent of the pill disentangled sex from both reproduction and heterosexual marriage but left in place an older misogyny in which women's sexual subservience and availability were assumed. Feminist resistance to sexual objectification dashed the playboy's hopes that the emerging counterculture would channel sexual liberation into the perfect accompaniment to the bachelor lifestyle.[28] For many men, the counterculture's emphasis on sexual liberation and the feminist movement's demand for sexual autonomy cultivated both a confusing mixture of pleasurable enticement and daunting fear of an active female sexuality. Kimmel writes that "if women could now be more fully sexual, then men might fear sexual activity as a constant test, a 'trial of manliness' that would find men perpetually wanting."[29] The prospect of male feminization in the bedroom and the workplace, or worse, that sex might become a test of masculinity, led some heterosexual men to vacillate toward homosocial bonding in spaces without the emasculating presence of women (bars, men's lodges, gymnasiums, fraternal orders, and clubs).

Ultimately, the playboy vision of bachelorhood sowed more self-doubt in men than it did confidence. Carrie Pitzulo observes that "in an era of expanding consumption and shifting gender standards, *Playboy* prodded male readers to scrutinize themselves, and potentially each other, with a self-consciousness usually reserved for women."[30] Playboy masculinity was plagued by a consumerist compulsion for self-improvement, a relentless pursuit to demonstrate use value and attractiveness to the discerning modern woman. As a precursor to the modern metrosexual lifestyle, the imperatives of contemporary bachelorhood in some ways feminized men by forcing them to attend to their personal appearance, home decor, and consumer goods. Faludi characterize the unraveling of postwar masculinity as a product of "ornamental culture," where institutions that made men indispensable—industrial labor, politics, and military service—were replaced with visual spectacles of glamour, entertainment, and consumerism. Indeed, "the more productive aspects of manhood, such as building or cultivating or contributing to a society, couldn't establish a foothold on the shiny flat surface of a commercial culture, a looking glass before which men could only act out a crude semblance of masculinity."[31]

This transformation in hegemonic masculinity makes sense of the contemporary man-boy: an enfeebled postindustrial male who finds purpose in modeling celebrity images of manhood and chasing consumerist fantasies of compulsive self-improvement, his focus directed toward sex, play, and leisure. The residual effect of feminism, sexual liberation, and ornamental masculinity, this perplexing mix of excitement and revulsion continues to addle the cinematic man-boy of the post–sexual revolution era. The man-boy, a staple of the contemporary neotraditional romantic comedy, is a sex enthusiast who takes feminism as a given yet remains anxious about his place in the heterosexual order and confused about how to respond to women's power and equality. Obsessed with some combination of play, self-interest, homosocial bonding, and serial dating, the cinematic man-boy repudiates traditional breadwinner masculinity by extending the youthful pleasures of adolescence into adulthood. In one sense, the man-boy refuses feminization by engaging in "bromance," a rediscovery of recuperative male bonding that counteracts the emasculating pressures of marriage and parenting in an age of nominal equality.[32] Appropriating feminine character traits enables these men to overcome their deep ambivalence about postfeminism masculinity with a nod to the idea that both traditional masculinity and feminism have created a happiness deficit for men as well as women. And when it comes to happiness and fulfillment, the man-boy can be just as sensitive as a woman.[33]

What is unstated is that both of these moves counteract the agency and empowerment imparted by certain aspects of sexual liberation and proscribes the old patriarchy as the way out for men enfeebled by feminism. Though without explicitly stating so, these films suggest that the oversexing of the American female outside the traditional family has ruined and confused men. But these films' deployment of irreverence and gross-out humor belies their neoconservative impulses. Whereas a film such as *Annie Hall* (1974) concludes with the humorous undesirability of traditional coupling, a neotraditional romantic comedy such as *The 40-Year-Old-Virgin* concludes with the undesirability of perpetual adolescence for men and the need for them to grow into heterosexual monogamy, be they playboys or virgins.[34] Ultimately, secondary virginity promises to remake American cinema's flawed man-boys. Audiences are invited to view Andy's late-in-life abstinence as a model of stability in a culture obsessed with sex and casual dating.

Boys Gone Mild

The 40-Year-Old-Virgin is unique among neotraditional romantic comedies because it portrays the man-boy on both ends of a reactionary spectrum. On one end is the sex-obsessed, unattached male (Jay, Cal, and David) who has been rendered dysfunctional and perpetually adolescent by his disavowal of traditional work and family life. These men are juvenile and self-interested, working in ostensibly dead-end service-industry jobs, and their primary preoccupation is serial dating and male bonding. They are the 1960s "playboy" without any of his "sophistication." These characters translate their insecurity over destabilized gender roles and their lack of upward mobility into juvenile hijinks and sexual adventurism. On the other end of the spectrum is the callow and frightened male (Andy) whose response to women's empowerment has been to retreat into the childlike behaviors of adolescent boys: toys, action figures, comic books, and video games. Andy's late-in-life virginity is the result of an unclear model of masculinity and the presence of a confusing and active female sexuality. By the end of the film, his abstinence is an attribute that forms the basis of a new expression of wholesome masculinity.

Andy's stunted personal development is reflected in the film's mise-en-scène. While the title cues audiences to the film's central comedic tension, the

FIGURE 5. Andy and Trish have a wholesome, old-fashioned date. *The 40-Year-Old Virgin*. DVD. Directed by Judd Apatow. Universal City, CA: Universal Home Entertainment, 2005.

establishing shots of Andy's apartment reveal his repressed adolescent melancholy. Meticulously constructed of boyhood film and television memorabilia, vintage toys, comic books, video games, and action figures, Andy's teenage bedroom is full of objects related to the forms of play and leisure that preoccupy boys before teenage sexual exploration.[35] His immaturity and repressed sexual desire are grafted onto his bodily habits and the walls of his apartment. Audiences are introduced to Andy as he awakens beneath a five-foot-tall poster of a cylindrical spaceship, its phallic imagery playfully mirroring Andy's own painfully inconvenient morning erection. Andy alleviates the pain of his unacknowledged physical urges and maintains his bodily vitality with comically retro exercise routines and a meticulously self-prepared breakfast.

These establishing shots illustrate that adolescent play and pleasure are both the cause and consequence of Andy's "problem." Namely, Andy has overinvested in adolescence as compensation for his deficits. As Cal (Seth Rogen) explains to him later in the film, "You've got to see this through the eyes of a woman. What is she going to think when she comes in here?" After all, he concludes, "none of this shit is sexy." Andy's asexuality is amplified by the fact that he rides a bike, works at a low-skilled job in an electronics megastore, and spends his leisure time either alone playing video games or drinking soda and watching reality television with his elderly neighbors. Even his octogenarian friends lament, "That guy needs to get laid." Yet as much as audiences may desire to see Andy finally lose his virginity, it is precisely his sexual inexperience that makes him endearing, not to mention that he is also kind, independent, and handsome. It is this tension that prompts audiences to sympathize with his prolonged lack of intimacy but without desiring him to lose his wholesomeness and vitality. In light of the fact that nearly everyone in the film is preoccupied with sex, something noble and virtuous remains about Andy's abstinence. Moreover, the initial alternatives to abstinence Andy's co-workers offer are so extreme that when the laughter subsides, the audience is left to ponder whether there is a better way to reintroduce Andy to the rituals of heterosexuality.

The sexual debauchery of Andy's co-workers provides a radical counterpoint to Andy's endearing yet disabling anxieties. Indeed, the opposite end of the spectrum—characterized by casual sex, perversion, and philandering—offers little reprieve. The man-boy's polarity is introduced when Andy and Cal share their weekend experiences at work. While Andy reveals that he spent his weekend attempting to make an egg salad sandwich, Cal relays an account of attending a "donkey show" in Tijuana, which despite the fact that it involved a "woman fucking a horse" was not "as cool as it sounds." Whereas Andy disguises his discomfort with such frank sex talk, Cal openly mocks Andy's banality by pretending to shoot himself in the head. The contrast between Andy and his co-workers comes to a head at the group's poker game, when Andy's inability to contribute a credible sex story exposes how far he lags behind the sexual experience of the average contemporary male. While the group's expression of confused sympathy and outrage suggests that male virginity is a condition or psychosis that must be overcome in order for men to function properly, each of Andy's friends displays extreme dysfunction up until the film's denouement, when they are introduced to the empowerment of secondary virginity and neo-traditional romance.

The sex stories of each member of the group reveals that these men use sex and dating to mask their deep-seated insecurities and project an image of virility that attempts to conceal their lack of upward mobility. For instance, Jay reveals that he must leave the card game early so he can cheat on his long-time girlfriend with a woman he affectionately refers to as a sexual "freak." Cal shares a personal anecdote with elements of bestiality while David recounts a moment of sexual bliss with an ex-girlfriend he continues to stalk. In this failed moment of male bonding, the film illustrates that all of these men—whether oversexed or chaste—have dysfunctional relationships with women that stem from the putatively perplexing nature of pleasure and women's sexuality. Thus, Jay proposes that Andy overcompensate for his years of abstinence by entering the gross-out cult of male dating. As the camera closes in on Andy to display his feelings of emasculation, Jay pronounces, "I want to get you laid. From now on your dick is my dick. I'm getting you some pussy." Of course, Jay's proposed solution to Andy's virginity is to simply move from disavowing women to engaging in active and depersonalized conquest in which men and women are symbolically reduced to their genitalia. Either way, the lesson is that men flounder when confronted with the modern woman, a mysterious Other who must be conquered.

Woman as Other

The film's sociopolitical explanations for its construction of woman-as-Other are rooted in the phallocentric ideology of patriarchy.[36] The film mistakes the man-boy's pathological and even abject fear of women for kind-hearted respect and reverence. Thus, Andy's horror at the sight of women—which often takes the form of gross-out humor—registers as chivalry and modesty as opposed to the kind of soft-spoken and insidious misogyny of abstinence culture. The unintelligibility of women and the dread they inspire provides the context in which Andy and his friends police and subjugate active female desire.

It is instructive that Andy's supposed respect for women never translated into platonic friendships or even pleasant banter with female customers, whom he also visibly avoids in several scenes.[37] Instead, Andy goes to great lengths to construct a world in which women are ostensibly absent. Yet Andy insists that he holds women in high esteem. He tells David, "You know what, I respect women. I respect them so much that I completely stay away from them." However, even as Andy insists that he has a more fulfilling life without women, the camera cuts to scenes of him playing a tuba and marching by himself, painting miniature figurines, playing video games, singing karaoke solo, and reading comic books. He tells David that when it comes to sex, "it just never happened. When I was young, I tried and it didn't happen. And, then I got older and I got more nervous because it hadn't happened and then I got kind of weirded out about it and then it really didn't happen. Then, I don't know I just kind of stopped trying." His celibacy is not without reason or explanation; Andy admits that early-in-life confusion about sex and courtship rituals fomented a reactionary impulse to run away from women entirely.

Andy, who is age 40 in 2005, would have come of age in the early 1980s, when women's liberation encountered the backlash of the Reagan Revolution. While the film only makes oblique references to Andy's past, it is significant that the time period for Andy's sexual experimentation was at the dawn of the post–sexual revolution era, a time when conservatives actively sought to contain women's sexual agency and independence. Andy fears a specific type of figure: the sexually empowered woman. A flashback montage in which a youthful Andy is humiliated by his encounters with sexually active women confirms the unique source of his pathology. Scenes include an encounter with a young girl whose brace-filled mouth invokes the specter of painful oral sex. Another scene features a woman who scoffs at Andy's failed attempts to remove her bra followed by an embarrassing episode of premature ejaculation. The final cut portrays coitus interrupted when a ticklish Andy accidentally kicks a sexually adventuresome young woman in the face. Andy is haunted by her admonishment that he "give up forever." Andy's misadventures indict the culture of dating and hookups, providing a rationale for avoiding the painful and embarrassing first time while one is young and unmarried.

Perhaps what is most striking is the fact that the film implies that Andy's fear of women also stems from a more universal castration anxiety—be it literal (in the cutting mouth of a young girl) or symbolic (the comic loss of his phallic potency in the presence of a judgmental and sexually attractive young woman). The film even attributes Andy's present youthfulness and physical vitality to his avoidance of castrating women. David remarks to Cal, "He looks younger than us but he's ten years older. You know why? It's because he's never had a relationship. No she-devil sucked his life-force out yet." The sexually empowered female born of women's liberation is thus akin to the mythic succubus who drains men's potency for its perverse pleasures. In some ways, Andy's male comrades can empathize with this universal fear of the castrating bitch. As it is represented, casual sex can drain a man's life force and potency.

The film's humor belies its phallocentric misogyny. As Andy enters the cult of male dating, he is confronted by an image of woman as threatening Other, or in Creed's terms, a vision of "woman that is shocking, terrifying, horrific, abject."[38] Throughout the film, this threat comes in a variety of forms: castration anxiety, the toxicity of bodily fluids, and the simultaneously horrifying and arousing sight of female genitalia. In psychoanalytical terms, this notion of abjection refers to a state of filth, degradation, and monstrosity, a hidden or taboo element that must be repressed or cast off from the self in early childhood subject formation. Julia Kristeva explains that the self must separate from that which destroys life, the "immoral, sinister, scheming, and shady: a terror that dissembles, a hatred that smiles, a passion that uses the body for barter instead of inflaming it, a debtor who sells you up, a friend who stabs you."[39] Creed adds that abjection takes the form of "sexual immorality and perversion; corporeal alteration, decay and death; human sacrifice; murder, the corpse; bodily wastes; the feminine body and incest."[40] Here I am interested in the forms of abjection that cultivate an imperative to discipline or excise the sexual threat of the feminine, namely the monstrous image of the castrated and castrat*ing* female body. From the vantage point of the male gaze, the woman as sexual vampire or succubus registers a sexual difference and active desire that deprive the phallus of its power and potency.[41] Without providing a totalizing psychoanalytical interpretation, I will simply note that the male gaze and phallocentric ideology that develop from feminist film theory explain how this particular film amplifies the sexual threat of the liberated woman. The film traffics in the "primal uncanny" to identify what might be so threatening and horrifying about the feminine that a virile heterosexual male would opt for sexual abstinence.[42]

The film begins with shots of Andy's clothed but fully erect penis. Continuing scenes of Andy's painful morning erections reassure spectators that despite being abstinent, Andy has not been castrated and is indeed capable of intercourse. His phallus is also invoked symbolically in his refusal to play with his "hermetically sealed" collectibles because a toy, in Andy's words, "lose[s] its value if you take it out of its packaging." In the same breath that David suggests to Andy that he masturbates because he is "wound up," he compares Andy's penis (and his own) to his action figures by quipping, "I'm just saying let it out, give it some air, man, play with it." Andy panics as David reaches to open one of his action figures, for like his phallus, it will lose its potency and value after it has been used. Andy experiences this phallic panic again later in the film when his new girlfriend Trish tries to seduce him after twenty sexless dates. Trish initiates sex with Andy while his collectibles sit in boxes on her bed, ready to be shipped and sold as part of an effort to help Andy grow up. When the boxes tip, Andy retreats from Trish, obsessed with the collectibles' physical integrity.

A confused Trish exclaims: "I'm throwing myself at you and all you can think of is fucking toys." Trish, however, is mistaken in her assessment. Andy is less concerned about losing his toys than he is about the emasculation represented by breaching the toys' (and his own) virginal integrity.

In attempting to help Andy grow up, Trish threatens to excise the metonymic stand-ins for Andy's youthful vitality. Andy explains: "These are not fucking toys. This is Iron Man. I got this when I was in second grade. Do you know how hard it is for a kid to not open that? This is important. These are my things and you are trying to make me sell them and I don't want to and you're making me. You're encouraging me to quit my job. You want me to open a store. You want me to sell everything. . . . I don't just change like that. I don't just change for you." With the looming threat of sexual defilement, Trish transforms into a castrating monster who wants to separate Andy from the symbols to which he has divested his phallic power in lieu of sex. As the active sexual initiator, Trish also exerts phallic power over Andy and threatens to eviscerate his potency and demote his rank in the symbolic order. Trish will have to delay her sexual gratification until marriage, at which point Andy will have assumed his proper place atop the sex/gender hierarchy. The threat of castration/emasculation is finally ameliorated when Andy successfully consummates their marriage. The final scene leaves spectators with an image of Andy as potent and Trish as a passive but visibly satiated recipient of pleasure following two hours of lovemaking. In short, the film begins and ends with Andy's phallic potency.

Throughout the film, castration anxiety is also accompanied by disparate and troubling images of both blatant sexuality—women's bodies, female genitalia—and the messy physicality of sex and bodily function. It promotes the idea that the world of dating is gross and embarrassing. For instance, Andy's first attempt to seduce a drunken woman at a nightclub leaves him predictably covered in vomit. The presence of abject bodily fluids prompts Andy to "pass on the sex."[43] More important, Andy's numerous other attempts to navigate the dating world leave him both aroused and horrified by the blatant presence of women's reproductive organs. In one scene, Andy attempts to traverse a busy Los Angeles street without thinking about sex. To his chagrin, the sidewalk is populated with attractive scantily clad women, sexually suggestive advertisements, and magazine stands littered with sexually explicit content and pornographic imagery. In an attempt to avoid the active gaze of women, Andy lowers his eyes only to be confronted with a horrifying onslaught of breasts, midriffs, and buttocks. While the soundtrack plays James Brown's sexually charged "I Got Ants in My Pants" the camera splices anonymous women into a stream of sex organs that aggressively pummel the anxiety-ridden protagonist. Andy finally collides with and inadvertently grabs an attractive woman by the waist. Shocked and horrified, Andy retreats from the sex-saturated scene only to be followed by a bus carrying an explicit cologne advertisement that reads "You know you want it: Eruption." In another scene, Andy is unable to watch the pornographic videos bequeathed to him by David not only because he is horrified by their graphic nature but also because he is horrified by the thought that touching his own penis in a sexual manner might be an indication of latent homosexual desire.

But it is the film's latent kolpophobia—fear of female genitals—that is particularly striking. Characters' frequent deployment of the term "pussy" to refer to sex, women, and emasculated men points to how the semiotics of the feminine—symbolized by the vagina—must be tamed or negated to maintain phallic power. In one scene, Andy's co-worker Mooj equates the vagina with a whole host of abject and taboo pleasures, telling Andy that "life isn't about sex. . . . It's not about fucking and balls and pussy, it's about love. It's about people. It's about connection. . . . It's not about cock and ass and tits. Butthole pleasures." Mooj's continuing list of euphemisms for sexual-scatological play again links sex and female bodies ("pussy") with filth and taboo.

Whereas the sexually active male characters use terms such as pussy and "punani" to domesticate the threat of women's sexual difference, thus providing a "terministic screen" that enables them to encounter female abjection, Andy's refusal to utter any reference to female genitalia reveals the inner presence of a sublime terror that has rendered him unable to enter the film's libidinal economy.[44] Jay aptly names this fear in mythical terms when he tells Andy, "You're putting the pussy up on this pedestal. Building the pussy up, man. You're making the pussy into this great big Greek goddess named Pussalia. And you're psyching yourself out into thinking it's some impossible thing." While it is unlikely that it was the intention of the filmmakers, Jay's metaphor closely resembles the Greek figure of the Medusa, whose head of writhing serpents, Freud argued, is linked to the abject sight of female genitalia.[45] The "pussy" as a synecdoche for sexual difference, sutured to monstrosity, grounds both Jay's impulse to conquer in his words "drunk bitches" and Andy's instinct to hide from most women in terror.[46]

Throughout his dating experiences, Andy's view of vaginas vacillates between horror and puzzlement, eventually resulting in domestication. A fitting scene shows Andy in a family health clinic fumbling with a three-dimensional plastic model of a vagina. With stunning naiveté, he whispers to himself, "where does the penis go?" as the model shatters into several pieces that seem to no longer fit together. Despite his studies, the vagina remains shrouded in mystery. When Trish discovers that Andy has taken the model home for study, he defensively explains that it is "for medicinal purposes . . . to learn." His efforts to study the vagina reveal that Andy has a sense that in order to lose his virginity he must ultimately conquer his fear of the feminine. He finally achieves this by dating a woman who insists on sexual abstinence until love (which eventually becomes abstinence until marriage) and avoiding women with transparent sexual desires. He engages in a prolonged and wholesome courtship with Trish, represented by a montage of dates that include home-cooked family meals and leisurely bike rides.

When his refusal to have sex with Trish nearly destroys their relationship, Andy finds himself the target of a sexually promiscuous woman who works in a local bookstore. Beth (Elizabeth Banks) takes an inebriated Andy back to her apartment, where she gets in the mood by masturbating with a shower massager. Andy recoils in horror at the sight of her unashamed pleasure. As he flees the scene, Jay, Cal, and David arrive to confront Andy about his decision to abandon his relationship with Trish for "a freak." Andy confesses, "I don't even know what I'm doing anymore. I'm not sure who I am anymore. All I know is, that woman scares the shit out of me and I just want to go home, okay?" Continuing his stable and wholesome relationship with Trish becomes the only path to allaying his fear and overcoming his pathological avoidance of women, their bodies, and their pleasures.

While Beth serves as a relational foil to Trish, she also embodies many of the horror-inducing and abject qualities of woman-as-Other. Her uninhibited sexual desire threatens to defile Andy, reminding him that the only safe expression of sexual desire is within a monogamous relationship and, most important, with a woman who is willing to subordinate her desires to the needs of men. The image of nymphomania assures spectators that sex with Trish as "man and wife" is Andy's only psychological remedy. Cloaked in chivalry, Andy's fear and its on-screen remedy suggest that women's sexuality must be tamed, disciplined, and brought under the sign of the phallus if man-boys are to recover their status as men.

Sexual Bootstrapping

The 40-Year-Old Virgin portrays contemporary liberated women as demanding and sexually aggressive. Their newly expressed wants and needs make dating a confusing social ritual for men. Throughout the film, Andy encounters bachelorette parties with sex toys; speed-dating with angry and demented women; a boss (Jane Lynch) who proposes that they become, to use her words, "fuck buddies"; and attractive women with sexual appetites that match those of the film's male characters. As active and empowered participants in dating culture, these postfeminist women have the luxury of being selective, pursuing their interests, expressing sexual desire, and presuming relational equality. They have the expectation that men must work as hard as they do at being desirable and interesting. To be sure, there is something progressive about this depiction of women; they contrast starkly with the 1950s model of femininity offered in antiquated dating advice books that instructed women to be demure ego-strokers.[47] With a new set of expectations before him, the postfeminist male must adopt many of the feminine conventions of self-care, including personal grooming (i.e., "manscaping"), careful attention to fashion, and acquiring knowledge about how to please his romantic partners. For Andy, women's active interest in sex makes virginity a more comfortable option.

For the men in this film, dating is labor. With traditional gender roles upended, heterosexual courtship confronts these men with the constant risk of humiliation. In response, the film folds sex and dating into the Protestant work ethic in which labor and constant self-improvement are thought to reap inevitable rewards and success. Whether it is to find a mate or experience sexual ecstasy, one must be willing to endure hard work, pain, and sacrifice. In the language of American Dream mythology, Andy must learn to pull himself up by his bootstraps if he is to enter the contemporary cult of manhood. The lesson is that the demand for dating equality has desacralized sex by subjecting it to economic logics. With men and women both entitled to mutual sexual availability and what typically have been understood as pleasures reserved only for men, males must actively labor to avoid being feminized. In this sexual labor market, abstinence for men is maligned as feminine passivity or portrayed as opting out of heterosexuality altogether. The historical association between virginity and femininity makes Andy more suitable for marriage than casual dating.

Schooled in the typologies of female desire, Andy's friends offer several and often contradictory pathways to sexual fulfillment. For example, Jay introduces Andy to the dating rituals of the sexually aggressively alpha male. In one scene, Jay grabs his crotch and suggests to Andy that he follow his "instincts" and that, like a "lion tackling a gazelle," he needs to "tackle drunk bitches." In another scene, he enlists the services of a transgender sex worker to overcome Andy's resistance to alpha-male behavior. He also insists that Andy wax his chest and engage in intense personal grooming to attract women. While Jay argues that it only hurts "if you're a bitch," the chest-waxing scene leaves Andy writhing in pain and unable to complete the procedure.[48] Jay's advice suggests that being a sexually attractive man is difficult, painful work and that the illusion of manhood is achieved only by sexually subjugating women. In addition, he uses precarious and vulnerable women to level the playing field for Andy. Here the unacknowledged subtext of rape is supposed to offer Andy a leg up in the world of aggressive but discerning women.

Whereas Jay's strategy is to lower women's value, Cal's approach is to invest Andy with greater value by making him more interesting and mysterious. Cal is a self-proclaimed "novelist" who acknowledges that he is "ugly as fuck" but nonetheless able to attract women. As Cal explains, "the problem most men have is they don't know how to talk to women." While Andy insists his problem is that he is simply not interesting—with hobbies like yo-yoing and ventriloquism—Cal insists that women are now so self-absorbed that he only needs to create an air of mystery about himself and let them do all the talking. Perhaps most noteworthy is Cal's insistence that he "play the odds" by "planting seeds" with a variety of women. Cal's economic metaphor suggests that dating success is achieved through entrepreneurialism and that like the gambler or investor, Andy needs to diversify his portfolio and hedge his bets in the sexual marketplace. Male virginity and monogamy need to be desacralized and abandoned to market forces. In contrast, David suggests that Andy's problem is that he is frigid and repressed. David's bequeathal of an oversized box of pornography not only suggests that raunch culture might open up a "Pandora's Box of love" but also that Andy needs to work on his sexuality on his own before he can ever hope to have sex with women. Similar to Jay's strategy of leveling the field, the suggestion of pornography implies that Andy can attain a sex and dating education vicariously through simulated environments in which women are sexually available nymphomaniacs. Of course, the irony of all these approaches is that they are rooted in a Protestant ideology of self-improvement.

The group criticizes Andy's efforts to strike out on his own and pursue a traditional relationship with Trish. Instead, the group's overall advice is that he should be promiscuous before approaching a woman he genuinely adores. Cal summarizes the group's advice: "You're gonna be so bad at sex the first time, you don't want to have sex with someone you like, they'll think you're a weirdo for being so lame at it. You want to have sex with 'hood rats' first so that by the time you get to a girl you do like you won't be terrible at sex, you'll be mediocre at, probably still pretty bad though." As this passage suggests, traditional romantic love is simply inadequate for the contemporary discerning woman. Women are constantly gauging the value of men's performance and prowess, leaving them susceptible to shame and ridicule. The persnickety woman and the demands of dating equality have reduced men to perverse economic calculations and the misguided pursuit of sexual self-improvement. Andy's friends expend more energy attempting to attract women than they do trying to advance their careers. Jay even describes the Smart Tech sales floor as more of an "aphrodisiac" than a place to earn money to support his family.

Although Andy's dating methods are initially presented as antiquated and even feminine, the film ultimately rebukes sexual bootstrapping, judging it to be an inappropriate response to active female desire. Instead, each of the characters' sophisticated dating methods unravels, and the film reveals that Andy's nostalgia for traditional romance is the answer men should have been looking for all along. In essence, his success provides a defense of secondary virginity over casual sex. Every time Andy puts the group's dating advice into action, it produces a comic spectacle in which he either gets hurt or embarrassed. When the group attends a speed-dating event, Jay is exposed as a philandering misogynist, Cal no longer appears to be the perceptive character study he once proclaimed, and David experiences an emotional breakdown at the sight of his ex-girlfriend.

Ultimately, their decline corresponds with Andy's ascendance. As each of his friends experience personal crises, Andy abandons their advice and begins dating Trish. While he struggles with how he will disclose his virginity to her, his success in dating is attributed to his ascent to breadwinner masculinity and traditional romance without sex. And the film's portrayal suggests that by abstaining from sex, Trish and Andy are able to get to know each other better and set a good example for Trish's sexually curious teenage daughter. The film's ultimate rejection of sexual bootstrapping is less about the problem of trying to domesticate sexually active women and more about the inefficacy of the approach. Andy's eventual dating success suggests that secondary virginity might reacquaint men with how to be *gentle*men and women with how to be ladies.

Born-Again Virgins

Once Andy starts on his pathway to marriage, he blossoms into the breadwinning male and eventually becomes deserving of sex from his wife. His dates with Trish illustrate his growth from adolescence into adulthood. Trish teaches Andy how to drive, how to be a parent, and how to translate his fascination with collectibles into enough money to start his own business. At the same time, Andy teaches Trish the benefits of late-in-life chastity. One benefit portrayed in the film is that the two get to know each other better by holding off on a physical relationship. But the more significant benefit is that Andy's purity enables Trish to reassert moral authority over her daughter Marla and prevent her from repeating the same mistakes she made. As Andy steps into a fatherly role, he helps Trish rediscover the importance of family values and find the moral strength to deter Marla from having sex with her boyfriend. The film implies that Trish was a teenage mother, had a series of failed relationships with men of dubious moral character, and is now struggling to prevent Marla from the same fate. Delaying sex and accepting the guidance of a burgeoning father figure allow Trish to atone for her past mistakes and bring stability to her home. Indeed, in abstinence culture the single mother who made mistakes in her past is the prototype for secondary virginity.[49]

Despite Marla's skepticism, Andy assumes a very important role in her life. In one scene, Andy even offers to take Marla to a family health clinic to get information about sex so that she can make the right decision. At the clinic, the other fathers are buffoonish caricatures who seem to lack basic parenting skills and knowledge about sexual reproduction. One dad even asks the counselor how he can shut down his daughter's reproductive system because she is "dumb." Another father wants to know how he can get his wife to perform sex acts that only his son's girlfriends are willing to do. Andy then reveals his virginity in order to provide a good model for Marla, allay her embarrassment, and repudiate the other fathers who surround him who are foils to Andy the emerging breadwinner father.

Andy's success in dating eventually prompts his fellow man-boys to also reclaim their masculine virtue. David observes Andy's youthful vitality and resolves to "retire" his penis in response to his relationship failures. He declares to Cal that "celibacy is the way to go, Andy had it right." Jay, after he is caught cheating on his longtime girlfriend, also concedes that Andy was right when he confesses to him in tears that "if you want to have a meaningful relationship you got to leave the sex out of it." While Cal continues to mock celibacy by equating it with homosexuality, he eventually joins Jay and David in order to stop Andy from having sex with Beth near the climax of the film. All are rewarded for their faith in Andy with monogamous relationships of their own. Jay becomes a father and learns that the real purpose of sex is procreation, David couples with a similarly jaded woman who begins working at Smart Tech, and Cal finds Beth to be a fitting match to his sexual perversions. While each of these budding relationships carry the implication of sex, it is all within the confines of stable monogamous relationships. The audience is also assured that virginity is preparation for marriage and monogamy.[50]

Although the central tension of their romance is Andy's secret, Trish is remarkably delighted to discover that his bizarre aversion to sex is only the result of his inexperience. Before he discloses his virginity, Trish becomes paranoid that Andy might be a "sex pervert," a "sexual deviant," or even a serial killer. She interprets his secrecy, his unwanted collection of pornography, and his sexual learning aids as signs that he is actually "buttering" her up for some kind of depraved sex act. Presumably, her reaction is predicated on the dearth of nice guys like Andy who are demure and shy about their sexual desires. Andy discloses the truth after he crashes his bike into the same Eruption advertisement that haunted him earlier in the film. Signifying Andy's final and inevitable confrontation with the sexual real, he lies on the street, immobilized, with Trish at his side. Although Andy is petrified that he will disappoint her sexually, Trish affirms, "of course it'll be good, we love each other." Andy responds, "For so long, I thought there was something wrong with me because it had never happened but I realize now it was because I was waiting for you." Andy realizes that he was not defective; he was merely waiting for true love and marriage to achieve sexual ecstasy.

In the end, Andy's virginity is a valuable asset. His quest to overcome his virginity is ostensibly training for assuming traditional breadwinner masculinity. His virginity is not a stigma to the extent that it helps him retrieve an older and more stable masculinity that will be consummated on his wedding night and sustained by his personal ambition and work ethic. He is the model for the man-boy's way out of perpetual childishness. In fact, his courtship with Trish rebrands the sexual bootstraps narrative. He uses the sale of his action figures—his surrogate phallus—to open up his own stereo store and become a self-made businessman. Andy's asceticism and Trish's feminine care enable him to abandon sexual bootstrapping for to the more traditional notion of the Protestant work ethic in which he spends his time earning for his family, not chasing women.

The Age of Aquarius

The modest amount of scholarly attention given to *The 40-Year-Old Virgin* has focused on the film's resolution, in which the entire cast performs "The Age of Aquarius" to symbolize Andy's newfound sexual ecstasy.[51] This performance assimilates both characters and spectators into a world of "posts" in which men's sexual anxieties are reconciled with what Celestino Deleyto characterizes as a "postmodern, post–sexual revolution, and postfeminist society."[52] In one sense, the film's conclusion discards the sexual politics introduced by feminism and the counterculture in favor of neotraditional romance and monogamy. In another sense, this scene makes the exploration of sexual pleasure and desire compatible with marriage and monogamy. As Michel Foucault observed in *The History of Sexuality*, discourses of sexual revolution are subject to a double movement in which once-stigmatized practices and identities are emancipated only to be subjected to new regimes of discipline and control.[53] This insight certainly troubles progressive narratives of sexual enlightenment and explains how it is that newly emancipated desires are so swiftly normalized by society's hegemonic institutions. But in this case we have an explicit example of cooptation whereby the very anthem of the counterculture is deployed in defense of what it once challenged. In other words, rebranding abstinence until marriage and monogamy as the pathways to sexual liberation absorbs and redirects any potential counterhegemonic challenge. As Herbert Marcuse presciently observed, dissident rhetorics of resistance are more frequently than not appropriated and inverted by the state and by capital to diffuse social upheaval.[54] The conclusion to this film evinces a series of cooptive strategies that redefine instruments of repression as the new harbingers of liberation.

First, the film's ending suggests that abstinence until marriage is the key that unlocks what was once taboo sexual desire. While Andy's first attempt at sex post-marriage is short and uneventful, the success of his second try demonstrates that the mastery of sexual pleasure is intuitive so long as it is within marriage. For waiting, Andy and Trish are rewarded with sexual bliss. Andy's stellar performance dispels the notion presented earlier in the film that trial and error with multiple sexual partners is the key to sexual fulfillment. Sex is not something you work at, but something that comes naturally (or even divinely) with true love. The couple's satisfaction confirms that the traditional courtship ritual is not broken but was merely enfeebled by confusion over the inner workings of sexual pleasure, its causes and consequences. This notion circulates ad nauseam in the rhetoric of the purity movement in its literature, on its websites, and in its school curricula, suggesting that great sex is the reward for following the morally righteous path to marriage.[55] The shift from condemning sexual desire to taking it into account certainly gives abstinence a much stronger appeal. And like abstinence advocates, *The 40-Year-Old Virgin* suggests that for both moral and practical purposes sex is worth the wait, even for middle-aged adults.

Second, Trish's capitulation to abstinence until marriage illustrates the benefits of secondary abstinence for women. Secondary virginity, secondhand abstinence, and other attendant neologisms refer to a state achieved by those who recommit to the imperatives of abstinence even after they have had sex outside marriage. One abstinence site asks, "Do you now feel like 'second-hand goods' and no longer worthy to be cherished? Do you ever wish you could re-wrap it and give it only to your future husband or wife? Guess what . . . ? You can decide today to commit to abstinence, wrapping a brand-new gift of virginity to present to your husband or wife on your wedding night."[56] As a recruiting tool, secondary virginity offers to expand the base of potential adherents to those who may have strayed or have been traumatized by their past dating experiences. For Trish, becoming chaste enables her to secure a stable husband and save her family. She is reacquainted with the simple and wholesome pleasures of romantic relationships that seem to be overshadowed by her physical relationships. Abstinence until marriage becomes the prescription that replaces Trish's misguided attempts to find fulfillment without true love and commitment.

Finally, the full-cast performance of "The Age of Aquarius" constitutes a repetition with a difference that introduces a new sexual revolution. This performance announces the end of the 1960s sexual revolution, serving as a kind of sexual counterrevolution that ends the sexual misadventures of these man-boys through secondary virginity and marriage. This full-cast performance adopts the signifiers of sexual liberation, this time to celebrate the realignment of the heterosexual universe. All the characters are depicted as coupled and in a state of euphoric sexual ecstasy. This new "Age of Aquarius" features responsible men and women. The pleasures of the counterculture have been appropriated and subsumed by conservative adjustments to the norms of heterosexual coupling.

The conclusion announces the end of the sexual revolution and its discontents, a kind of counterrevolution where both sexual ecstasy and social stability are accommodated and accounted for within the same rituals and institutions that produce alienation and oppression. The ubiquity of sex and the demands of liberated women have ruined the male characters, turning them into man-boys who are either obsessed with infantile sexual pleasures or frightened into chastity by female sexual power. Abstinence, coupling, and monogamy become the solution to an overactive women's sexuality and the man-boy's state of permanent adolescence. Great sex is the reward for marriage and monogamy, the remedy for the meaningless and hollow pleasures of sexual liberation. Abstinence until marriage, or at the very least monogamy, offers man-boys a path to finally growing up and reestablishing a sense of stable manhood. Abstinence also tames women's active sexuality and autonomy, bringing the whole spectrum of sexual desire under the control of traditional heterosexual courtship rituals. "The Age of Aquarius" offers spectators the promise of emancipation from the burdens and sometimes abject horror of their own desires.

3

Monstrous Girls
and Absentee Fathers

The Possession (2012)

The abstinence-until-marriage movement traffics in images of absentee fathers and young girls in crisis. For instance, Randy Wilson of the Family Research Council writes, "There is a lost generation of girls out there that has resulted primarily from the absence of committed fathers. Many men are uninvolved and disengaged at home."[1] As one of the movement's founders, Wilson calls on men to "restore what has been abdicated in our culture and then to renew and reestablish: the father-daughter relationship."[2] For abstinence advocates, sexual purity is as much about restoring the proper role of fathers in the family and society as it is about protecting young girls' chastity. Anecdotes of vulnerable young girls and absentee fathers are by no means confined to sexual purity discourse. American popular culture is replete with representations of young girls who have been abandoned by their fathers and are embattled by malevolent forces. Many recent horror films feature young girls in the grip of evil, targeted by demonic spirits determined to defile their purity and innocence. In *Dark Water* (2005), *The Exorcism of Emily Rose* (2005), *Silent Hill* (2006), *Case 39* (2009), *The Last Exorcism* (2010), *Let Me In* (2010), and *Apartment 143* (2011), crumbling family structures render young women vulnerable to possession by supernatural powers.

The Possession (2012) provides perhaps one of the most strident contemporary examples of horror amid a withering father-daughter relationship. A dybbuk (a demon from Jewish folklore) takes up residence inside a prepubescent girl's (Em's) chest cavity while her absent father (Clyde) is distracted by his personal ambitions. Read allegorically, the vulnerability and violation of Em and the many other young female characters in contemporary horror films oddly parallel the rhetoric of sexual purity. With their emphasis on the threats to young women's physical and moral integrity, the dangers of lost fatherhood, and the protections of religious faith and the heterosexual family, possession films also project collective fears about the perceived vulnerability of young women. Robin Wood argues that horror films resonate with popular audiences because they project the mainstream culture's "collective nightmares."[3] If that is the case, contemporary horror films about possessed young girls evince a more pervasive cultural panic about young women's sexuality and the failure of their fathers to provide adequate protection. These new films rely on a very old reason for the return of patriarchal order to the home: the vulnerable young girl.

In the context of these persistent social anxieties, possession films are productive texts for observing the features of the conservative panic about lost fatherhood and the uses of the image of the young girl in crisis. While possession films and purity culture may not share an apparent connection, this chapter uses a comparative analysis to illustrate how these two disparate discourses articulate what is presently impotent about fathers and monstrous about young women. *The Possession* illustrates precisely how occult movies resonate with abstinence culture's fear that without paternal protection, burgeoning young women might precipitate a crisis in the traditional family. Unlike past horror films, *The Possession* literalizes the experience of possession by giving the demon a material form capable of both spiritual and physical penetration. This transformation reflects a fundamentalist turn in popular demonology in which evil is invited into the corporeal world by moral transgressions that disrupt traditional Judeo-Christian institutions and violate the principle of bodily purity. *The Possession* registers a growing sexual panic that prescribes a return to traditional roles for fathers and daughters as the antidote to the horror of contemporary social ills, including real demons. It is important for feminist scholarship on horror films to account for a contextual shift in the meaning of demonic possession to address how the genre has become sutured to increasingly conservative ideologies about fatherhood, the traditional family, and the proper place of young women.

Women, Horror, and Possession

Horror films provide insights into dominant cultural ideals about femininity and often index what is currently articulated in public discourse as monstrousness in young girls. Within the genre, the possession film is where the collapse of family structures portends the entrance of evil into home and society. Like Hesiod's myth of Pandora or Eve in the Book of Genesis, a young woman's expressions of curiosity or desire, her unauthorized enactments of agency, and her vulnerability to moral and physical corruption invite sin into the world. Possession films locate the battle between good and evil in the body of young women, whose salvation is necessary for the restoration of moral order and the male-centered nuclear family.[4] Carol Clover argues that in horror, "the female may not be the exclusive port of entry for the satanic, but she has been since Eve the favored one."[5] With their emphasis on vulnerable and violated young women, possession films thus offer critical insights into what young womanhood means in our contemporary moment.

After a decade of some of the most iconic horror films in the history of the genre, from the early 1970s through the mid-1980s, feminist film scholars such as Barbara Creed, Carol Clover, and Robin Wood argued that the genre's portrayal of woman-as-monster signified how the feminine subject of patriarchal culture was constructed as an abject Other.[6] Feminist horror critics suggested that the genre fulfilled the scopic pleasures of male spectators, who revel in taboo behaviors before obliterating the threat of the feminine.[7] Creed argued that the horror film reveals that every culture has its concept of the "monstrous feminine."[8] When these works were written, the threat of second-wave feminism to male primacy was chief among the anxieties of neoconservative men. Much of the popular horror genre not only indexed patriarchal fears of women's power and autonomy but also featured punishment of women who violated dominant gender expectations (e.g., the slasher film).

Thus far, feminist analysis of the horror film aligns more closely with a meta-critical, psychoanalytical account of possession rather than a context-centered analysis that accounts for changes in the political struggle over girlhood. With their emphasis on repressed desire and deferred meanings, exclusively psychoanalytical approaches might overlook how films speak through and rework the ideologies that are active in a particular cultural context. For instance, Projanksy contends that scholarly criticism of popular culture often suggests that depictions of girlhood stand in for some other anxiety (in this case theories of abjection or repressed libidinal desire). In this process, the cultural meaning of girlhood itself is deferred. If depictions of vulnerable and violated girl's bodies are always interpreted as a sign standing for a more significant referent, critical attention is diverted from the ongoing and regressive transformations in the cultural narrative of femininity and masculinity.

Recently, there has been a politically significant transition in the horror-film genre that moves toward a very literal notion of possession. This transformation reflects an evolution of popular demonology in which literal demons are now imagined to invade our bodies when they become addled with desire. While rooted in both Jewish and Catholic perspectives on exorcism, *The Possession* most closely mirrors the evangelical movement's emphasis on real, material evil and the unique vulnerability of young women. Leaders in the purity movement suggest that the devil exists in the physical world and that specific actions are to blame for inviting demonic forces into our bodies. In light of this transformation, it is important to think about demonic possession films politically and account for the unique conjuncture of discourses about girls, fatherhood, and sexual purity.

The nature and substance of celluloid demons continue to evolve alongside political and religious struggles over feminism. In past feature films, demons were malevolent spirits that commandeer the body but have no specific corporeal form. However, in *The Possession* the demon has its own corporeal form that must physically enter and reside within a human host. The film distinguishes itself from the genre by representing the physicality of demons and making young girls and absent fathers ultimately responsible for the experience of possession.

What appears to be an unimaginative elaboration of a hackneyed genre in fact marks a significant transformation in the relationship between women and horror. First, in Clover's analysis, possession films "materialize abstractions, turning ideas and feelings into things, and represent gender if not by sex then by the figurative apparatus of sex."[9] She notes how in *The Exorcist* and its knock-offs, medical expertise and diagnostics fail to detect the presence of the spiritual forces that have taken over the body. The prescription for exorcism, then, forces the female body to "externalize its inner workings, to speak its secrets, to give a material account of itself—in short, to give literal and visible *evidence*."[10] Demons are spiritual forces whose presence is manifest in physical signs of bodily possession. Demonic invasion has heretofore been portrayed as a spiritual ailment (or "black magic") with physical symptoms that are indecipherable to "white science."[11] The recent attempt to give demons a physical form that is distinct from that of their host reflects a different conception of bodily vulnerability and its spiritual remedies. *The Possession* is unique in that it simultaneously engages in both the materializing of abstractions and the abstracting of materialization by giving demons the ability to spiritually *and* physically possess young women. The film literalizes the possession experience, reflecting the notion that demons have material essence and actually live inside vulnerable bodies.

Another key difference is that recent cinematic representations of demons hold individuals responsible for their openness to evil. While representations of Catholic demonology attributed possession to an atmosphere or corruption (i.e., *The Exorcist*), other films such as *The Possession* revolve around the specific moral failures of young girls and their fathers. In part, this transformation can be attributed to the rise in evangelical Protestantism. For instance, Joshua Gunn notes the growing sect of evangelical Protestants who practice "deliverance," a doctrine of faith healing premised on the literal existence of demons that holds them responsible for every type of personal and social ill.[12] This view of evil also appears in the writings of purity advocates such as Dannah Gresh, Joshua Harris, Jane Owens, and Jim Burns. Christian abstinence literature emphasizes

FIGURE 6. The demon resides in Em's changing body. *The Possession*. DVD. Directed by Ole Bornedal. Santa Monica, CA: Lionsgate Entertainment, 2013.

that impure thoughts, sexually suggestive music, and even seemingly benign acts of coveting invite satanic forces into the home. According to these authors, absentee and permissive parents (not to mention sex educators) are ultimately responsible for the demonic corruption of children and young adults.

Finally, protestant influence demonology attributes agency to "occult" objects and symbols. For those who practice deliverance, the body is vulnerable to demonic possession when it comes into contact not only with Ouija boards, horoscopes, tarot cards but other items that symbolize dark desires (sex-laden music, television, films, books, and clothing). In addition to resorting to the extremity of exorcism, adherents recommend removing dangerous items from the home as a remedy for psychological and spiritual disturbances. Demonology is surprisingly prevalent in current U.S. culture. A 2012 study conducted by Public Policy Polling found that 63 percent of Americans age 18 to 29 believe that demons are capable of taking control of a human body and that demons are the root cause of many contemporary social problems.[13] Fundamentalist Christian abstinence-until-marriage campaigns insist on the real existence of demons in the corporeal world and place heavy emphasis on human responsibility. Purity advocate Jane Owens writes that in addition to sex, it is "books, magazines, pictures, music, and statuary of idols that have invited demons of darkness into your homes."[14] Although *The Possession* draws from Jewish folklore and relies on the audience's familiarity with the Catholic rite of exorcism, its depiction of demons most closely aligns with the Protestant doctrine of deliverance.

In light of popular belief in demons, it is no surprise that Hollywood continues to recycle the genre. Directors such as Eli Roth and William Friedkin and film critics argue that the genre remains profitable because audiences are captivated by the idea of an innocent girl overwhelmed by evil and the mystery of religious mythology.[15] *The Exorcist* is one of the highest-grossing films of all time ($441 million), and recent derivations have been immensely profitable.[16] Directors note that recent iterations of the genre reach a younger audience that is enamored with demon-possession films despite negative reviews.

Both demonic corporeality and human agency are largely absent from *The Exorcist* and similar films. While young women may be vulnerable to possession on account of troubling circumstances or by virtue of a patriarchal axiom that women are naturally enterable, the specific actions of young girls are not to blame. Instead, Creed notes that *The Exorcist* mirrors the biblical story of Sodom and Gomorrah in that "the moral climate is so corrupt that the devil is able to take possession of the young with the greatest of ease."[17] In *The Possession*, the decline in familial values is only the backdrop to specific acts of coveting and lust that invite demonic possession. Whereas in *The Exorcist* Regan's body is an ideal stage for a battle between God and Satan, in *The Possession* it is Em's desire itself for a mysterious box that invites dark desires in return. *The Possession* suggests that there is a more profound connection between human agency and demonic forces. Of course, while human actions are responsible, conquest over the evil forces through spiritual warfare remains the only remedy for possession. Thus, the film aligns with and advances the pop demonology that is woven throughout contemporary purity literature.

The Horrors of Girlhood

The Possession depicts father-daughter relationships in crisis and the perilous journey young women face as they enter adulthood. Directed by Ole Bornedal and produced by Sam Raimi, *The Possession* presents a recently divorced couple, Clyde and Stephanie (Jeffrey Dean Morgan and Kyra Sedgwick), who are negotiating parenting responsibilities for their two young daughters, Emily (Em) and Hannah (Natasha Calis and Madison Davenport). Most popular film critics argue that despite the appearance of a demon from Jewish folklore, *The Possession* is a formulaic update of all previous films of the genre. After noting the intriguing mythology surrounding dybbuks, Tirdad Derakhshani laments, "The rest, you've seen 100 times already."[18] Another critic writes that "whether the perp is Satan, a random devil or, as in this case, a dybbuk—a malicious spirit in Jewish folklore—demonic-possession movies are cut from the same diabolically familiar cloth. A malevolent force captures the soul of an innocent child, and sinister mayhem ensues."[19] Despite the generally poor reception by critics, the film grossed nearly $50 million.[20] The generic, formulaic, and banal structure of the film offers entree into the rhetorical structure of the crisis in the family social conservatives speak of in their discourses of purity that is characterized by lost relationships between fathers and daughters. My analysis elucidates why *The Possession* constructs a corporeal demon that is capable of new kinds of mayhem. In the remainder of this chapter, I map how discourses of evangelical deliverance and sexual purity converge in *The Possession*. This analysis shows how the new nature of evil presented in the film reasserts traditional family values as the solution to the "demons" of a secular, permissive, and sex-saturated culture.

Narratives of Purity

Since both the purity movement and possession films use the broken fatherless family as the entry point for evil, lust, and temptation, my analysis identifies symmetry between their rhetorical structures to show how themes of purity and deliverance operate inferentially in film. For many evangelicals, the household without a father is the root of most contemporary social ills. In *Fatherless America* (1995), an iconic text for many in the purity movement, David Blankenhorn argues that sex out of wedlock begins in the fatherless home and that young girls will naturally seek out father figures in the form of false idols. Blankenhorn instructs, "Instead of good fathers, [settling] for child-support payments, divorce reform, and other attempts to salvage something from the wreckage . . . search for adequate substitutes for fathers."[21] Purity advocates place mothers in a tertiary role and see father-daughter relations as the key variable that predicts whether girls will remain abstinent. Blankenhorn's call to restore lost father resonates with evangelical Protestants, particularly with members of organizations such as Promise Keepers whose sole emphasis is remaking Christian men into strong and devoted domestic patriarchs.[22]

The family depicted in *The Possession* is particularly vulnerable to moral pollution. Divorced for nearly a year, Clyde and Stephanie struggle to raise their young girls as they come into adulthood. Adolescence is the time of greatest concern to purity advocates because it is when young girls are beginning to have sexual desires and curiosity. Purity advocate Jim Burns argues that "the problem is at the same time that your body is changing and you are rapidly moving from childhood to adulthood, your relationship with God is probably changing."[23] Rachel Lovingood adds to the argument: "The culture of middle schoolers is very sexual—from their music, to the television shows they watch, to their hallway conversations."[24] There is a strong belief within the purity movement that upon reaching puberty, young girls will be tempted by sin and impurity. This is the time when purity advocates believe that fathers need to be heavily involved in their daughters' lives. True Love Waits points to the dangers of absent, distracted, and inconsistent parenting: "An abundance of unsupervised free time can lead to undesirable behavior, and even solid Christian teens can make bad decisions when faced with repeated temptation in unsupervised environments."[25] Only by shielding and protecting young women from temptation can fathers be sure that their daughters will stay committed to abstinence until marriage. Purity advocates construct the bodies of preteen and early teenage girls as a battleground between good and evil.[26]

Clyde and Stephanie's family suffers from inconsistent parenting and vacillating family roles. Stephanie is the parent most concerned with protecting the girls from impure foods and outside influences. While Stephanie is involved, fastidious, and strict with the girls' schedule and diet, Clyde is permissive, career-centered, and lighthearted about his parenting responsibilities. He orders pizza for the girls even when Stephanie expressly prohibits it, he buys them whatever they want, and he cares more about his career as a basketball coach than about his role as a parent. While Clyde still clings to the hope that he and Stephanie can work out their differences and reunite as a family, Stephanie has moved on to a relationship with Brett, who she believes is a more upstanding father figure.

The film's central antagonism emerges as a result of Clyde's permissiveness and lack of presence in his daughters' lives. It begins with a peccadillo, a small and seemingly innocuous act of coveting. Without thought, Clyde permits Em to purchase a strange antique wooden box at a weekend yard sale. Unbeknown to Clyde, the box contains an ancient malevolent spirit that seeks to attach itself to the innocent souls who covet the box. Though the box seems fairly innocuous, its presence in Clyde's house coincides with odd changes in Em's behavior. After she deciphers how to open the box, Em finds a weird assortment of dark items, including a mysterious ring, locks of hair, a carved wooden figurine, and a human tooth. Em develops an unhealthy obsession with the box and even claims that she communicates with the spirit inside. She acts out at home and in school and grows listless, detached, and even violent as the demonic spirit begins to take hold of her. In the course of the film, Clyde learns that the box was created to contain a dybbuk, a creature in Jewish folklore that seeks to inhabit the bodies of the living. The spirit possessing Em calls itself Abyzou, "the taker of children." The film implicitly connects Clyde's paternal absence with Em's corruption. Stephanie can only do so much to prevent their daughters from being invaded by impurities; it is ultimately a father's duty to protect their physical and moral integrity.

Portals of Evil

The monster of *The Possession* is primal, supernatural, and malevolent. Since the fifteenth century, Jewish mystics, cabalists, and rabbis have recounted tales of young girls' bodies invaded by dybbuks or malevolent spirits that attach themselves to living humans. As with the Catholic concept of possession, the Jewish exorcism ritual focuses almost exclusively on young women and reflects the culture's anxiety about their sexuality. Yoram Bilu explains that in Jewish folklore "women were excessively vulnerable to possession because 'the impurity stemming from the serpent still abounds in them.' Here an allusion is made to Eve's primordial sin or succumbing to the temptation of the snake, the nature of which temptation was blatantly sexual."[27] Bilu writes that Jewish folklore frequently constructed dybbuk possession as not only induced by but similar to sexual penetration. Tracing women's lineage to Eve and primordial sin, both Jewish and Christian folklore find women more easily seduced by evil and more likely targets of demonic possession.

Although the film draws from Jewish mysticism, Em is a contemporary composite of mythical female icons seduced by evil. In Genesis, Eve is responsible for the fall of humanity, tempted by the serpent to eat the forbidden fruit from the tree of knowledge in the Garden of Eden. In Greek mythology, Zeus gives Pandora a large jar containing all worldly evils. Like Eve, Pandora was the first woman on earth and her curiosity resulted in the pain and misery of all humankind. As it was for Eve and Pandora, Em's desire and curiosity invite evil into her family's world. Like an apple from the tree of knowledge, the dybbuk box is a seemingly innocuous though curious item. At a yard sale, Clyde lets Em sift through items without supervision. Em dresses up in a formal woman's hat and white satin gloves and while posing declares, "Dad, look, *I'm a lady*." Though a comical moment, it reminds the audience of Em's burgeoning femininity and draws attention to what kinds of items arouse her curiosity and interest. Like Eve and Pandora, Em becomes enthralled with a mysterious item harboring forbidden qualities, an item that represents desire and temptation. As Em's attention turns to an antique wooden box engraved with Hebrew, the camera closes in on her eyes. The close-up reveals a gaze of intense desire, the lustful coveting of a material item. When she asks Clyde if she can have the box, he replies without consideration, "Whatever you want, kiddo." Throughout the film, the box serves as a stand-in for a number of forbidden desires: idolatry, coveting, and lust. It is important to note that the box is not the portal by which evil enters the world but is instead its container. The choices made by those in the box's presence determine whether evil can be admitted into human affairs. Thus, it is Em's attachment to the box that transforms her into a portal. Clyde's lack of vigilance about female curiosity enables Em to become tempted and fractures the already fragile Edenic state of innocence.

The film's construction of evil closely aligns with the purity movement's focus on the problem of lust. Purity advocate Joshua Harris writes that lust "covets the forbidden. Lust grasps for, with our eyes, hearts, imagination or bodies, what God has said not to."[28] For purity advocates, it's a father's duty to pay attention to what cultivates lust in his daughters and specifically to what kind of material items they bring home. While much of this certainly appears to be practical parenting advice, purity advocates assume that young women are uniquely vulnerable to evil and that they tend to indulge lustful impulses unless their fathers exercise strict control. In Dannah Gresh's *And the Bride Wore White*, women's weakness and vulnerability are blamed for original sin: "[Satan] caused Eve to believe that she had the intellect to draw her own morality—or to determine what was right for her. Oh, if only Eve had stood firmly on the truth of what God said. . . . She decided she was smart enough to debate the devil. And because Eve was busy talking, he found her weakness . . . touch. She had told him God said they couldn't even touch it. Perhaps this gave him an idea."[29] Film and folklore alike construct women as moral gateways. Their value is commensurate with their physical and spiritual purity. The fact that Em is on the cusp of puberty is vital to the construction of her as portal. This is the age when she will begin to experience sexual and physiological changes that make her susceptible to being invaded by evil. Em's possession projects latent fears that physiological changes in young women bring the potential loss of innocence, purity, and virginity.

FIGURE 7. A portrait of monstrous girlhood. *The Possession*. DVD. Directed by Ole Bornedal. Santa Monica, CA: Lionsgate Entertainment, 2013.

Body and Home

The central antagonism between Clyde and Stephanie is over the proper control of young women's bodies and their environment. Quite literally, the film is orally fixated. Stephanie is obsessed with what her daughters eat, Brett (a dentist) wants to fix Hannah's teeth against Clyde's wishes, and the demon enters Em through her mouth and resides in her throat and chest cavity, routinely inducing gagging, voice projection, and compulsive eating. This oral fixation also focuses the audience's attention on the protection and violation of Em's physical integrity. The film suggests that parents need to monitor what goes inside their daughters' bodies. The contrast between Stephanie's regimented home life and Clyde's permissiveness coheres with the abstinence movement's insistence that sexual purity begins with clean living in controlled environments. Of course, sex is only one aspect of purity; True Love Waits asserts that "it's what our minds probably go to first, but God calls us to be pure and to live with integrity in every area of life."[30] Burns claims that those who do not follow the purity code "fill their bodies with unwholesome ingredients, including alcohol and drugs. They might even cut themselves and do other types of self-injury. These people are not bad people, but they surely are not taking care of their bodies. Honoring God with your body is the most important step in living out the Purity Code."[31] Abstinence rhetoric prioritizes highly structured home environments and disciplined care of the self, including no unsupervised time for children, prohibitions on nonreligious entertainment, and careful monitoring of children's food choices.

Stephanie and Brett's home is an ideal space for the promotion of purity. Stephanie maintains a regimented household and strictly controls what Em and Hannah eat and wear. She lays out their daily outfits, monitors their food allergies, worries about germs, and berates Clyde for not taking control of the girls' health and safety. Stephanie's new partner Brett is a dentist obsessed with germs, insisting that guests take off their shoes when they enter the house because "you won't believe the bacteria that get dragged into the house." Stephanie insists that Hannah and Em only eat "healthy foods . . . stuff that grows on trees." As the youngest and most impressionable, Em takes to her mother's strict diet and is a self-proclaimed vegetarian, a lifestyle practice that indicates that she maintains the highest standards of bodily purity. When Em and Hannah are depicted at home with Stephanie, they are studying for school or spending quality time with their mother. They are heavily involved in school activities: Em lobbies the school administration for "meatless Mondays" and Hannah is a member of the dance squad. Their time appears to be highly structured, and their physical and mental states are tightly controlled and monitored. Stephanie and Brett extol the virtues of clean, antiseptic living characterized by hard work, self-discipline, and bodily purity.

In contrast, Clyde maintains a home that is vulnerable to immoral influences. His newly constructed suburban home is perfectly clean and well organized, but it is the house of someone who spends most of his or her time at work. At Clyde's house, the girls are allowed to eat pizza, drink soda, and have pancakes for breakfast. Em and Hannah are often depicted together while Clyde works or alone in their rooms. Any time they spend with Clyde is interrupted by work-related phone calls or fights about his divorce. Clyde's house is constructed as the kind of permissive environment in which demons might flourish. In one sense, the presence of the dybbuk box in Clyde's home is a synecdoche for the evils unleashed by absent parenting and poor household management. In fact, the demon takes hold of Em when she is alone in her room with the box. There, the demon inside tells her that she is special as it begins to explore various ways to control her body. She becomes obsessed with the box, frequently asking Clyde about its well-being while she is at Stephanie's house. She wears the dark-colored ring she found inside the box, symbolizing the perverse spiritual union she has formed with the demon inside. The demon takes hold of Em because Clyde fails to carefully monitor what comes into the house and adequately structure her free time.

In a different sense, the demon inside the box also symbolizes the impure forces outside the home that desire to corrupt young girls. After Em sleeps with the box in her bed, the demon begins to take control of her body. The next day, as gray storm clouds close in, she confesses to Hannah that she does not feel like herself. In another scene, while Clyde's house becomes infested with moths, Em sits alone in the dark, on her bed, petting the box. This scene suggests that the demon is able to take hold of Em because she invites it into her most physically and spiritually intimate spaces. The demon and Em share an intimate moment "in bed" while chaos invades the home. After the demon physically penetrates Em, it maintains control of her mind through disingenuous expressions of love and affection. In essence, the demon fills the place of her father's absent love and guidance. The implicit sexualization of the relationship between Em and Abyzou constructs young girls as vulnerable to lust and desire even before puberty. The film also implies that young girls will seek out father substitutes if the father is not present in the home. It suggests that one misguided moment of curiosity opens up female bodies to complete exploitation by their father substitutes. Merely removing the box from Clyde's home does not release the demon's grip; Em runs away and finds the box in a dumpster. This is when the demon takes full possession of Em, an act that is symbolized by the moths that leave the box and enter her body against her will.

It is important to note that the demon concentrates most of its malevolence against the film's father figures. Under its direction, Em attacks her father with a fork, rips all the teeth out of Brett's mouth, and violently attacks the rabbi (Tzadok) who performs her exorcism. Although the demon also attacks women throughout the film, its focus on men suggests that corrupting agents understand that strong father figures pose a significant barrier to their success. As Tzadok informs Clyde, "The dybbuk looks for innocence. A pure soul. It will move back and forth from the box, searching for a proper host. . . . All of this is the deception of the spirit. To protect the host and drive others away . . . it will feed and take until there is nothing left. It wants only the thing, that which it does not have: Life." Thus, the demon focuses on removing the only male figures who can save Em. The demon even strikes Em to create the appearance that Clyde is abusive, compelling the police to order a temporary injunction against his visitation rights. Each stage in the possession escalates the amount of control the demon can exercise over Em in comparison to Clyde. It seeks to supplant Clyde altogether as the authority over her mind and body. For example, Clyde discovers Em staring into a mirror inside the box and observes one of her eyes rolled back into her head before she awakens from a trance with no recollection. Scenes depicting the stages of possession indicate that the demon is exploring her body and figuring out ways to control it. Em suddenly develops a supernaturally large appetite to feed the demon that takes up residence inside her body. In several scenes, Em eats violently, shoving pancakes, French fries, and eventually raw red meat down her throat like a ravenous animal.

The film's emphasis on bodily integrity resounds with the fears of abstinence culture. Unlike with other possession films, the dybbuk character physically enters Em as a flock of moths forcing themselves down her throat in rapid succession. The film includes a number of scenes in which Em gags or convulses violently when the demon seems to want more control of her body. In one scene, Em looks into the mirror to understand her changing body only to find the demon's fingers climbing up her esophagus. In another chilling scene, a full-body CAT scan reveals that the demon literally resides inside her chest cavity as a kind of perverse pregnancy. The physicality of the demon literalizes the experience of possession in a way that draws attention to the imperatives of physical purity. In other words, we are what we eat.

Fatherhood in Crisis

As Clover observes, "Behind the female 'cover' is always the story of a man in crisis, and that crisis is what the occult film . . . [is] about."[32] Indeed, Clyde is a man in crisis. He has been supplanted by Brett as the male head of the household and only gets to see his daughters on weekends. Stephanie has stepped in as the dominant parent, enforcing strict study habits, mandating rigid dietary restrictions, and requiring that Clyde follow the rules if he wants to continue seeing his daughters. Clyde romanticizes the nuclear family and holds out hope that he and Stephanie will eventually reunite. He is also torn between his career as successful basketball coach and being an active parent. His job frequently causes him to be late to his daughters' school functions, and a potentially glamorous job as a college coach distracts him from his plans to reconnect with his estranged family.

Ultimately, the film folds Em's possession into a narrative masculine crisis and resolution. In other words, her condition is both the result of Clyde's poor parenting and an opportunity to restore his position as the leader of his family. While her older sister Hannah was able to negotiate her first few tumultuous years after puberty within the confines of the traditional family, Em must do so without that structure. Overworked and emasculated, Clyde is no longer in a position to protect his Em throughout the most vulnerable years of adolescence. Much like *The Exorcist* and *The Last Exorcism*, in *The Possession*, malevolent forces seek to exploit the weakness of the broken family. While Clyde is aware that the changes in his daughter's behavior may defy rational explanation, Stephanie remains naive and blames him. Stephanie's constant emasculation and disapproval of Clyde drive a wedge between him and his daughters that ultimately weakens his ability to control them and protect them from the demon. This portrayal of evil within the family coheres with the discourses of the abstinence movement that emphasize strong and overbearing father-daughter relationships, including ritualized pledges of purity and obedience.

In *The Possession*, the remedy of exorcism helps Clyde reassert control over his daughters and reunite his family. Once Clyde realizes that he is battling supernatural forces, he turns to male experts in possession, first a professor of folklore and then a group of Hasidic rabbis. The rabbis are absolutely petrified by the dybbuk box and the demon it used to contain. Because the source of the evil is supernatural, the expertise for dealing with female possession lies in the hands of religious fundamentalists instead of medical professionals. The film constructs men, religious fundamentalists in particular, as experts on the dangers that young women face (especially their changing bodies). If possession represents repressed fears of teenage girls' sexuality, then the religious rite of exorcism is an attempt to reassert male control over the female body.

With the whole family present and armed with Holy Scripture, Tzadok begins a lengthy and violent exorcism during which the demon actually enters Clyde before being forced back into the box. In an act of self-sacrifice, Clyde takes the demon into himself. I read this act as Clyde saving Em from the pains and hardships of womanhood; perhaps the demon represents an even more generalizable fear of the dangerous world outside the home. Clyde is ultimately redeemed because he has taken a direct and active role in protecting Em and his family from malevolent forces. Here the film constructs a cycle of masculine crisis and resolution that results in Clyde returning to the role of the male center of his family. Aided by spiritual expertise, Clyde battles the demons and expels them from his daughter. Ultimately, cycles of crisis and redemption are fundamental to the restoration of masculine subjectivity. Tania Modleski argues that "however much male subjectivity may currently be 'in crisis,' as certain optimistic feminists are now declaring, we need to consider the extent to which male power is actually consolidated through cycles of crisis and resolution, whereby men ultimately deal with the threat of female power by incorporating it."[33] In this spirit, the film concludes with Clyde, Stephanie, Hannah, and Em reunited as a family and eating breakfast together in their old home, their bonds of love and affection restored. Although the dybbuk is contained in the box once again, Tzadok is killed in a car accident before he can dispose of it properly. The film ends with a close-up shot of the box and the faint whispers of the dybbuk chanting inside.

Compelling Coherence

In the rhetoric of the purity movement, Hollywood is often blamed for promulgating sexual immorality and promoting sex out of wedlock. For instance, Psalidas argues that "with everything going on in today's society, particularly in Hollywood with its celebrity-oriented press, pregnancies outside of marriage being considered the norm, sexual immorality displayed on TV shows, in movies, and written about in women's magazines, purity is almost non-existent."[34] Many purity advocates say that they do not have cable TV or watch films unless they have a religiously uplifting message. They offer practical advice about how to avoid sexually suggestive images in television and movies, including "eye-bouncing" to give "your mind less time to take a picture—a picture that can never be deleted."[35] The irony is that despite the violence, gore, and sexually explicit content in many Hollywood films, their narrative structure coheres with more conservative cultural discourses about the literal demons facing the family. Despite the fact that purity advocates have not embraced the horror genre as family friendly, the discursive linkage between these two discourses suggests something about the disturbing salience of each text, even when those claims are marred by patriarchy, misogyny, and sexual repression. How does the purity movement continue to garner so much public support and influence in public policy? In her rhetorical study of the purity movement, Gardner suggests that part of the movement's success is attributable to its cooptation of secular and sometimes even feminist ideals.[36] The purity movement's critique of the sexualization of young girls and pornography aligns well with certain threads of feminist thought. While these two social critiques arise from vastly different motivations and do not share the same political ideology, their alignment on some key issues suggests that purity is more valorized in the structure of Hollywood films than was once thought. Both discourses share some common assumptions about young women's sexuality and the importance of family values.

Emerging scholarship on the rhetoric of horror films and the rhetoric of trauma and sacrifice in disaster films highlights how the larger ideological and psychological investments that pervade public culture are worked through, often reaffirmed but sometimes challenged, on the big screen.[37] This chapter suggests that a comparison of films and public discourses about young women's sexuality points to deeper-rooted assumptions that make its similarity in rhetorical structures salient. The specific case of possession films and purity culture illustrates the evangelical Protestant moorings of our popular culture's representation of the "monstrous feminine." Possession films exert their power because of a history of discourses linking women's sexuality and autonomy with evil and because of the growing popular acceptance of Protestant demonology. They resonate with a culture that assigns women value according to their sexual behavior and in which true womanhood is articulated by innocence, virtue, domesticity, and purity. While *The Exorcist* may have inspired audiences to call their local diocese or synagogue to perform exorcisms, the substantive and material fear accessed by *The Possession* appeals to an emerging common sense about the real threat of the demonic and the proper role of fathers and daughters in delivering us from evil. While the demon has been cast out of Clyde's family, when will it visit yours?

4

Abstinence, the Global Sex
Industry, and Racial Violence

Taken (2008)

In the 2008 film *Taken*, retired CIA agent Bryan Mills (Liam Neeson) uses his espionage and counterterrorism training to rescue his teenage daughter Kim (Maggie Grace) from a French-Albanian crime syndicate that abducts, drugs, and sells young white women into forced prostitution. Rather than wait for the police, Bryan takes matters into his own hands. He travels to Paris and brutally assaults, tortures, and murders nearly everyone associated with his daughter's abduction. All totaled, Bryan kills thirty-five people during the course of the film. Ultimately, he is able to save Kim and exact revenge on her captors. At the film's climax, Bryan executes the wealthy Arab sheik who purchased Kim, preventing him from consummating an act of sexual violation. After a long estrangement, Bryan's display of heroism brings the two closer and compensates for his absence during her childhood. *Taken*, which grossed over $145 million, was one of the most popular action-adventure films of 2008.[1] The film was followed by two big-budget sequels that to date have earned nearly a quarter of billion dollars.[2] Though critical of producer Luc Besson's fondness for spectacular violence, many reviewers noted that *Taken* was a guilty pleasure. Christy Lemire provided perhaps the best summation: "It's all sordid and unseemly but if you can get past that, 'Taken' is also unexpectedly fun in a guilty-pleasure sort of way."[3] Mick LaSalle wrote that "the placement of an archetypal American character, the avenging action hero, wreaking havoc through the Paris streets has some dark appeal."[4] Some critics expressed mild hesitation about the film's xenophobic undertones but admitted that they were attracted to the film's preposterous narrative.

Beyond the satiation of guilty desires, what makes the protagonist redeemable is his heroic defense of his daughter's purity against a dark and sexually marauding enemy. In this sense, *Taken* is an old story retold. The motifs of revenge and innocence expressed in the film resemble the structure of other troubling narratives that have served as historic rationalizations for white masculine violence against racial Others, including "captivity narratives" of Puritan women abducted by "savages" on the colonial frontier,[5] the prescription of lynching to defend white women's virtue against the American South's mythic black rapist,[6] and the early twentieth-century repressive panic over "white slavery" in which young women were purportedly abducted by foreign vice trusts and sold into prostitution.[7] During these panics, the violation of white women's purity by dark and foreign elements provided an occasion for purification, redemption, and the restoration of moral order through masculine violence. Eric King Watts argues that the "Great White protector" is a long-standing myth in Western culture that is often used as a pretense for preserving white masculine supremacy over women and people of color.[8] He writes, "White masculinity is charged with the moral obligation to confront and conquer dark threats to white purity and innocence. White spirit requires sublimation as dark forces encroach upon it. In particular, white women need protection and control because sexual relations invite 'impurities' in the form of dark desires. Thus, white women are conceived paradoxically as 'virgin/whores,' as both innocent and fallen."[9] The ongoing salience of these tropes in the film *Taken* points to how both archaic demands for patriarchy and a racial fixation on whiteness and conquest still pervade our cinematic landscape. According to Kent Ono, contemporary film and television are saturated with neocolonial narratives that revise, update, and refashion historical justifications for racism, colonialism, and white male supremacy in new contexts.[10] Thus, the "dark appeal" of *Taken* can be explained in part by its reliance on familiar discourses, imagery, and axioms that legitimate the ongoing need for a great white male protector to defend against the threat of rape by foreigners. The film is a neocolonial narrative that forwards a racist appeal to white males to protect vulnerable and morally virtuous young women.

For many Christians, *Taken* is an appealing film because it highlights a contemporary social issue that many faith-based advocacy groups are passionate about: human trafficking. Since the passage of the Trafficking Victims Protection Act in 2000, organizations such as the A21 Campaign, Sold No More, Shared Hope International, and Stop Child Sex Trafficking Now have accepted federal money to expand domestic Christian abstinence campaigns to include eliminating sexual exploitation abroad.[11] Arina Grossu of the Family Research Council illustrates the strong connection between abstinence-until-marriage and anti-trafficking campaigns: "Sex trafficking will not be eliminated until the demand is eliminated. The demand will not be eliminated until the roots of disordered sexual desire are eliminated. . . . This modern-day slavery has an even deeper slavery, an enslavement and addiction to sexual sin."[12] Similarly, the National Abstinence Clearinghouse features many articles and links to human trafficking reports that blame the sexualization of American culture for a global sexual exploitation crisis.[13] Sold No More even requires its volunteers and paid staff "to commit to a lifestyle of sexual purity, which includes abstaining from sexually immoral acts and avoiding all forms of pornography."[14] Dominated by evangelical and Catholic organizations, U.S. anti-sex-trafficking campaigns have explicitly religious overtones and, like abstinence-until-marriage discourse, often proselytize about the need for sexual purity.

While *Taken* film is free of religious directives, some Christian and conservative news outlets have treated the film as if it were an accurate representation of the global sex industry and a portrait of the negative consequences of the liberalization of sexual attitudes. For instance, the website WorldNetDaily writes: "Consciously suppressing their sexual lusts[,] our forebears built a society that protected the vulnerable. Six decades of 'sexual liberation' would change all that. In his recent Fox thriller, '*Taken*,' actor Liam Neeson tackles the inevitable result of that change, for sexual predators are the natural pedigree of sexually libertine societies."[15] The website treats *Taken* as a "wake-up call" that is "brutally honest about the 'high end' of the growing global sex slave traffic."[16] Similarly, A21 Campaign founder Christine Caine says she was inspired to action by the film: "Thank God for the movie *Taken* with Liam Neeson because that sort of gives the men something to hold on to. It's kind of a Hollywood take, but that's OK, whatever it takes."[17] Others have rallied around the film because it connects sexual immorality and the breakdown of the family in America with the growth of the global sexual industry. An article in the *American Catholic* opines,

> With the growth of the global business economy there seems to be an increase in human trafficking for sick sexual purposes like is seen in "Taken." I suppose it is the lethal brew of liberalism—economic and sexual. When sex is reduced down to a mere pleasure activity, a recreational past time, or romantic obsession—well that unleashes many demons. Add to this the extreme nature of unbridled consumerism, and you have many bad outcomes waiting to happen. If sex is just a means to someone's pleasure, then it can be made into a commodity, something that is for sale, or can be used to sell something else.[18]

For Christians who are passionate about anti-trafficking advocacy, *Taken* has achieved the status of a social problem film, a kind of ripped-from-the-headlines story that seems to integrate larger social conflicts with a fictional narrative that alerts the public to the human trafficking epidemic.

The gospel of *Taken*, however, is premised on a dangerous mythology. Bryan Mills's get-tough approach to sex trafficking was been popularized not only by the film but by the public advocacy of Christian anti-trafficking organizations, particularly the work of William Hillar, on whom the film was loosely based.

Hillar claimed to be a retired colonel from the U.S. Special Forces and that his daughter had been abducted by a human trafficking ring in Thailand. Bolstered by the popularity of the film, Hillar worked as a highly paid consultant to several anti-trafficking groups and nongovernmental organizations. However, in 2011, Hillar was convicted of fraud. He admitted that he had fabricated both his military credentials and the story of his daughter's abduction for financial gain.[19] Nevertheless, Christian enthusiasm for *Taken*'s "wake-up call" has contributed to the militarization of anti-trafficking campaigns. Stop Child Sex Trafficking Now models Mills and Hillar's "special set of skills" by employing private military operatives who boast training and experience in paramilitary and anti-terrorist operations.[20] The widespread misperception that *Taken* is an exposé of the global sex industry or, worse, a training video on how to end human trafficking has contributed to the growing militancy of Christian campaigns against sexual exploitation.

Taken resonates with the clarion call of the abstinence movement: protect the nation's daughters. Like faith-based anti-trafficking campaigns, the film suggests that libertine attitudes and the breakdown of the traditional family are responsible for the emergence of a global criminal sex trade. Throughout the film, the lackadaisical parenting of teenage girls and the erosion of sexual decency invite sexual aggression from foreign and morally inferior men. Thus, the potential violation of Bryan's daughter's sexual purity legitimizes a brutal campaign of masculine violence to obliterate this threat and reestablish a patriarchal moral order. The film elaborates on two central tropes in abstinence discourse. The first element is the notion that virginal white women who violate patriarchal directives invite sexual aggression.[21] This mythical premise calls for daughters to remain chaste and fathers to protect their daughters' sexual purity at all costs. The second trope is drawn from the contemporary politics of abstinence culture. A faith-based analysis of the global sex industry starts from the premise that recreational sex outside wedlock feeds the global demand for forced prostitution. In short, *Taken*'s portrait of sex trafficking promulgates both the mythos of young women's virtue and the ideological presupposition that permissiveness fuels sexual exploitation. In this chapter, I illustrate how *Taken* advances repressive and misinformed approaches to protecting young girls from sexual exploitation by drawing parallels between the film's narrative discourses that celebrate young women's purity, white male heroism, and racialized fears of sexual contamination.

The Great Protector and Action-Adventure Ideology

In *Taken*, the threat of "dark" masculinity from the East summons forth a white hero (Bryan) to slay the enemies of civilization and protect the sexual purity of white women. The film implies that the protection of white feminine purity legitimates both white masculine revenge-seeking and the overbearing protection of young women. While on its surface *Taken* is the story of a father willing to do anything to rescue his daughter, the narrative shares a likeness in structure to the discourses of historical sex panics in which violence and repression were seen as essential for protecting white women from dark-skinned predators. The film uses an icon of feminine virtue to excuse the use of force against uncivilized men and invites popular audiences to sympathize with extreme acts of cruelty. In particular, the film's representation of sex trafficking as a superlative evil and omnipresent danger to young women who leave the safety of home and country establishes the need for strong male protection against uncivilized, foreign, and racialized enemies. *Taken* is part of an action-adventure genre that subscribes to myths about masculinity, femininity, and whiteness.

Long-standing racial myths are updated and amplified when they enter the medium of film because cinematic representations have the power to give substance and form to everyday discourses. *Taken* is illustrative of a variety of myths and anxieties about the perceived frailty of whiteness and masculinity. It is a text in which broader discourses that valorize white masculine protection and feminine purity are discursively codified as reasonable commitments to taken-for-granted belief structures. Hernan Vera and Andrew Gordon use the term "sincere fictions" to describe how hegemonic whiteness and masculinity operate not as the overt message of Hollywood films but as taken-for-granted assumptions that take on the appearance of being innate, unchanging, and necessary structures of social existence.[22] This concept of film builds on Stuart Hall's earlier contention that racist ideologies in the media function "inferentially," drawing from a history of unquestioned racist assumptions that naturalize the existing social order.[23]

An analysis of *Taken* thus offers insights into circulating ideologies of whiteness and masculinity. As Richard Dyer demonstrates, the blockbuster U.S. action film typically venerates and reaffirms hegemonic (if not spiritual) conceptions of masculine whiteness.[24] Throughout the genre, the threat of "dark" masculinity to white femininity summons forth the mythic white hero whose masculinity is tested and forged through trial and triumph over racial Others. Cinematic revenge narratives draw from the mythos of white heroism to legitimize violence as the exclusive terrain of the white male, as something that is necessary for the proper functioning of law and order. Thomas Nakayama and Robert Krizek argue that the power of whiteness is that it makes white identities and practices "the norm by which Others are marked."[25] In revenge narratives, "saving women" often provides the ultimate test of masculinity, as such rescues symbolize the restoration of moral order. Sharing a common root with purity culture, *Taken* is an exemplary text for showcasing how revenge-seeking in popular culture is implicitly racialized and gendered.

More than any other genre, the popular American action film puts mythic white masculinity on display as a heroic response to the direct threat of dark masculinity. This trope reaches back to the dawn of modern cinema. In D. W. Griffith's *Birth of a Nation* (1915), the Ku Klux Klan heroically triumphs over the sexually aggressive black male of the Reconstruction South. In John Ford's genre-defining western *Stagecoach* (1939), the archetypal Western hero (John Wayne) single-handedly defends a group of white passengers against a horde of blood-thirsty Indians. Ford's *The Searchers* (1956) features Wayne again as a triumphant hero who must save his innocent niece from her violent Comanche captors. *Taken* can be situated in a series of similar contemporary films that demonstrate a cultural commitment to mythic white masculinity and feminine purity. The action-adventure blockbuster frequently summons white men to adventure and conquest in foreign lands (*Conan the Barbarian, Dune, Indiana Jones and the Temple of Doom, Rambo II, Star Wars, The Expendables, The Lord of the Rings*), valorizes white masculine triumph over foreign or alien enemies (*Big Trouble in Little China, Blackhawk Down, Commando, Predator, Stargate*), lionizes lone male vigilantes (*Death Wish, Die Hard, Dirty Harry, Falling Down, Lethal Weapon, Rambo, Robocop*), or creates a need for white men to protect white women against dark masculinity (*Flash Gordon, Romancing the Stone, The Limey, The Professional*). Each section of the analysis that follows elaborates on a series of ideological commitments to white masculinity and femininity expressed in *Taken* and connects them to the social contexts from which they draw and to which they contribute.

In *Taken*, female characters are either passive objects in need of protection or fallen women who haplessly invite violence and pain onto themselves and others. Women are either "good girls" who deserve male protection or "bad women" whose pursuit of autonomy invites violence and sexual aggression. Kim is the film's "good girl": chaste, innocent, passive, and in need of male protection. At seventeen, she has the physical maturity and cognition of an adult but lacks the agency to make her own choices. Her poor decisions and childish mannerisms, behavior, and dress accentuate her innocence. This trait is highlighted most of all by the film's focus on her virginity. For instance, Kim's traveling companion Amanda tells her that she intends to sleep with a young man they meet on their trip to Paris. Kim, who admits that she is a virgin, clearly disapproves. Amanda has a much more casual attitude and comments, "You got to lose it [virginity] sometime; it might as well be in Paris." The contrast between the two amplifies Kim's innocence and naiveté. By following Amanda to Paris, Kim forsakes the protection of her father and renders herself vulnerable to the world's cruelty. As the film's Jezebel, Amanda places Kim in harm's way. Later in the movie, Amanda pays for her transgressions with her life at the hands of sex-trafficking thugs.

Taken constructs ideal femininity—or the type of womanhood worthy of male protection—around an antiquated notion of "true womanhood" that constructs white women as the emblems of civilization's moral virtue that derives from a Victorian discourse of true womanhood that emphasized women's natural submissiveness, passivity, domesticity, and moral prudence.[26] As the "fairer sex," women were viewed as the protectors of society's moral fabric, particularly in the home. As a metonym for the values of Euro-American civilization, the subject of true womanhood was also implicitly white. Therefore, she was always embattled by the savage and lustful impulses of nonwhite, uncivilized men. Given the stake invested in true womanhood, gender transgressions often involved severe censure, ranging from the "unsexing" of women who sought autonomy to the loss of male protection from sexual violence. In fact, it was believed that without male protection, women's sexual victimization was virtually guaranteed.[27] Saving women provided an ideal test of white masculine power, granting men the opportunity to both save the icon of civilization and triumph over its external enemies.

These types of feminine attributes are amplified in the first half of the film by Bryan's sentimental effort to recover his lost relationship with Kim, an endeavor designed to delay her transition to adulthood and reassert his paternal authority. For Bryan, Kim is still the child he left behind for his career in intelligence. Lenore (Bryan's ex-wife) and Stuart (Lenore's new husband) are comfortable with Kim "growing up," and they encourage her to experience the world. After he retires, Bryan moves to Los Angeles to rekindle his relationship with his estranged daughter. The film begins with Bryan preparing for Kim's seventeenth birthday. He purchases a karaoke machine and wraps it in childish paper. These establishing shots lay the foundation for the fundamental clash between Bryan and Lenore, which is ultimately a moral conflict over Kim's burgeoning womanhood. While Kim is excited to see Bryan and is pleased by the gift, Lenore is visibly irritated. Kim embraces Bryan and whispers, "I still want to be a singer; just don't tell mom." This exchange illustrates that although Kim will enter adulthood, she retains some childlike innocence. But the moment is disrupted when Stuart presents Kim with a pet horse. Stuart quips, "She's not a little girl anymore," to which Bryan responds ruefully, "I guess not." Overall, the film cultivates discomfort with Lenore and Stuart's desire to support Kim's transition to womanhood.

Lenore threatens Bryan's efforts to shield Kim from the dangers of the outside world. While Bryan relates to Kim exclusively through her childhood, Lenore pushes her headlong into adulthood. Bryan and Lenore's struggle over Kim's burgeoning womanhood develops in a series of exchanges over Bryan's future role in her life and Kim's desire to travel to Europe. Kim is willing to indulge Bryan's sentimental desire to nurture and protect her childlike qualities. However, she also wants to experience the world. Not surprisingly, Bryan is shocked by Kim's request to travel to Paris with Amanda. He responds by asserting his paternal authority: "I am not comfortable with this. I know the world, sweetie. . . . I don't think a seventeen-year-old should be traveling alone." In contrast, Lenore displays a misguided faith in Kim's maturity and independence. She thwarts Bryan's renewed efforts to play a role in Kim's upbringing and dismisses his concerns for Kim's safety as paranoid and overbearing. Her glib attitude about Kim's development makes Lenore appear to be reckless about her parenting responsibilities. Exchanges between Bryan and Lenore about issues related to parenting suggest that although Lenore may have been able to raise Kim in Bryan's absence, only he knows how to keep their daughter safe. Here the film makes an interesting statement about proper parenting and motherhood. Even though Bryan was an absent father and husband, Lenore is the one who is portrayed as the uncaring, hapless parent who is not properly concerned about Kim's safety. Lenore's skepticism toward Bryan's return to Kim's life is depicted as neither concern nor protection. Instead, Lenore is constructed as an unfit mother, an emasculating shrew who challenges Bryan's authority at every turn.

Bryan and Lenore's struggle over Kim implies that the protection and autonomy of both women come at a price. Iris Young notes that "central to the logic of masculinist protection is the subordinate relation of those in the protected position. In return for male protection, the woman concedes critical distance and decision-making autonomy."[28] In assuming the role of protector, Bryan demands women's submission and adoration as the price for his shielding of them from the harms of the outside world. "Good girls" accept the need for protection, but "bad women" who move without the guidance of men invite aggression from the cruel outside world. The film's depiction of Bryan's relationship with Lenore and Kim mimics the logic of "protection rackets," an analogy Susan Rae Peterson uses in her analysis of women's relationship to men as gang-style extortion: women who seek autonomy from their husbands or fathers forgo their protection.[29] *Taken* affirms the necessity of protection rackets by punishing the female characters who move about in the world without Bryan's support and validation. In contrast, women who stay true to the film's expectations of their gender are rewarded with protection and salvation.

Sexual Liberation and Its Victims

In Bryan's search for Kim after her abduction, the film spotlights sex trafficking as a contemporary threat that women who leave the protection of the home face. Like Kim, the victims of sex trafficking are depicted as young, innocent, and passive victims of male lust. Like faith-based anti-trafficking activists, *Taken* depicts legal and tolerated prostitution as partially responsible for the rise of the illicit sex trade and thus as responsible for Kim's abduction. Here the film presents a regressive view of sexual liberation. It attributes sexual coercion and forced prostitution to the erosion of traditional gender roles brought on by the impurity of women and the moral weakness of men. It not only reifies patriarchal norms but also tacitly rejects the notion that women exercise any agency in the sex industry. It thus cultivates a strong sentiment in favor of neotraditional gender roles and the overbearing protection of young women.

The setting of Paris enables the film to connect casual attitudes toward sexuality with violence and exploitation. In popular and literary culture, Paris is historically associated with the bohemian lifestyles and social attitudes of artists, writers, actors, musicians, and vagabonds. It is often seen as an epicenter of unconventional thought, anti-orthodoxy, and free love. The bohemian backdrop suggests that Kim and Amanda lack protection because they have entered a foreign culture that is permissive toward moral deviance, free love, and prostitution. In part, the weakness of French men is to blame: their tolerance for immorality, their effeminacy, and their inability to repress their dark sexual desires create an atmosphere in which women's exploitation hides in plain sight.

The film portrays the prevalence of sex trafficking in Paris as a problem of moral permissiveness. After Kim is abducted, the film focuses on Bryan's efforts to infiltrate a foreign human trafficking ring that kidnaps American girls to be sold for sex around the world. Using his CIA contacts, Bryan ascertains that the group focuses on exploiting American tourists. The film places special emphasis on the purportedly new and innocent victims of prostitution; it represents the global sex industry as populated by individuals who are the figures of Victorian true womanhood, including young girls. It suggests that a culture that entertains dark desires and permits the degradation of women through prostitution will cannibalize even its most prized symbols of purity. This depiction calls for the eradication of prostitution in order to save the innocent from being swept up in its wake.

The image of the young innocent victim of prostitution also legitimizes extreme and moralizing responses to contemporary sexual exploitation. Jo Doezema explains that this image of naive girls who are abducted or coerced by evil traffickers "bears as little resemblance to women migrating for work in the sex industry as did her historical counterpart, the 'white slave.'"[30] Empirical data demonstrate that most of the women engaged in sex trafficking are there by choice. In addition the traffic flows from East to West rather than vice versa, and it exists within the garment, restaurant, and service industries.[31]

There is no documentation of a systemic trade in abducted Western women in Eastern Europe or the Middle East. While it is of course true that films should not be critiqued merely for their lack of verisimilitude, *Taken*'s framing of prostitution as a modern slave trade composed of innocent white women accentuates the importance of traditional sexual morality and the strength of men as women's protectors.

The film tacitly endorses an abolitionist view of the global sex industry, a perspective that all sex work is exploitation. Abolitionists oppose legal prostitution, contending that it creates a welcoming environment for violence against women.[32] Bryan begins his search for Kim by infiltrating the world of tolerated prostitution in Paris. Law enforcement personnel in Paris are portrayed as having little concern about or control over the exploitation of women. Scenes of the city show ubiquitous advertisements featuring scantily clothed models and women walking the street in sexually suggestive clothing. The film suggests that this is an environment in which illicit trafficking could plausibly exist.

The film also uses the setting of France to contrast rugged American masculinity with the effeminacy of European men. While Bryan is framed as the icon of manhood, European men are portrayed as weak, infirm, sexually immoral, or sexually aggressive. For example, Bryan uncovers a vast trafficking ring connected to legal prostitution, high-class socialites, and corrupt public officials. He meets with his longtime contact in French intelligence, Jean-Claude, who informs him that immigrants control all aspects of the Parisian sex trade. Despite Jean-Claude's awareness of the problem, it is curious that he does not offer any special police attention. He seems more concerned with his status when he reminds Bryan to "remember who he's talking to." Like other members of French law enforcement in the film, Jean-Claude is arrogant yet impotent. As the narrative continues, the film reveals that Jean-Claude actually receives large bribes to protect illicit trafficking in Paris.

This representation of French society as weak and immoral is plausible because it builds on existing cultural imagery. As Anna Cornelia Fahey notes, it is not uncommon for French men to be represented as elitist, emasculated, impotent, and morally corrupt.[33] Films such as *National Lampoon's European Vacation*, *French Kiss*, *Forget Paris*, and *EuroTrip* exemplify how French men are typically categorized as sexual dilettantes, arrogant waiters, drunkards, and criminals. In *The Pink Panther* (1963), Peter Sellers's portrayal of Inspector Clouseau elaborates on popular perceptions that French men also suffer from conceit and bumbling weakness. In *Talladega Nights*, Sacha Baron Cohen portrays a sexually charged gay race car driver who confirms for audiences that French men are hypereffeminate, homosexual, and sexually aggressive. Overall, American films reflect a very low opinion of the French. In fact, a 2009 Pew Research Center study confirmed that American attitudes toward France were the worst among all attitudes toward America's European allies. Anti-French prejudice in the United States has been amplified by France's opposition to the U.S. invasion of Iraq in 2003.[34] In addition to withholding state visits and cooperation with France on substantive policy issues, Republican lawmakers symbolically censured France by changing the term "French fries" to "freedom fries" in the House of Representatives cafeteria.[35] In an environment in which the French are so despised, French immorality and weakness provide a fitting foil to rugged American masculinity.

Bryan finds that it is the French tolerance for immorality that enables an illicit sex trade. Posing as an inquisitive client, Bryan discovers a brothel at a public construction site with makeshift rooms and dirty mattresses where dozens of kidnapped women are housed. Construction workers ignore or perhaps even join the long line of suspicious-looking johns waiting outside for their turn. By situating spectacular acts of exploitation within a mundane setting, the film blurs distinctions between conditions of voluntary and forced prostitution in several ways. First, this scene infers that tolerated or legal prostitution attracts unwelcome outsiders who will take advantage of tolerance to exploit women. The film suggests that the legal and illicit portions of the sex industry are intimately connected: where prostitution is tolerated publicly, sex slavery will flourish secretly. Second, this scene implies that once sexual exploitation becomes commonplace, its most extreme forms will flourish in everyday settings. The ringleaders operate openly in front of workers who either barely take notice or perhaps participate as collaborators or customers. The audience is left with the impression that the workers find nothing wrong with the operation. The film depicts a society so thoroughly corrupted by deviant sexual morality that it cannot tell the difference between prostitution and slavery. Finally, this scene emphasizes the severe cruelty of the perpetrators and the innocence of the victims. The scene's arrangement implies that the traffickers convert women into dehumanized commercial products. The coercive, dirty, and unwelcoming environment encourages audiences to disassociate prostitution from sexual pleasure or autonomy.

Justice for the Perpetrators

The film uses French weakness and sexual immorality to frame Bryan's vigilante law enforcement campaign as a necessary endeavor. The film expresses reverences for its object of purity. The film's framing of revenge as heroism invites the audience to witness, rationalize, and vicariously experience (and even enjoy) the act of violent retribution. It cultivates a desire for vengeance, a wish to see the crimes perpetrated against young girls to be revisited on their kidnappers. Even excessive rage is portrayed as merely balancing the scales of justice. As Derek Buescher and Kent Ono observe, such narratives "construct the audience as *a sympathizer with acts of vengeance*."[36] The film also reinforces whiteness by normalizing white masculine violence as a protective and necessary recourse for the proper functioning of global law and order.

Taken constructs extreme violence as a routine and necessary part of Western law enforcement. Its sympathetic embrace of torture illustrates the logical limits of the white male revenge narrative. When Bryan finally captures the man responsible for kidnapping Kim (Marko), he conducts a lengthy and violent interrogation. In a dark and filthy basement, Bryan stabs two metal rods into Marko's legs and attaches two jumper cables connected to a light switch. When Marko spits in Bryan's face and refuses to answer any questions, Bryan calmly flips the light switch. This is followed by the sound of humming electric current and the sight of Marko writhing in pain. Bryan's cavalier attitude and remarkable composure during this brutal electrocution presents torture as a commonplace tactic of Western law enforcement operations, particularly when innocent girls' lives are at stake. Marko's eventual capitulation confirms that torture produces results and may be necessary to protect innocents against society's most sinister criminals.

More important, the film represents retribution and sadism as acceptable expressions of white masculine rage. Torture becomes a fitting end for uncivilized men who exploit women. Lynn Arnault notes that women are frequently cited as the justification for extreme acts of violence against non-Western men. For bystanders, the abject cruelty of foreign violence against women can "predispose us to become infected with the desire for excessive retribution."[37] In other words, only excessive violence can adequately compensate for women's suffering and communicate the appropriate amount of moral condemnation of its non-Western male perpetrators. *Taken* thus lends support to the idea that violence and conquest in the name of saving women are the natural impulses of the white male hero. For Dana Cloud, the danger of such a discourse is that it contorts Western feminism into an all-encompassing rationalization for military interventions in the global South (e.g., the Taliban's oppression of women is used to justify America's ongoing war in Afghanistan).[38] Bryan's desire for excessive retribution seems to be the natural impulse of the enlightened Western male.

Bryan's detachment from Marko's suffering emphasizes this point. His calm demeanor as Marko writhes in agony communicates that he does not feel ambivalence about inflicting pain on guilty parties. With Kim's life in the balance and Marko's guilt a foregone conclusion, audiences are asked to suspend any moral apprehensions that they may have about cruelty and view Marko's torture as practically and morally necessary to the attainment of justice. When Marko gives him the information he needs, the interrogation phase concludes and the judgment and sentencing phase begins. Begging for his life, Marko pleads that he has given Bryan all the information he knows. Bryan responds, "I believe you . . . but it's not going to save you," then he executes Marko by flipping the light switch and walking away. In this case, justice for victims of sex crimes means vengeance on their perpetrators. Justice could be portrayed as the due process of law, rehabilitation through the legal system, assistance to survivors of sexual exploitation, or preventative measures that empower women to avoid entering the sex trade. Instead, the film conflates white male violence against non-Western men with justice and women's liberation.

Emancipating the Harem

The film's depiction of international trafficking illustrates how the filmmakers link the abduction of young white women with the craven sexual appetites of dark-skinned men. The "purest" of girls are saved for a high-end auction for wealthy international clients. Near the film's climax, the audience learns that Kim and several other girls are destined for the harem of a wealthy Arab man. This depiction of sex trafficking relies on Western imagery of the mythical Eastern harem, an exotic collection of female concubines who serve the sexual desires of men. Trafficking is portrayed as the means of stocking these harems with young white women who will be made to serve the exotic sexual whims of men of the Orient. This depiction accesses Orientalist tropes of Eastern mystery and backwardness. Edward Said argues that Orientalism is a solipsistic representational system of making the East present to Western eyes "by making statements about, authorizing views of it, describing it, by teaching it, settling it, ruling over it."[39] The harem has a history in Orientalist discourse as a kind of brothel containing sensual young women whose sole purpose is to pleasure powerful men. The harem is a projection of Western male sexual fantasies onto the East, an imaging of the Orient as a place of sexual adventure and conquest.[40] However, instead of using the harem as a projection of Western sexual desire, *Taken* uses it to construct the East as a sexual threat. Instead of entering the harem to gain exclusive access to exotic pleasure, Bryan seeks entry to emancipate its denizens from sexual oppression and to punish its Oriental perpetrators.

The film posits that Arab men place an astronomically high value on virginal white women. This connection can be seen in the underground auction block where clients bid on young girls from the luxury of lavish private rooms with two-way mirrors. The facility is presented as a modern-day high-tech slave auction. A female announcer describes the "merchandise" to men in business attire, who casually press buttons to bid hundreds of thousands of dollars for girls. All the girls on display are white, and all of the buyers are Arab, as audiences can infer from their language, dress, and physical features. The man who purchases Kim also buys two other women, suggesting that they are part of a white harem. The scene emphasizes that young white women are valuable to Arab men because they are embodiments of purity. When Kim appears on the auction block in a scanty bikini, the female announcer boasts, "We saved the best for last . . . certified pure." In this scene, Kim's chastity and innocence become the object of sex fetishization for Arab men. Portraits of her disturbingly eroticized body purport to show Kim through the scopic pleasure of a racial Other.

This scene relies on the myth that Arab men fetishize virgins and that they are sexually domineering toward women. These stereotypes persist in large part as a result of the portrayal of Arabs by the U.S. film industry. In a survey of 900 U.S. films, Jack Sheehan finds that Arab men are persistently identified as sexually threatening, criminal, and violent toward women.[41] *Taken*'s auction scene bears a remarkable likeness to scene in the spy thriller *Never Say Never Again* where a young white girl is taken prisoner by Muslim terrorists, stripped naked, and sold on an auction block to an Arab sheik. Arab men abduct or purchase white slaves in a series of other films, including *The Jewel of the Nile* and *Sahara*; in both films, sheik-like figures sexually torment the female lead. Other films across genres and era reinforce the general perception that Arab men domineer and threaten women, including Disney's *Aladdin*, which is riddled with violent and threatening caricatures; Elvis Presley's light-hearted Orientalism in *Harum*

FIGURE 8. Kim's purity on auction to the highest bidder. *Taken*. DVD. Directed by Pierre Moral. Los Angeles, CA: 20th Century Fox Home Entertainment, 2009.

Scarum; and the violence and exoticism of *The Thief of Baghdad*, *Raiders of the Lost Ark*, and *True Lies*. *Taken* relies on this familiar but negative imagery to accentuate the danger and evil Bryan faces.

In sum, the contrast of white women's purity with the hypersexuality of Arab men emphasizes the supposedly fundamental difference between Western culture and the Orient. The harem imagery confers legitimacy on the notion that the demand for trafficked women is driven by the deviant and uncontrollable sexual impulses of non-Western men. In this final scene, the film uses harem imagery to amplify the evil of the purveyors, the innocence of their victims, and the righteousness of Bryan's revenge. The harem structure of the film's climax is accentuated by the filmmakers' construction of its mise-en-scène. As Alloula and Dubrofsky contend, visual settings most powerfully signify the qualities of the harem, which is often characterized by "sumptuous, boudoir-like furniture; the array of sitting rooms with stuffed couches, throw rugs, and oversized pillows; and wall hangings in rich dark colors."[42] Kim's fated destination is precisely such a space: a lavish yacht with a grand staircase, dark-colored tapestries, labyrinthine hallways, white walls, gold trim, and oversized furniture. After the auction concludes, the three newly purchased girls are shuttled onto the boat wearing white veils and see-through nightgowns. Unlike the drugged girls in Parisian brothels, these girls resemble the tantalizing girls of the harem made to fit the unique tastes of powerful men. The guards exchange lines in Arabic and brandish their guns in anticipation of Bryan's rescue attempt. A sheik-like figure lounges on a round bed dressed in a sultan's robe embroidered with stylized Arabic patterns. The surrounding decor is composed of minimalist white walls and furniture, both accented with gold trim, assorted vases, and antiquities. The scene's physical composition helps audiences visualize the harem as a heavily guarded palace where the sexual desires of powerful men are fulfilled.

The obliteration of the harem and the death of its sheik mark the triumph of civilization over barbarism. By destroying the demand for trafficked girls, Bryan restores moral order and reestablishes his role as paternal protector. During the film's climax, Bryan conquers the ship's guards with lethal force and finds the sheik holding a curved blade to Kim's throat. Bryan shoots the sheik in the forehead with a single shot. As Bryan and Kim embrace, the camera pulls away to show the boat in ruins, strewn with the debris from Bryan's destruction. Their embrace in the context of the harem's destruction signifies the unfortunate but necessary cost of Kim's salvation. The restoration of order is appropriately signified by a quick cut to a well-lit and vibrant Los Angeles airport, where Kim and Bryan walk together down the tarmac. Despite the toll of his destruction, Bryan is able to return home with Kim. Lenore thanks Bryan for rescuing Kim and, amid tears, embraces him affectionately. Lenore appears humbled and more appreciative of Bryan's protective role. She is confronted with the difficult truth that protection comes at the expense of autonomy.

A Return to Purity and Whiteness

My analysis of *Taken* illustrates how blockbuster Hollywood films structure adherence to popular myths and ideological assumptions about race and gender hierarchies. While the film offers a preposterous narrative, it gives presence to taken-for-granted assumptions about the proper social roles of white men and women. *Taken* reasserts a demand for a white male protector to serve as both guardian and avenger of white women's purity against the violent and sexual impulses of racial Others. It draws from a reservoir of historic justifications for white male supremacy and conquest to legitimate the protagonist's use of violence and revenge to defend white women's honor. The continuing valorization of male revenge-seeking against the threat of rape by racial Others normalizes white male violence as protective and just. *Taken* invites its audiences to set aside their own predispositions against violence and instead trust in actions of the male protector. This analysis also elaborates on how an obsession with abstinence until marriage and women's purity might be used as a justification for repression and violence.

This critical examination of *Taken* highlights the renewed salience of troubling popular discourses about the virtues of women's purity in the context of international relations and anti-trafficking campaigns. The film contributes to a cultural atmosphere that reduces the value of young women to their chastity and crafts social policy around preserving girls' innocence at the cost of their agency. *Taken* also confirms the legitimacy of purity as a social ideal for young women and overbearing protection as a political ideal for chivalrous men. The lesson for young women is that they should delay their transition to adulthood as long as possible and sacrifice their autonomy in exchange for protection. "Good girls" assent to socially acceptable gender roles and move only with the guidance of male protectors. "Bad girls" invite sexual victimization when they forsake their prescribed social roles and usurp male power. My analysis shows how revenge narratives instruct audiences about the appropriateness of traditional gender roles. They present a stable society is one in which white men are protectors, the white women they seek to defend embody society's virtue, and foreign or dark-skinned men represent the omnipresent threat posed to civilization by dark desires that must be kept at bay through the moral and physical strength of the great protector.

5

Sexploitation in Abstinence Satires

From depictions of car cruises in the 1950s to the ubiquitous portrayals of shopping malls in the 1980s, teen cinema exploits the protean desires of youth that wax and wane over time.[1] Hollywood perpetually gauges social trends and repackages them as authentic expressions of youth culture. When the trend stagnates or ceases to be profitable, the culture industries move on to the next phenomenon.[2] However, some features of youth culture remain constant in teen cinema, including fantasies of independence and mobility, the travails of puberty, and the looming specter of sexual initiation. Constructed as a timeless and unavoidable teenage ritual, virginity loss has evolved into Hollywood's most convenient pretext for exploiting teenage sexuality. Typically, this takes the form of the light-hearted sex-quest film in which teenage protagonists make pacts to lose their virginity before they go to college or enter adulthood or wagers about doing so (e.g., *American Pie*, *Little Darlings*, *Sex Drive*, *The Last American Virgin*, and *Very Good Girls*). At the same time, teen cinema also provides earnestly somber portraits of the negative consequences of teen sexual exploration (*Juno*, *The Ballad of Jack and Rose*, *Skipped Parts*, and *Thirteen*). There is a tension in Hollywood between accepting and titillating portrayals of teenage libidinal energy and anxious representations of youth in sexual crisis.

This ambivalent tension is emblematic of contemporary struggles over the value of abstinence. Timothy Shary contends that it is unlikely that pro-abstinence discourse will prevail over what he perceives as a progressive arc in teen cinema. He writes that "even as social trends in virginity fluctuate and conservative groups continue to promote chastity . . . young people will always to be eager to explore sexual practice and will always find some level of profound feeling when they do."[3] However, Hollywood has opted to resolve the social tension between permissive and neoconservative ideologies by exploiting both sex and abstinence within the same text. The abstinence satire is an emerging subgenre of teen cinema that features wholesome virgins navigating an oversexed culture. Big-budget teen comedies such as *Easy A* (2010) and *Superbad* (2007) portray high school virgins who are so beleaguered by sex that they ultimately opt for neotraditional romance over sexual exploration. These films take as a given that losing one's virginity in a sex-saturated culture leads to the shame, defilement, and the desire run amok. While these films are irreverent in their portrayal of abstinence culture—they mock chastity clubs and self-righteous virgins—they translate the teen sex romp into a nostalgic recovery of wholesome youthful courtship. The abstinence satire is less a sign of irrepressible progress than a reflection of the confusing mixture of hypersexuality and moral panic that constitutes sexual discourse in the United States today.

Hollywood's attempt to satirize abstinence in the teen sex-quest-cum-virgin comedy has also created the optimal conditions in which low-budget films can join the chorus. Attempting to capitalize on Hollywood virgin blockbusters, low-budget productions such as *American Virgin* (2000), *American Virgin* (2009), *I Am Virgin* (2010), and *18-Year-Old Virgin* (2012) combine graphic portrayals of often depraved sex acts—pornographic mimicries of teen sex-quest films—with the message that "true love waits." These recent low-budget features are ambivalent about the status of virgins in a world where pornographic sex acts are considered mainstream. Characters that aspire to remain wholesome are unable to achieve this goal because sexual initiation inevitably deprives them of agency and self-restraint. The only solutions are to either remain a virgin or commit to traditional monogamy. The emergence of abstinence satires suggests that Hollywood and its shadow entertainment industries are not insulated from the political struggles over sexuality present in contemporary public culture. Quite the contrary: Hollywood revels in it.

This chapter examines the trend toward exploiting the abstinence movement in contemporary teen sex comedies. In order to succeed, raunchy teen comedies and their low-budget knock-offs must cash in on either a public preoccupation with a topic of current concern or a profitable film trend before its popularity wanes.[4] The emergence of abstinence satires as a subgenre indicates that both of these conditions have been satisfied. In fact, because exploitation producers unapologetically use public anxieties for profit, more than any other mainstream genre the abstinence satire makes transparent the sociopolitical process of cinematic transcoding. In short, the public and cinematic struggles over the meaning of virginity have made abstinence until marriage an exploitable concept. And because discussing sexual inexperience is fraught with fantasies and repressed desires, abstinence can be seamlessly integrated into classic sexploitation films without any apparent contradiction. Indeed, the notion that chastity is sexy has not been lost on Hollywood and the exploitation film industry.[5]

I argue that both high- and low-budget abstinence satires are an anemic and counterproductive cultural challenge to pro-virginity discourses. Integrating comic spoofs of abstinence themes into sexually charged teen comedies reduces the sexuality of youth to the simplistic polarities of virgins and whores. I examine *Easy A* and *Superbad* alongside a series of low-budget spoofs that integrate abstinent characters into quasi-pornographic narratives, including *American Virgin* (2000), *American Virgin* (2009), *I Am Virgin*, and *18-Year-Old Virgin*, to illustrate how exploiting both abstinence and sex in the same text ultimately invites identification with normative heterosexuality. First, while these films mock abstinence, they ultimately affirm the conservative proposition that American culture is too sexually permissive. As a result, abstinent characters are depicted as merely seeking out reasonable ways to navigate a confounding landscape of physical desire. Second, abstinence satires constitute what Paul Booth calls "hyper-articulations" of sexuality that reinforce the virgin/whore dichotomy,[6] by which he means that pornographic spoofs of mainstream films tend to cultivate overidentification instead of disrupting normative sexual practices. While some feminist film scholars see traditional sexploitation as a challenge to conventional heteronormative sex acts, I argue that abstinence sexploitations invite a search for normalcy amid a sex-saturated culture.[7] Although the virgin/whore dichotomy has always been a staple of the sexploitation subgenre, recent attempts to capitalize on society's preoccupation with virginity do less to menace social taboos than they do to ultimately solidify moral prohibitions against nonmonogamous sex or sex outside marriage.

Abstinence: An Exploitable Concept

In response to teen promiscuity and the attendant rituals of "slut shaming," the film *Easy A* suggests that women can maintain an aura of respectability when it comes to virginity loss and the performance of sexual identity. This recent instantiation is an overtly self-conscious version of the teen sex comedy but one in which the protagonists ultimately remain abstinent (with the exception of an illicit teacher-student affair). In this film, Olive Penderghast (Emma Stone) is an overachieving but relatively unknown high school student who becomes the subject of false rumors about the loss of her virginity to a college student. Her precociousness compels her to engage the spectacle of the high school rumor mill with an irreverent reenactment of *The Scarlet Letter*, agreeing to let a select group of high school boys lie about losing their virginity to her in exchange for money and gift cards to retail stores. While Olive gives these young men sexual bragging rights, she becomes a symbol of her high school's promiscuity crisis. Even though she never actually loses her virginity, she ends up defiled by her ironically stylized persona. While the film critiques the hypocrisies of abstinence culture—including hyperbolic caricatures of the high school chastity club—it cleans up the teen sex comedy without jettisoning its gross-out humor and titillating portrayals of teenage girls. It is a film that is both chaste and sexy.

To its credit, the film concludes that on-screen virginity loss is, in Olive's words, "nobody's goddamn business." Nonetheless, her sentimental attachment to a time when chivalry was alive and well is indicative of the film's underlying conservatism. When Olive's ironic appropriation of the slut persona leads boys to treat her in a degrading manner, Olive expresses nostalgic longing for the kind of respectable teen romance depicted in the teen films of the 1980s, particularly those directed by John Hughes.[8] As a montage of iconic scenes from *Can't Buy Me Love, Ferris Bueller's Day Off, Say Anything, Sixteen Candles*, and *The Breakfast Club* play over a sentimental cover of the Thompson Twins' "If You Were Here," Olive pines: "Whatever happened to chivalry? Did it only exist in eighties movies? I want John Cusack holding a boom box outside my window. I want to ride off on a lawnmower with Patrick Dempsey. I want Jake from *Sixteen Candles* waiting outside the church for me. I want Judd Nelson thrusting his fist in the air because he knows he got me just once. I want my life to be like an eighties movie." Despite her nostalgic longing, the failure of Olive's hijinks has little to do with her the fact that her life is not being directed by John Hughes. Instead, her failures stem from the notion that girls who do not act like ladies do not receive the respect they deserve. While audience members are given insight into Olive's true nature, the film moves toward a resolution that restores her reputation so that she can finally connect with Todd, her primary love interest. Her nostalgia for a simulacrum of teenage romance cultivates attachment to a supposedly simpler time when the pressure to have sex did not complicate teen relationships. Ultimately, Olive lives out her eighties teen film fantasy with the performance of a musical number that restores her reputation, a thoughtful soliloquy that summarizes lessons learned, and a lawnmower ride with Todd to the tune of an updated rendition of Simple Minds' "Don't You Forget about Me." The return of male chivalry enables Olive to have a traditional teen romance without the complications of sex. In this way, the film indicts the oversexualized teenager of contemporary cinema and suggests that a teen film can be sexy without losing its wholesome appeal.

Superbad (2007) is another recent Hollywood adaptation of the teen virginity quest that adheres to sexual respectability as a pathway to a more wholesome and fulfilling version of teen romance. This film even adopts many of the stylistic features of exploitation films, with a soundtrack reminiscent of classic Blaxploitation films and a significant number of references to pornographic stag films (but of course without their explicit material). In this film, Seth (Jonah

Hill) and Evan (Michael Cera) are determined to find girlfriends for the summer before they leave for college. Their hope is that they can gain the sexual
and relationship experience they need for the next phase of their life without
jeopardizing their ongoing bromance. Despite the fact that both protagonists
consider themselves pornography aficionados, they represent opposite poles of
teen romance. While Seth wants to put his pornographic fantasies into practice
with his longtime female love interest (Jules), Evan wants a wholesome relationship with his friend Becca that is based on respect for women's virtue. The
film thus sets up the "all-or-nothing" binary between chastity and pornography
that low-budget knock-offs exploit. Although Jules initially rebuffs Seth for not
following the proper pathway to wholesome teen romance, Evan spurns Becca's sexual advances because he sees himself as a gentleman and has too much
respect for her. Neither character loses his virginity, but both learn the benefits
of taking things slow so they can develop more meaningful relationships with
their respective love interests. Although the film includes explicit references to
pornography, graphic sex talk, and extreme gross-out humor, it concludes that
the pursuit of sex complicates the development of deeper and more meaningful
relationships. In the end, Seth abandons his pornographic fantasies so he can
court Jules in an appropriate manner.

   While abstinence satires capitalize on a number of contemporary trends in
teen films, these two successful Hollywood features typify the contemporary cinematic terrain of what is exploitable about virginity and abstinence. Moreover,
they establish the mise-en-scènes, the narrative structure, and the thematic elements that give textual meaning to the struggle between sex and abstinence in
contemporary cinema. These films place virgins engaged in wholesome teen
romance against the backdrop of the teen sex romp (sexually charged teen parties, the repressed good girl, the pornographic fantasy, and graphic gross-out
humor), where their purity and innocence can be simultaneously valorized and
sexually exploited.

Abstinence Culture Meets Sexploitation

Although abstinence satires are relatively new, virginity has always been an
exploitable cinematic concept. Low-budget sexploitation films feature scenar-
ios such as the following: stranded in the woods, three virgins are abducted
by a swamp monster and forced into sexual servitude; an innocent young virgin is abducted off the street and sold into white slavery; two virgins' dreams
of becoming fashion models are dashed when they are duped into becoming
part a witches' coven; a hunter must save a damsel virgin from being sacrificed
by a primitive jungle tribe; a scantily-clad all-female virgin biker gang exacts

revenge on a drug kingpin. These film descriptions illustrate that the history of the exploitation film and B-movie double feature is replete with titillating and salacious tales of virgin women who become nymphomaniacs (*Damaged Goods, Entrails of a Virgin, Protect Your Daughter, The Cheerleaders, Virgin in Hollywood*), banded together as vigilantes (*Revenge of the Virgins, Virgins from Hell*), are seduced by the occult (*Attacks of the Virgin Mummies, The Virgins of Sherwood Forest, Virgin Witch, Virgins among the Living Dead*), are sold as chattel by foreign vice trusts (*Is Any Daughter Safe?, Traffic in Souls*), and are ritualistically sacrificed by jungle tribes (*Brides of Blood, Virgin Sacrifice*).[9] In these lurid low-budget features, female virgins are exploited and fetishized in order to arouse male fantasies of erotic conquest. The composite figure of woman as virgin/whore registers latent male desire for a female subject who is innocent and chaste while also being sexually craven.

As the titles above suggest, Hollywood productions have always been accompanied by a shadow industry of low-budget features that explicitly sacrifice art for profit. Historically, the classic exploitation film either mirrored Hollywood trends or covered subjects that were considered taboo or so salacious (i.e., sex, drug use, and juvenile delinquency) that they were unsuitable for distribution in accordance with the Motion Picture Production Code. To capitalize on the popularity of a film trend or topic, exploitation films were produced quickly on a low budget, typically with a cast of relatively unknown actors. The film's promotional materials compensated for low production values, bad acting, and lack of star power by wallowing in sensationalism and spectacle, promising audiences shocking revelations and cheap thrills.[10] To avoid censorship, some producers used the guise of education to show what was typically considered inappropriate material.[11] For instance, iconic films such as *Reefer Madness* (1936) claimed to inform the public about the threat of marijuana use with preposterous portrayals of drug-induced sex and violence. But as social taboos and exploitable film trends continued to evolve, exploitation cinema encompassed a vast array of titillating subgenres (biker films, Blaxploitation films, cannibal films, carsploitation, Canuxploitation films, CGIsploitation films, mockbusters, Mondo films, Nazisploitation films, nudie features, rape/revenge films, splatter flicks, monster movies, sexploitation films, and women-in-prison films).[12]

Although the exploitation film industry stood in contradistinction to mainstream Hollywood, its lurid subject matter was often accompanied by heavy-handed moralizing. In this regard, sex and sexual morality have always been the most readily exploitable phenomena, rarely if ever going out of style. Films such as *Sex Madness* (1938), *Mom and Dad* (1945), and *She Shoulda Said No!* (1949) warned parents and their teenagers about the dangers of premarital sex, including pregnancy, venereal disease, and social disintegration. The mixture of erotic visuals and prudish admonishments of sexual activity these films presented, although confusing, prefigures conservative impulses within some subgenres of the contemporary exploitation film industry.

When abstinence enters the realm of cinematic exploitation, it provides a confusing portrait of teenage desire. Low-budget abstinence satires are derived from Hollywood's recent emphasis on virgins finding their way to romance in a sex-saturated culture. This narrative capitalizes on abstinence advocates' emphatic assertion that virgins are beleaguered victims of a sex-obsessed culture. For instance, the Heritage Foundation contends that "today's teenagers live in a sex-saturated culture. Teen virgins are treated as oddities or misfits in popular media and even in sex education. This negative representation of teen virginity is obviously harmful."[13] The films examined in the remainder of this chapter frequently contrast the protagonists' sexual inexperience with a culture of normalized pornography and sexual inhibition. Although this juxtaposition provides directors with an occasion to show what is ostensibly pornographic material, the virgins' curiosity about sex is frequently tempered by repeated exposure to graphic and comically embarrassing acts of sexual depravity.

Unlike earlier sexploitation films' take on the virgin/whore archetype, these films focus not on the voyeuristic pleasures of the virgin-turned-whore but instead on the victimized virgin who resists the temptation to adopt the norms of his or her sex-crazed compatriots. The virgin protagonist peering over the threshold of sexual inexperience observes a slippery slope to complete moral degradation and retreats to the safe and morally superior position of traditional monogamy. These films adopt a male gaze through which spectators may access the promiscuous, sexually available woman of pornographic fantasies but maintain their fidelity to the chaste woman who is worthy of marriage and monogamy. They also capitalize on the abstinence movement's reliance on a virgin/whore dichotomy in which girls are forced to choose between two extremes: purity or promiscuity.[14] This hyperarticulation ultimately cultivates sympathy for those beleaguered by the libertine values of contemporary American culture without sacrificing their sex appeal.

Virgins in a Pornographic World

18-Year-Old Virgin (directed by Tamara Olson), an example of a sexploitation film par excellence represents virginity loss as an induction into raunch culture in which deviant sexuality (including bondage, tantric sex, and orgies) is mainstream if not banal.[15] Asylum Pictures—a production company that is renowned for its highly profitable low-budget straight-to-DVD knock-offs—released the film in 2009 to capitalize on the popularity of teen virgin comedies and titles such as The 40-Year-Old Virgin.[16] The film's cast of relatively unknown actors, low production values, explicit sexual content, and transparent appropriations of Hollywood teen films is indicative of how exploitation productions capitalize on sexual abstinence. It depicts Katie Powers's numerous failed attempts to lose her virginity at a high school graduation party. Her primary love interest (Ryan) refuses to sleep with her until she loses her virginity because his extensive sexual experience has taught him that virgins are simply "too much drama." In contrast, Todd, a longtime admirer of Katie, is unable to achieve arousal when a romantic rendezvous between the two turns into a pornographic encounter. While Ryan wants a girl with vast sexual experience, Todd fantasizes about an innocent kiss the two shared as young children and primarily admires Katie for her intelligence and academic accomplishments. These two contrasting tales of teenage desire illustrate that Katie is desirable to men only as a virgin or a whore. Virginity loss is depicted in extreme binary terms. For women in particular, there is no pathway to sexual experience that does not entail defilement.

The virgin/whore dichotomy is exaggerated by Katie's attempts to transform from debate team captain to X-rated vixen. To become more desirable to boys, Katie and her sexually experienced friend Rose make her over in accordance with the beauty standards of women featured in a pornographic magazine. She shaves her pubic hair, stuffs her bra with chicken breasts, and makes a special effort to make boys feel smarter than her. Despite her new porn-star

FIGURE 9. Poster for *The 18-Year-Old Virgin*. DVD. Directed by Tamara Olson. Burbank, CA: The Asylum, 2010. Design © 2009 The Asylum Home Entertainment.

affect, Katie is humiliated through a series of failed intimate encounters involving group sex, sex toys, masturbation, sadomasochism, and tantric sex. At one point Katie declares, "This whole sex thing is so much more disturbing than I expected it to be. I'll be happy if I never see a penis again." Katie's repudiation of sex is premised on the assumption presented throughout the film that pleasure is fundamentally taboo. In addition, the film portrays virginity loss as fundamentally devoid of female agency. Since Katie just wants to "get it over with," she is willing to put her own desire in the background—even enduring pain and embarrassment—to conform to the expectations established in the male pornographic fantasy. Never materializing into an explicitly sexual fantasy, her desire for Ryan is framed in vague childlike terms based on her misguided belief that the two were destined to be together. The film suggests that it is impossible for Katie to both have sex and retain her good-girl status. This point is accentuated by the fact that Katie's exploits put her in danger of losing her high school's good citizenship award. The film's raunchy high school party becomes an occasion for young female characters to choose a side of the virgin/whore binary.

18-Year-Old Virgin exploits every aspect of the contemporary Hollywood virgin feature: sexualized chastity, graphic gross-out humor, repressed good girls, and sex-obsessed boys. Despite its pornographic interludes, the film also mirrors the latent conservatism of mainstream films. Confused and alienated by the perversity of sexual desire, Katie opts for a relationship with Todd instead of Ryan. Katie loses interest in Ryan after she learns that he is secretly bisexual and has no interest in a long-term relationship. It dawns on her that Todd has always been her love interest because he values her most wholesome traits. Sex with Ryan seems to be unfulfilling and requires an unnecessary loss of self. While the film implies that Katie and Todd may ultimately lose their virginity to each other, the audience is reassured that this is permissible if they are guided by true love within the confines of a traditional heterosexual relationship. In short, a relationship with a fellow virgin offers an escape from defilement. In another sense, the film's conservatism lies in its adherence to the myth that virgins are taunted and victimized by a culture unmoored from traditional sexual morality. The film takes as a given that pornography is the telos of sexual liberation and that women cannot pursue sexual pleasure without losing their identity. Katie is sympathetic because she is powerless against liberationist forces that have rendered virginity obsolete. Her only reprieve comes through adherence to her core values. She is a virgin lost in a pornographic culture, seeking a like-minded wholesome man with whom she can have morally appropriate sex, guided by the spirit of true love.

I Am Virgin (directed by Sean Skelding) is another recent low-budget production that capitalizes on the victimized virgin seeking relationship fulfillment in a culture devoid of sexual morality. In this sexploitation spoof of the

FIGURE 10. Poster for *I Am Virgin*. DVD. Directed by Sean Skelding. Portland, OR: IMD-Films, 2010.

post-apocalyptic film *I Am Legend* (2007), Robby believes that he is quite literally the last virgin on Earth.[17] He appears to be one of the only remaining survivors of a global pandemic that has transformed most of humanity into sex-crazed vampires. The narrative follows Robby and his basset hound companion Bill as they scour a metropolitan landscape looking for a wholesome girl with whom he can share his life and hopefully lose his virginity. Throughout the film, he encounters bands of nymphomaniac vampires who desire nothing more than to deflower virgins. From his fortified suburban home, Robby broadcasts a video journal of his exploits in the hope that he will find a mate who is not afflicted by the sex virus. Despite his desire to meet a fellow virgin, Robby spends most of his time either watching pornography at home or peeping into the vampire orgies that take place in dark corners of the city. Thus, lengthy pornographic sex scenes continually interrupt the narrative and invite the audience to adopt Robby's erotic voyeurism. Despite his fascination with pornography, Robby's virginity renders him immune to the lustful urges of the infected.

I Am Virgin embeds a socially conservative message within an irreverent sexploitation feature. On its surface, the protagonist's erotic fascination with pornography and voyeurism seems to be at odds with his desire to meet a wholesome virginal woman. But Robby's deep ambivalence about sex suggests that men need not reconcile the contradiction. Instead, the film implies that men can take pleasure in the sexual degradation of women while maintaining an expectation that the women they marry will be pure and innocent. This iteration of the virgin/whore dichotomy suggests that there is no hypocrisy in the fact that men demand that women remain abstinent until marriage while at the same time engaging in their own sexual indiscretions. Here, the male ideal is to have a wholesome woman in the daylight and a fallen woman in the shadows. But Robby's ingrained sense of guilt and shame makes it impossible for him to do more than vicariously take part in the new society's sexual pleasures. Scenes from Robby's childhood reveal that his parents are sexual prudes who berated him about the evils of women and insisted that it was imperative that he remain abstinent until marriage. Although his parents first appear as preposterous caricatures of abstinence proponents, the reality of the sexual apocalypse ultimately validates their anti-sex ideology. Robby curses his virginity, yet his parents' guilt-laden admonishments are what protect him from the infected and compel him to continue his search for the right woman instead of succumbing to desire. Sexual vampires may be titillating, but they cannot offer Robby the relationship fulfillment he believes he would experience with a wholesome girl.

Like Hollywood abstinence films, *I Am Virgin* constructs sexual desire as an infectious liability. It suggest that without a sense of propriety, shame, and guilt, sex is a slippery slope to the myopic pursuit of base pleasures at the expense of one's humanity. The film's female vampires are incapable of expressing any other thought or desire aside from their vulgar and all-consuming sexual urges. Near the end of the film, Robby encounters a male vampire (played by porn icon Ron Jeremy) who finally discloses the nature of vampire infection. He tells Robby that it is possible to have casual sex without succumbing to the disease so long as one discards one's sense of guilt. He contends, "It's not the sex that changes you, it's how you feel that makes a difference." Robby is excited by the prospect that he can have sex and retain his humanity. Yet at the film's climax he forgoes guaranteed sexual pleasure because, as he confesses, there is no such thing as guilt-free sex. As they are in *18-Year-Old Virgin*, audiences are confronted by the binary of sexual abstinence and promiscuity. The film concludes that there is no middle ground between virginity and unbridled sexual expression. Once one succumbs to desire, one will always be a prisoner of his or her own urges. Desire is monstrous. Only the protagonist's stalwart morality protects him from losing his humanity. Like early exploitation films that titillated while teaching moral lessons, *I Am Virgin* teaches that abstinence is the only remedy for a sex-saturated culture. However, in the process, the film revels in its own hypocrisy by showing graphic sex scenes while imploring spectators to avert their gaze.

In *I Am Virgin*, we also see the recurring fear of female vampires, horrifying villains that illustrate the mythic monstrosity of female sexual desire. The film's sex scenes feature close-up shots of the characters' menacing fangs that remind spectators of the constant risk of penetration. The toothed mouth of the female vampire invokes the primal fear of the castrating woman and the need to contain the threat of female sexual desire. Robby is simultaneously aroused and terrified at the sight of the female monster. The female vampire is menacing because she represents the danger of unbridled female sexuality that leads to the potential loss of male sexual power and potency. The vampires want to deflower Robby and rob him of his humanity for their own perverse pleasures. Robby must refuse sex to curtail the threat of female domination. He tells the vampires, "I'm looking for a sweet girl who will love me for me. . . . I want my first time to be with the right woman and you are not the right woman." His purity intact, Robby leaves the city to find a girl among the prudish outcasts of the North. Although the film refuses to take itself seriously, its juxtaposition of the exploitation of powerful female sexuality with the victimized and ostracized virgin registers anxiety about the extreme risks of sexual activity. Robby resigns himself to the fact that virginity and monogamy are incommensurate with the values of the new dystopian society and opts to live safely in exile with those who retain the old traditionalism.

Countless other straight-to-DVD releases exploit the sexual motifs present in these films, but these two films are exemplary for their narratives of victimization. Virginity is portrayed as obsolete in a dystopian society without sexual inhibition. These texts imply that sexual pleasure is not worth the price of total defilement. Spectators are temporarily allowed to revel in sexual voyeurism, sometimes to the point of disgust, only to reveal that pleasure is necessarily accompanied by pain and embarrassment. When the choice is between unbridled sexual activity and abstinence (or at least traditional monogamy), a return to sexual morality is made to appear the more appealing.

As American as Virginity

In the titles of teen films, the adjective "American" often satirizes the national mythos of youth coming of age. For instance, films such as *American Graffiti* (1973), *The Last American Virgin* (1982), and *American Pie* (1999) spoof the dating rituals of the American teenage male in a time of lost innocence.[18] In the titles of many Hollywood films, the word "American" is less a declaration of heritage than it is an invitation to distantly gaze at the corruption, disintegration, or unattainability of some quintessential element of the American Dream such as idyllic small-town America (*American Graffiti*), equality and upward mobility (*American History X, American Violet, American Girl*), the suburb (*American Beauty*), or consumerism and neoliberal capitalism (*American Psycho, American Hustle, American Gigolo, American Gangster*). "American" films often ask spectators not for reverence but for a critical reflection—sometimes comedic—on a dysfunctional aspect of American life.

The ubiquity of the "American" designation provides low-budget producers with ample opportunities to ride the promotional coattails of iconic Hollywood features. Since 2000, two separate sexploitation films have shared the clichéd title of *American Virgin*. Although their plots are different, both movies ostensibly blame the decline of youthful innocence on the pornification of everyday life. Graphic gross-out humor notwithstanding, the disillusionment registered in these two films capitalizes on recurring moral panic over the loss of the wholesome vitality of youth. To a certain extent, the films capture how the pornography industry seized upon the concept of sexual liberation in order to exploit and sexualize youth culture.[19] While the films quite hypocritically engage in the very process they indict, they invite spectators to adopt a paternalistic stance toward the films' female protagonists. The films suggest that pornography loses its eroticism when both male characters and the male audience are forced to imagine its subjects as daughters. Invoking the taboos of incest and pedophilia, this presentation of young women as hypersexualized ultimately attempts to cultivate in the audience a nostalgia for an overprotective ethos. The films purport to recover youthful innocence from the mainstreaming of pornography, saving the victimized virgin protagonist from personal defilement. Both iterations of

American Virgin exploit parents' nightmares about degraded youth, detailing the precariousness of female innocence in pornographic culture.

The first iteration of *American Virgin* (directed by Jean-Pierre Marois) depicts the efforts of a teenage daughter of a famous pornographer to expose her father's hypocritical expressions of overbearing protectionism. Prior to the film's 2000 release date, the film's lead (Mena Suvari) went from relative obscurity to instant stardom with her acclaimed performances in *American Pie* and *American Beauty* (1999). In the final stages of production, the producers decided to cash in on Suvari's newfound celebrity and iconic on-screen virginity by changing the name from *Live Virgin* to *American Virgin*.[20] In this film, Katrina exacts revenge on her father, Ronny Bartolotti (Robert Loggia), by attempting to lose her virginity on live television. Produced by Ronny's rival, Joey Quinn (Bob Hoskins), the live broadcast spectacle is designed to capitalize on the popular fetishizing of female virginity. Included with the pay-per-view feature is a virtual-reality sex suit that enables customers to vicariously have sex with Katrina. While Suvari, as Katrina, is billed as the feature's lead, the film gives far less attention to the theme of the daughter indicting her overbearing father than it does to Ronny and his hypocritical efforts to thwart the live TV airing.

Predictably, the 2000 version of *American Virgin* sacrifices a potential critique of the virgin/whore dichotomy to exploit the mythic notion of a father's worst nightmare. Despite years of exploiting women in his films, Ronny expects his daughter to attend college and become a lawyer, all while remaining sexually abstinent. The moral bifurcation of his work and his home life is represented by the division of his home into a film studio on the one side and a simulacra of domesticity on the other. Ronny has struck a delicate balance in which he can both profit from the adult film industry and expect his daughter to remain pure and sheltered. Katrina's response to Ronny's hypocrisy is to collapse the tenuous boundaries between his work and personal life by entering the pornography industry in spectacular fashion. Hypothetically, losing her virginity on pay-per-view TV would expose Ronny's failings as a father and indict pornography's creation of disposable women. Despite the potential for social critique, the film gives less attention to the rationale for Katrina's decision than it does to the struggle between Ronny and Joey over who will control the fate of her virginity. Through a series of physically brutal though slapstick encounters between the two, the narrative devolves into a macho contest over a young woman's sexuality. This masculine test of wills is matched by the filmmaker's conspicuous use of phallic imagery, including scenes where the two mercilessly assault each other with large penis-shaped objects. In addition, the fantasy of humiliating Ronny and rebooting his own career in pornography in the process enables Joey to overcome his sexual impotence.

The film diverges from the theme of Katrina's indictment of sexual double standards into a depiction of a father in crisis, besieged by lecherous men who find pleasure and fulfillment in deflowering innocent young girls. When the film transforms into a male contest, it becomes significantly easier for audiences to identify with a father who wants to protect his daughter from the ultimate act of personal defilement. At these points of intense competition, the audience is encouraged to adopt a paternalistic gaze and identify with Ronny as he attempts to stop the production of *Live Virgin* and commits to abandoning the pornography industry. Although his overprotectiveness is what initiates the film's central antagonism, it develops into a point of identification that, in part, contributes to his redemption. He never fully regains his moral status as a father, but he is most sympathetic when he expresses a desire to protect his daughter from sexually craven men. His real failing as a father is that he lacks the moral authority to keep his daughter from making bad decisions about her body. This overemphasis on what is presented as a father's worst nightmare leaves Katrina's sexual agency underexplored and quite often negated.

American Virgin's portrayal of the pay-per-view special *Live Virgin* aligns with many key elements of contemporary virgin lore. Foremost among the mythologies presented in the film is the overinflated social and erotic value of female virginity. The patrons of *Live Virgin* eagerly anticipate what has been advertised as a gratifying though virtual sexual experience with a young woman with no sexual experience. Katrina is cast as Joan of Arc. In that role, the iconic chastity of her character presents customers with the opportunity to deflower and subjugate one of history's most well-known female virgins. The portrayal of *Live Virgin* implies that male pleasure derives from power and domination. Joey writes the scene as a rape that turns into a mutually gratifying and consensual sexual encounter. He instructs her to resist but eventually succumb to her assailant's overpowering force. *Live Virgin* purportedly reaches men who desire a female who is an inexperienced girl, someone whose pleasure is ancillary to the sexual experience. In essence, the film confirms that chastity is sexy, or that the ultimate subject of male fantasy is the inexperienced adolescent female body tied to a subject who is incapable of fully articulating mature adult desires. The customers are depicted as emasculated working-class males teeming with unfulfilled perverse desires; the promise of vicariously deflowering a virgin offers them a chance to feel newly powerful. As *Live Virgin* approaches its climax, the camera cuts between three different men—including another cameo from Ron Jeremy—at home in space-age sex suits staring directly at the camera, visibly addled by their desire. The presence of futuristic cyborg technology suggests that these men, along with millions of others, are now equipped to conquer a new frontier as they collectively traverse the boundaries of female sexual inexperience.

The depiction of the young girl as the sexual ideal is not merely an expression of predatory and pedophilic desire but also a depiction of the adult woman as used, unclean, and unattractive. This theme is a staple of abstinence-only curricula that frequently involves exercises where a teacher circulates a piece of candy and then tells students, "no one wants food that has been passed around. Neither would you want your future husband or wife to have been passed around."[21] The notion that used women are not valuable is reflected throughout the film. For instance, one customer is poised to deflower Katrina as his wife looks on with inexplicable enthusiasm. Despite her excitement, the husband appears altogether sexually and emotionally uninterested in his middle-aged wife. It is telling that the pay-per-view event does not involve a pornographic celebrity or even an adult woman who at the very least could be a helpful and knowledgeable participant in this simulated sexual encounter. The film's message is that adult women with sexual experience have diminished social and erotic value. Hyperawareness of Katrina's virginity and the pleasures of male conquest trumps a more meaningful, and perhaps more erotic, portrait about what women desire both before and after they cross the threshold of inexperience. The film's exploitation of "chastity is sexy" renders all that comes after virginity ostensibly meaningless and devoid of pleasure for men.

The film resolves the dialectic between pornography and abstinence by situating the protagonist's first sexual encounter in the context of heterosexual monogamy. Katrina and her ex-boyfriend Brian spontaneously collaborate to undermine the production of *Live Virgin* by cutting the Internet connection and entering a sealed chamber to have sex without the vicarious participation of the pay-per-view customers. Katrina's resistance to her father's hypocrisy is dampened by what amounts to a spectacular announcement of monogamous love for her ongoing romantic interest. While Katrina subverts the show's production, she loses her virginity in a way that is much less threatening to her father's duplicitous moral code. By denying the millions of spectators their voyeuristic experience, she saves herself for a monogamous relationship with Brian. Her act of defiance ultimately reaffirms the notion that virginity and its loss are more unique and meaningful when explored in the context of committed relationships. It suggests that the mainstreaming of pornography has quite tragically translated the value of virginity loss into an economy of perverse male pleasure. If complete abstinence is untenable in a pornographic world, then the only act of resistance is to rearticulate the significance of virginity loss within a monogamous relationship. While it is true that Katrina recovers some degree of agency and pleasure, her actions have a more profound impact on Ronny's moral equivocation about pornography than on his hypocrisy about the proper expression of her sexual identity. In fact, her actions disrupt the commercial appeal of Joey's business and inspire Ronny to leave the pornography industry

for legitimate film. Monogamy, then, is presented as the most threatening oppo-
nent to the pornification of everyday life.

The second iteration of *American Virgin* (directed by Claire Kilner) also portrays the lone virgin imperiled by the normalization of pornographic sex acts.
Originally titled *Mardi Gras* and then *Virgin on Bourbon Street*, the film was written to be shot in New Orleans but changed locations to Detroit to take advantage
of local tax incentives.[22] But with a budget of approximately $4 million and some
recognizable though predominately B-list celebrities, *American Virgin* is a good
example of how the style of exploitation cinema has been absorbed into more
mainstream Hollywood productions.[23] However, as a straight-to-DVD release in
the U.S. market, the film's distribution was fundamentally the same as for most
exploitation features.

The 2009 *American Virgin* explicitly satirizes abstinence culture by contrasting the comic prudishness of the protagonist Priscilla (Jenna Dewan Tatum)
with a hackneyed portrayal of college life that includes parties, alcohol, drugs,
and casual sex. A devoted and outspoken virgin, Priscilla is able to attend college
with the support of a scholarship from a faith-based abstinence organization.
Priscilla's scholarship is jeopardized by the potential revelation that in a reluctantly inebriated state, she posed naked for *Chicks Go Crazy*, a thinly veiled parody of *Girls Gone Wild*. The plot focuses on Priscilla and her new friends' sexually
charged journey to recover the tape from pornography mogul Ed Curtzman (Rob
Schneider). Although the film mocks abstinence until marriage, its attempts at
irreverent humor are ultimately counterproductive. Although it suggests that
abstinence rhetoric inadequately prepares young women for adulthood. the
misguided warrant for this position is that pornography and raunch culture
are somehow the contemporary iteration of feminism. For example, Priscilla's
roommate Naz taunts Priscilla with vulgar sex talk and a nonchalant attitude
toward sex toys, group sex, masturbation, and drug abuse. Naz is a caricature
of pro-sex feminism so far removed from the politics of sexuality that her promiscuity is not a statement of bodily autonomy but instead a sign of moral turpitude. In the same vein as *American Virgin*, *18-Year-Old Virgin*, and *I Am Virgin*,
the ubiquity of pornographic sex acts throughout the film portray a culture that
has lost its moral foundations. Naz is depicted as the logical outcome of sexual
liberation on the contemporary college campus.

The depictions of the video series *Chicks Go Crazy* also take as a given that
pornography is the necessary outcome of sexual freedom. The film begins with
a spoof advertisement for videos of naked college girls in which an announcer
boasts that the product is unavailable in "sexless places" such as Utah. When
Curtzman visits college campuses, his pitch to get young women to disrobe frequently takes the form of a cynical postfeminist diatribe that lambastes religious
conservatives for making women feel ashamed of their bodies. For instance, he

tells two women that "these fundamentalists believe the Earth is only 5,000 years old, now how stupid is that, so don't let these morons tell you that you can't show your tits." Curtzman is particularly adept at appropriating feminist language to facilitate active participation from reluctant women. He tells a crowd of enthusiasts, "Don't burn your bras, just take them off." Positioned against repressive sexual norms and in favor of women's liberation, Chicks Go Crazy suggests that it is impossible to embrace sex positivity without traversing a slippery slope to exploitation. This moral descent is denoted between major scenes by stills of Priscilla posed on a Chicks Go Crazy advertisement that feature a meter that measures her declining percentage of sexual purity. The filmmakers' effort to satirize the pornography industry leaves little ground between abstinence and promiscuity. A confused and ambivalent text, the 2009 American Virgin both celebrates and laments the iconic loss of teenage innocence. Like other exploitation films, its mixed message offers the filmmakers the opportunity to moralize while showing gratuitous sex and shocking images.

The film attempts to make light of both abstinence culture and pornography but fails to make a powerful comedic statement against either. The filmmakers resolve Priscilla's troubles regarding Chicks Go Crazy with the same spirit of masculine protection promulgated in the first American Virgin. Specifically, Priscilla enlists Curtzman's teenage daughter to convince him to destroy the tape. In a dramatic confrontation, his daughter says, "You're taking advantage of these girls. It is not okay." This initial argument fails because Curtzman has bifurcated his home and work life, enabling him to demand respectable behavior from his daughter while exploiting girls who were not, in his estimation, "raised better." Similar to how Katrina confronts Ronny, Curtzman's daughter collapses the work/life boundary by exposing her breasts to her father. Curtzman is terrified by this act of abject defiance. And like the other version of American Virgin, it is at this point in the movie that the audience is encouraged to imagine the exploited girls of pornography as daughters rather than sex objects. Presumably, the eroticism of Chicks Go Crazy is lost when the audience adopts a parental gaze toward the videos' enthusiastic participants. This protective gaze directs audience outrage toward the exploitation of innocent girls.

Priscilla adds the pleasure of turning the tables on pornography to this protective ethos. She broadcasts one of Curtzman's private misogynistic diatribes to an audience of women waiting to break the world record for public breast exposures. Quite suddenly, the crowd loses its enthusiasm for exhibitionism, storms the stage, and publicly disrobes Curtzman. While the film concludes with the fulfillment of a satisfying revenge fantasy, the humiliating demise of Chicks Go Crazy merely clears the way for the return of traditional romance. This sudden development of feminist consciousness simply removes the tormenting presence of a sex-obsessed culture from a coming-of-age narrative. The wiser Priscilla who emerges also abandons abstinence culture, having witnessed throughout her ordeal the hypocrisies and cynicism of its so-called adherents. Her triumph over both pornography and abstinence stabilizes a world that putatively existed before sexual liberation made both necessary. Thus, she is free to pursue a romantic courtship with a love interest who shares her understanding that virginity loss is something special. The film recovers innocence as a corrective for the forces that took sexual liberation too far.

What is ostensibly "American" about these films is their ambivalence toward sexuality. As modified knock-off versions of the teenage coming-of-age narrative, both versions of *American Virgin* inadvertently and satirically mirror America's conflicted discourses about sexuality. Both films combine representations of taboo sexual desires with moralizing sentiments about the loss of youthful innocence. This deep ambivalence is also reflected in their sexualization of sexual inexperience. In other words, these texts invite audiences to desire the untouched female body while the narrative laments the decline of youth in corrupt times. The pornification of everyday life permits graphic displays of sexuality to exist, seemingly without contradiction, alongside appeals to a mythic time in which youth came into sexual experience without the pressures of sexual liberation. Monogamy and traditional teen romance emerge as modest solutions to the pornographic excesses of contemporary public culture.

Sex Negative/Sex Positive

While abstinence satires seem to indict abstinence culture by exposing conservative prudes to vulgar sex acts and embarrassing sexual experiences, they also affirm the virtues of committed monogamous sex for young adults. These films provide no middle ground between chastity and pornography. They offer no pathway for sexual experimentation outside traditional heterosexual monogamy that does not result in personal defilement or social disintegration. An examination of contemporary abstinence satires illustrates that despite their sexually explicit content, low-budget attempts to capitalize on the Hollywood virginity film reinforce a socially conservative position on sexual rites of passage. They present the notion that sexual experience outside traditional courtship is fraught with shame, embarrassment, and depravity. Even Hollywood's shadow industry, or its "displaced abject," affirms that sex is an all-or-nothing proposition.[24] The pornographic and often comedic content of virgin films belies the sex-negative assumptions that are at their core. Graphic sex aside, even the exploitation genre is not immune from the abstinence anxieties that pervade public culture.

Another significant drawback of these films is their profound whiteness. To the extent that these films include people of color, they are minor characters who fade into the background. As in many other teen films, in these films, virginity loss becomes primarily a suburban ritual for relatively affluent white teenagers. Abstinent white youth are treated as sufficiently safe for satire; they are a group who is privileged enough to take a joke. The erasure of nonwhite characters in these light-hearted spoofs infers that African American or Latino/a virginity loss is not a laughing matter. In a film like *Precious*, in which an African American female teenager's first sexual experience is rape resulting in pregnancy, the tone is somber tone. Or consider such films as *Cooley High* and *Boyz n the Hood*, which embed narratives of black virginity loss in subplots of urban crime and juvenile delinquency.[25] The whiteness and racial stereotypes of teen cinema are amplified when white youth are the subject of light-hearted parody while nonwhites who lose their virginity loss experience only peril.

Conclusion

Counternarratives

In 2002 and 2003, fourteen-year-old Elizabeth Smart was abducted and held captive for nine months, during which she was repeatedly raped and physically abused. During a 2013 human trafficking forum at Johns Hopkins University, Smart explained that while she had several opportunities to escape, she chose not to do so. In part, Smart had internalized one the most dangerous assumptions of abstinence education, that women who have sex outside marriage—even without consent—are impure and used. She explained, "I'm that chewed-up piece of gum. Nobody re-chews a piece of gum. You throw it away. And that's how easy it is to feel like you no longer have worth. You no longer have value. Why would it even be worth screaming out? Why would it even make a difference if you are rescued? Your life still has no value."[1] Smart's narrative illustrates how abstinence discourse cultivates loathing and self-doubt in young women, even to the extent that they blame themselves for the horrific actions of others. Her comments suggest that for all its valorization of women's virtue, abstinence culture teaches that women's bodies are shameful and unclean. Perhaps most revealing about Smart's reflection is the totalizing power of abstinence culture: she had internalized abstinence discourse and even used it to rationalize her traumatic experience.

The films I examined in this book also reveal the power of abstinence discourse as it becomes naturalized on the big screen. Because this vision has seeped into the popular Zeitgeist, it is imperative that feminist media scholars attend to the cultural proxy wars fought through American film and television. Cinema is one of the places where audiences acclimate to popular ideologies, and it is through film that the abstinence advocates' narrative of virginity loss is given significance. Despite its fictitious narratives, it is through cinematic spectacles that audiences might adopt the kinds of assumptions and value judgments that become the basis for behaviors, beliefs, and actions. Assumptions about the personal and political significance of abstinence until marriage have far-reaching effects on the social and political meaning of women's bodies, coming of age, girlhood, hegemonic masculinity, and the family. In light of the current challenges to nearly all forms of feminist politics, the emerging cultural narrative of virginity has profoundly negative consequence for both men and women.

Naturalizing abstinence on the big screen has profound implications for the personal and political lives of American audiences. Abstinence culture has made it a social imperative to perpetually retell, finesse, and reinvent the figure of the innocent young girl imperiled by the hypersexualization of American culture. Expressed in a wide variety of cultural mediums—film, television, news, political rhetoric, and popular fiction—the popular mythology surrounding the dangers of sex out of wedlock contributes to the conservative impulses in society that compel many to turn back the clock on women's political rights and reproductive freedoms, to return to an imagined moment of innocence that existed before feminists and sexual dissidents uprooted religious and familial order. In the name of Christian family values, abstinence culture valorizes girls who remain "pure" and virulently repudiates adult women for expressing desire and exercising their personal reproductive freedom. In doing so, virginity enthusiasts articulate a sociopolitical vision of women's place that has consequences that reach well beyond what type of sex education curriculum will be taught in public schools. Because of its emphasis on the physical and moral danger posed by female sexuality—and the fact that it pays little to no attention to young men—abstinence rhetoric translates systemic cultural misogyny into a social and religious imperative to control women's bodies. Aided by a postfeminist culture that has disarticulated the politics of women's liberation from the rhetoric of choice, abstinence has even been marketed as the new instantiation of feminist emancipation.

In another sense, abstinence discourse is but one (albeit very significant) facet of a larger religious movement to remake government and society, to legislate a familial and procreative sexuality to supplant the fundamentally feminist notions of sexual and reproductive freedom. This vision is manifest not only in continuing federal support for abstinence education but also in renewed opposition to Plan B emergency contraception, HPV vaccinations, access to legal abortions, and insurance coverage of women's birth control.[2] For example, during the 2012 Republican primary, candidates Mitt Romney, Newt Gingrich, Rick Santorum, Herman Cain, and Rick Perry publicly announced that if elected they would defund Planned Parenthood.[3] In the same year, when Georgetown law student Sandra Fluke testified before Congress about the importance of women's access to contraception, she was publicly insulted by conservative pundits such as Rush Limbaugh, who called her a "slut" who wanted taxpayers to foot the bill for her promiscuity.[4] In 2014, the Supreme Court ruled in *Burwell v. Hobby Lobby* that closely held corporations are not required to cover birth control for employee insurance plans under the Affordable Care Act.[5] One amicus brief filed on behalf of Hobby Lobby demanded that the Court take into account "the documented negative effects the widespread availability of contraceptives has on women's ability to enter into and maintain desired marital relationships."[6]

The conservative voices that resound against women's reproductive freedom share in common abstinence culture's insistence that sex outside marriage is not—and should not be—free of consequences. Abstinence culture is part of a more pervasive and reactionary response to feminism's politicization of personal inequities in home and family life. Women's sexual and reproductive freedom gave women greater control over when or if to start a family and a greater ability to have careers and ambitions outside of motherhood and it enabled them to more safely explore their own sexual needs and desires. Attempts to legislate women's sexuality, promulgate family values, and promote female virginity until marriage reveal an underlying cultural fear that women's independence threatens the institutions and practices that structure heterosexual intimacy.[7] In addition, such legislative measures reduce women to their bodies and seem to assume that their minds are less capable of governing their faculties than male policy makers.

The films examined in this book reinforce a series of interlocking oppressions that intersect in abstinence culture.[8] For instance, films such as *Twilight* sentimentalize the patriarchy and regressive sexuality of the conservative pre-1960s era. *The 40-Year-Old Virgin* presents an image of hegemonic masculinity embattled by contemporary feminism and women's sexual agency. *The Possession* and *Taken* renew the conservative movement's call for men to rediscover their essential nature as protective fathers and husbands. The irreverent abstinence comedy confirms the victimhood of virtuous young women and men who seek nothing more than a return to simpler times when sex did not complicate teen romance. All of these films are remarkable for both the persuasiveness of their abstinence message and their recovery of patriarchal family values. These films also negate a series of diverse sexual and racial identities. Not only do they provide little or no screen time to queer characters but also they construct virginity loss as a heterosexual rite of passage.[9] The erasure of queer sexuality in these films ignores the important challenges LGBT communities pose to both the concept of marriage and the concept of virginity loss. These films also reinforce the whiteness of abstinence culture. The innocent and virtuous virgin of contemporary cinema is invariably white and quite frequently embattled by what Pat MacPherson calls "offwhite" sexualities.[10] The erasure of difference in abstinence cinema constructs purity as a vaunted status that is attainable only by privileged white youth.

The struggle over abstinence in films is neither superfluous to nor simply reflective of the cultural wars waged through political discourse and governmental legislation. Films are part of the terrain, a site at which competing visions are simulated on the big screen. Although the films I analyze throughout this book illustrate the cultural hegemony of the sexual purity movement, it is important to conclude by noting the emergence of new cinematic rhetorics that in many ways challenge or subvert the master narrative of abstinence until marriage. In culture there are always fissures, contradictions, and slippages that open space for contesting the rhetorical common sense of dominant ideologies. As Terry Eagleton writes, "hegemony is never a once-and-for-all achievement" and therefore, "any governing power is thus forced to engage with counterhegemonic forces in ways which prove partly constitutive of its own rule."[11] While this means that hegemonic institutions are always engaging in the process of absorbing and reframing challenges, there is also a sense that cultural hegemony is a dialectical process in which oppositional ideational forces are always working to remake the dominant culture. As George Lipsitz observes, "Culture exists as a form of politics, as a means of reshaping individual and collective practice for specified interests, and as long as individuals perceive their interests as unfilled, culture retains an oppositional potential."[12] As a site of struggle over signification, cinema can also produce narratives and construct ways of seeing that cast doubt about the tenability and desirability of a dominant system of belief.[13] While Hollywood remains a hegemonic institution, there are filmmakers both within and outside the mainstream industrial structure whose vision of virginity offers a more empowering account of the coming-of-age narrative than the one that is being presented by abstinence culture.

While Hollywood films continue to exploit sex for financial gain, some emerging counternarratives feature the failures of abstinence and offer empowering models of girlhood that do not revolve around whether or not a girl has sex before marriage. Sex educators, activists, students, and feminist filmmakers have been outspoken about the damaging effects of abstinence culture on young women. For instance, in 2013, Katelyn Campbell, a senior at George Washington High School in Charleston, West Virginia, received an outpouring of public support when she was punished for protesting a mandatory abstinence assembly with virulent abstinence advocate Pam Stenzel.[14] Her story inspired Ann Werner and Kimberly A. Johnson to publish *The Virgin Diaries*, an anthology of seventy-two "first time" stories that illustrate the complexity of virginity loss without appeals to shame and defilement.[15]

Some filmmakers have taken notice of growing discontent with abstinence culture. The harms of abstinence have been analyzed in documentary films such as *Daddy's Little Girl* (2007), *The Purity Myth* (2010), *Miss Representation* (2011), and *How to Lose Your Virginity* (2013). To a certain extent, popular culture is beginning to take notice of this growing dissatisfaction with abstinence culture, the evidence experts provide of its inefficacy, and the demand for more empowered representations of sex and girlhood. Some independent films have broken through with competing conceptions of youth sexuality. *The To-Do List* (2013) and *The Virginity Hit* (2010) are independent films that satirize the hype surrounding virginity loss while offering an empowered pathway to sexual experience that does not fundamentally alter the protagonists' core values or self-worth. *Teeth* (2007) is an even more direct and subversive critique of abstinence culture, a critically acclaimed horror/drama about a teen abstinence spokesperson (Dawn) who becomes sexually empowered through a traumatic process of bodily self-discovery.[16] Although these are minor films, they reflect the notion that virginity is subject to dialectical struggle in the realm of popular culture.

In part, the transparent failures and contradictions of the abstinence movement have cultivated public desires for new cinematic narratives of virginity. When scores of young women publish their personal narratives of abuse and degradation by purity advocates, when the teenage daughters of prominent abstinence advocates begin having children out of wedlock, when international abstinence campaigns are linked with the spread of false and malicious information about sexuality, and when public health studies indict the claim that abstinence works, it becomes increasingly difficult to sustain abstinence until marriage as a cultural ideal.[17] Despite the fact that many popular films elide these contradictions in their depictions of virginity, feminist critiques of abstinence continue to make their way into popular culture. In this concluding chapter, I examine the implications of abstinence films and the emerging resistance to abstinence culture in cinema to note how dialectical struggle might produce new accounts of virginity on the big screen. My hope is to end this study with potentiality, or a sense that Hollywood's capitalization on virginity anxiety is the result of film's tenuous yet ongoing relationship with the sexual-political anxieties of the previous decade.

Reform: *The Virginity Hit* (2010)

In Hollywood, teenage sexuality is often depicted with ambivalence. The result is a composite portrait of salacious nubile bodies that filmmakers feel compelled to continually punish or repudiate for their youthful transgressions.[18] Teen sex-quest films have either presented teens as the subject of adult voyeuristic fantasy or have served as an occasion to moralize about the loss of youthful innocence. At times, Hollywood has attempted to displace the significance of sex to the coming-of-age narrative and at others it has suggested that the oversexing of the American teen calls for a return to more traditional romance. Very few films have attempted to challenge or reform the polarizing struggle between sexual purity and the pornification of everyday life that pervades the common sense of youth sexuality in contemporary cinema. In other words, film continues to portray a two-sided struggle for the soul of the teenager: on the one side is purity and on the other is defilement. The middle ground is rarely explored; there is little space on screen for a coming-of-age narrative about sex that is not teeming with sociopolitical anxieties about moral pollution.

One potential challenge to abstinence culture is in cinema that mediates the binary position on virginity. Such films acknowledge the importance of virginity loss to one's sense of self without reducing the importance and value of the individual to the simple question of whether or not they have sex or express sexual desire. Recognizing the importance of sexual rites of passage need not elevate the process to a definition of an individual's character or be accompanied by warnings of personal or social degradation. In the films examined in this book, sex outside marriage and monogamy, expressions of female sexual autonomy, and the loss of a young woman's purity resonate with a right-wing Christian vision of sex and society. More can be done in cinema to disarticulate virginity loss and sexual autonomy from dangerous and immoral consequences.

The Virginity Hit (dir. Huck Botko and Andrew Gurland) is a recent example of a teen sex-quest film about virginity loss that self-consciously chronicles the relatively mundane sexual anxieties of a virgin teenage male in world that is hyperconscious about sexual status. The film is a cinéma-vérité–style mockumentary that follows a group of four high school boys as they assist in their friend Matt's efforts to lose his virginity. In accordance with the performative rules of a social media age, the film is shot from the perspective of Matt's stepbrother Zack, who uses his personal camcorder to do to Matt's "virginity what Alfred Hitchcock did to birds." Throughout the film, Zack posts footage of the exhilarating but mostly embarrassing moments of Matt's efforts to gain sexual experience. To produce the aesthetic quality of social media videos, the directors gave the film's stars cameras with instructions to shoot many scenes on their own. Several of the film's more embarrassing scenes are shot from the viewpoint of a laptop user watching Zack's videos who also scrolls through the YouTube user comments about Matt's successive failures. While the film is fairly unoriginal in following the virginity-pact formula set forth in *Little Darlings* and *American Pie*, it is remarkable as a parody of the obsessive spectacle of virginity. The film's use of hypermediation and remediation—a proliferation of the screens (movie, computer, camera, phone) that mediate contemporary public culture—draws attention to the spectacle made of virginity loss in contemporary media, exaggerating the phenomenon to the point of absurdity.[19] Simulated YouTube videos of "Matt's First Condom," complete with interviews with a convenience store clerk, highlight the overinflated importance contemporary society places on virginity loss. By portraying everyday sexual anxieties as a public spectacle, the film invites critical reflection on how film exploits virginity and leaves audiences unnecessarily agitated about the status of the virginity loss ritual.

The film constructs a humanizing portrait of youth that diverges from cinematic convention. The use of cinéma-vérité techniques, amateur footage, and relatively unknown actors gives the film a kind of documentary realism that provides audiences with an empathetic and intimate connection to Matt and his friends. Audiences are allowed to vicariously experience Matt's failures, to be privy to the kind of earnest and seemingly unscripted moments of vulnerability that is not seen in other sex-quest films. The public nature of Matt's virginity-loss adventure makes him the victim of Internet phishing schemes and painful online ridicule. By providing access to Matt's most intimate insecurities, audiences are encouraged to empathize as a part of his friendship group rather than as simply voyeurs hiding behind their screens.

Above all, the film indicts the polarity between virginity and pornography that is taken as given in countless other teen films. For instance, Zack arranges for Matt to lose his virginity to his favorite adult film star, Sunny Leone (played by the actress of the same name), and hopes to capture the experience on camera. After meeting Matt and consulting with her boyfriend, Leone changes her mind and tells him, "You shouldn't lose your virginity like this." As the movie humanizes the adult film star, it suggests that losing one's virginity outside marriage need not be a slippery slope to personal defilement or an induction into the culture of pornography. Leone's appearance in the film as an ordinary compassionate individual—someone very different from her salacious on-screen persona—disrupts male pornographic fantasies without moralizing or inviting a paternalistic responses. Instead, Leone disabuses Matt of the notion that virginity loss must be a spectacular act of moral depravity. Like the audience, Matt breaks through the fourth wall to adjust the importance of sex and virginity to his own sense of self.

While the film does not directly address abstinence culture, *The Virginity Hit* concludes that virginity should be defined more by the participants than by the broader culture. Ultimately, Matt loses his virginity to his estranged girlfriend (Krysta), with whom he has a longtime intimate connection. After Matt and Krysta have sex for the first time, they are portrayed as satisfied but ultimately unchanged by the experience. A postcoital interview with Zach interview reveals that the experience was less significant to their emotional development and sense of self than their personal relationship with each other and their intimate connections with friends and loved ones. The film offers a relatively modest adjustment to the cultural narrative of virginity. It draws attention to the spectacle of cultural anxiety about youth sexuality and evacuates the narrative of moral judgment. At the same time, the film proposes only a minor repair and fails to address the disparate impact virginity culture has on young women. The film's potential lies in its suspension of judgment and its efforts to debunk the hyperanxiety surrounding the sexual status of youth.

Resistance: *Teeth* (2007)

Independent and cult filmmakers have offered some of the most direct challenges to abstinence culture.[20] Even in a highly conglomerated media market where many independent studios are subsidiaries of larger corporations (e.g., Fox Searchlight, United Artists), independent filmmakers have some ability to direct and produce subversive representations that counter the conventional scripts about sexual inexperience. Confrontational independent films can produce the kind of antagonism that might create space for a fundamental cinematic reevaluation of virginity in film. Although more provocative films are not a panacea, alternative cinema can capture the alienation from and dissatisfaction with virginity culture many men and women express and direct those energies toward countering abstinence until marriage as the de facto sexual norm.

However, there is an important distinction between subversive critique and earnest middle-of-the-road parodies of abstinence culture. Consider the United Artists film *Saved!* (2004), a dark comedy that points out the hypocrisies of chastity groups (e.g., "The Christian Jewels") and self-righteous behaviors in the name of organized religion. The film illuminates the troubling ironies of gay conversation therapy, high rates of teenage pregnancy in devoutly religious communities, and the mean-spiritedness of moral crusaders. Nonetheless, the film's resolution suggests that while purity culture goes too far, there is collective blame for antagonisms between religious fundamentalists and their detractors. For instance, *Saved!* settles the controversy over a pious teen's pregnancy and the misguided judgments of a community of moral crusaders with a birth that brings both sides together. The birth also brings the beleaguered protagonist (Mary) back to a more understanding and benevolent God who is loving and sympathetic, not judgmental. While the film offers mutual understanding and respect as a corrective, suspending judgment of pregnant teens is a relatively piecemeal challenge to abstinence culture. Tolerance has its limitations; it is a moderate stance that is frequently adopted as a way to permit difference to exist without fundamentally challenging power and privilege.[21]

By contrast, subversion is a strategy by which one attacks the values of a given system and subjects its ideological belief structure to contradiction and antagonism. To this extent, a much more direct and radical critique of abstinence culture appears in *Teeth* (dir. Mitchell Lichtenstein). In *Teeth*, Dawn is an enthusiastic envoy for The Promise, a religious advocacy group that promotes teen abstinence, female modesty, and sexual purity. Her convictions are tested by her sexual attraction to Tobey, and the two agree that they should stop seeing each other before they let their urges lead them to violate their abstinence pledges. When the two meet against their better judgment, Tobey rapes Dawn in a remote cave at a local swimming hole. During the sexual assault, Dawn discovers that she possesses the mythic *vagina dentata* and castrates Tobey, leaving him for dead. Dawn discards her purity ring and learns to control her monstrous private parts so that she can punish men who violate her personal bodily autonomy while exploring the vicissitudes of her sexual desire. What makes *Teeth* subversive is the filmmaker's appropriation of the "monstrous feminine" as a sign of feminine empowerment. In one sense, literalizing the mythic fear of women's bodies evinces the deep-rooted misogyny that pervades abstinence culture. The film illustrates that the impulse to control women's sexuality is premised on the assumption that women's bodies are monstrous, a source of mythic evil. It also presents the idea that women can refashion their monstrous bodies as sources of physical strength, pleasure, and autonomy. Men who are punished by the castrating vagina are portrayed as receiving their just reward for demanding entitled access to and control over women's bodies.[22]

In another sense, the literal *vagina dentata* serves as an allegory for bodily self-discovery and sexual liberation. Through the experience of physical sexual trauma, Dawn awakens to the fact that even the most well-meaning and pious men in her life feel entitled to her body. The fact that each physical trauma she experiences reveals the duplicity of the male authorities in her life reflects the fundamental contradictions of demanding that women remain pure while men do as they please (the virgin/whore dichotomy). Discovering and confronting her supposedly monstrous body facilitates the development of a feminist consciousness, an awareness of her own oppression, and later her physical power. Her newfound abilities and capacity for pleasure symbolize the strong relationship between bodily autonomy and sexual gratification. As Dawn overcomes her alienation from her own body, she destabilizes the patriarchal order. The film closes with Dawn looking suggestively at the camera as an oblivious would-be rapist is poised to receive his just deserts. This conclusion suggests that women's sovereignty menaces the phallocentric order. Depending on the audience, her seductive look might represent either the threat of castration or the possibilities of emancipation.

Teeth directly challenges the assumptions that structure abstinence culture. The film illustrates how the rhetoric of sexual purity is premised on fear of women's bodies and invites audiences to adopt a feminist consciousness that asserts the primacy of women's bodily autonomy and capacity for pleasure without shame. While the film literalizes male castration anxiety, when read allegorically, it subverts phallocentrism and misogyny with abstinence culture serving as a contemporary example of male dread of the feminine. With an avenging feminist heroine, *Teeth* is an example of how independent cinema can subvert the taken-for-granted misogyny of abstinence culture and mainstream Hollywood.

Redefinition: *The To-Do-List* (2013)

The recurring refrain in abstinence advocacy is that boys are governed by their physical impulses while girls are predominantly emotional and seek deep, meaningful, long-term relationships. Girls will reluctantly have sex to get to "I love you," while boys will say "I love you" to get to sex.[23] This viewpoint can be damaging because it suggests that even as young women enter adulthood their physical desires are unnatural and that they should adopt passivity as a feminine virtue. This assertion is also fraught with a "boys will be boys" attitude that places the responsibility for physical and moral restraint squarely on the shoulders of girls. The kind of gender essentialism that supports such a proposition also structures much of the teen sex-quest genre of film, which typically chronicles the humorous sexual exploits of young men in the process of coming of age. Young women in cinema are typically the objects of conquest, their virginity seldom treated with such light-heartedness as that of adolescent boys. The essentialisms that ground the disparate meaning of virginity loss must be made visible and must be questioned if cinema is to move forward with representations that unburden girls from damaging moral judgments.

The To-Do-List (dir. Maggie Carey) unpacks this aspect of the purity myth with portrayals of young women who have an active but thoughtful interest in sex that bypasses cinema's myopic focus on girls' emotional fulfillment. The film inverts the typical sex-quest formula by adopting the perspective of young women who are more concerned with gaining experience than with preserving their adolescence. Brandy Klark is an overachieving high school graduate who embarks on a quest for sexual experience before she leaves home to attend college. She indulges her penchant for organization and academic rigor by developing a "to-do-list" of sexual experiences that ends with her losing her virginity to her high school's most desirable male (Rusty Waters). The film is unique because it divests female sexuality of sentimentality to illustrate that female virginity loss can be more about personal discovery than a definitive mark of one's moral character. The comically overperiodized costume design and mise-en-scène of Boise, Idaho, in 1993 conveys a blithe sensibility about a sexual subject that is typically treated with heightened emotional intensity. More important, reversing the gender roles of teen sex-quest films gives primacy to young women's choices, sexual agency, and personal development. Meanwhile, the film's male characters adopt stereotypically feminine attributes: emotional attachment, dimwittedness, and flightiness. For instance, Cameron continually misinterprets his sexual encounters with Brandy as signs of love and is devastated to learn that they had not forged the deep emotional connection he sought. Rusty's fit physique accompanies his idiocy and general aloofness in response to Brandy's sexual pursuit. Between the men she pursues and the men who pursue her, the film presents the varied and overlapping meanings of sex for Brandy. Sex is merely one facet of her personal development, and her experiences with both Cameron and Rusty reveal how little it defines her character.

What distinguishes Brandy's moral integrity is not her attitude toward sex but how she treats her friends and love ones. The lesson Brandy derives from her sexual experiences is that she needs to be safe and responsible with her body and sensitive to the feelings of others. For instance, when Brandy's sexual experiments create jealousy and animosity within her friend group, she learns that she must balance her sexual relationships with her close female friendships. Unlike a film such as *Easy A*, which suggests that heterosexual intimacy and authentic female friendship are incompatible or the *Twilight* saga, in which female relationships must be sacrificed for "true love," this film defines women's friendship and solidarity as fundamental to healthy intimacy. Brandy also learns to empathize with her more sexually experienced sister and forges closer ties with her mother. While her father is comically overprotective and sexually prudish, Brandy's mother and sister ultimately accept her efforts to explore her desires and earnestly discuss sex without shaming and judging. The film illustrates how women can support one another in a social environment that often condemns women who take control of their sexual desires.

Finally, the film communicates the simple but rarely publicized message that women's sexual pleasure is acceptable and healthy.[24] In part, this aspect of the narrative accounts for why the film was reviewed poorly by professional critics. One reviewer called the film "a fake feminist comedy that pays lip service to female empowerment but inadvertently makes sex seem both demeaning and meaningless. Vulgar, cynical and rarely funny."[25] Because such sexual vulgarity and cynicism is relatively commonplace among gross-out bromance comedies, it is remarkable that a similar film with female protagonists would be criticized for presenting light-hearted but frank representations of sex. The charge of faux feminism belies a thinly veiled cinematic double standard in which women who mimic the sexual adventures of men are criticized for devaluing the meaning of sex. Meanwhile, critics praise "boys will be boys" comedies, such as *The 40-Year-Old Virgin*, that present women's sexuality as abject and utterly terrifying as crude but ultimately sweet and enduring. Male film directors are seldom lambasted for betraying the cause of feminism or desacralizing sexual intimacy. There is something implicitly threatening about a character such as Brandy, who declares in the film: "Ladies, we must take responsibility for our own sexual gratification." Far from cynicism, the film's underlying message is that women do not need to be ashamed for having sexual interests and for pursuing pleasure over romance. In this regard, the film is more explicit than vulgar. Surrounded by men who are confounded by women's pleasure, Brandy's mother explains the basics of not only safe sex but also pleasurable sex, accompanied by an awkward but sex-positive gift of lubricant. Even though her first experience with sexual intercourse involves Rusty, Brandy's first time is instructive but unsatisfying. In many ways, the loss of her virginity debunks the myth of the perfect first time and encourages the character to reassess her physical needs and desires. Perhaps the perception of vulgarity is premised on the fact that Brandy is interested in achieving orgasm—a goal she finally reaches with Cameron while at college. The challenge this film presents to abstinence culture is that it opens space for individuals to define the meaning of sex for themselves and gives women access to the kind of sexual pleasure almost exclusively enjoyed by boys on the big screen. The film reclaims a sex-positive message without over-determining the personal meaning of sex and virginity. As Brandy concludes: "Sex is a big deal and sometimes it's not a big deal."

Refutation: *How to Lose Your Virginity* (2013)

The cinéma-vérité participatory-style documentary—with its low financial and technical barriers—enables filmmakers to unfold truths through organic interactions with interview subjects. In this mode, voice-of-God narration provides context for and continuity between testimonials that reveal the nature of social problems from those with intimate experience or expert knowledge. Documentaries can give audiences an emotional engagement with their social world, sometimes meeting the viewer where they live.

Documentarian and film theorist Bill Nichols writes that the persuasiveness of documentary filmmaking is sutured to the ways they "invite engagement with their representation of the historical world."[26] Documentaries can convey a sense of authenticity that invites emotional connections between audience and subject; at their best, they cultivate political investment in the film's subject matter.

Therese Schechter's *How to Lose Your Virginity* is an activist participatory-style documentary that adopts an explicitly political stance against the abstinence movement. This film juxtaposes the voices of prominent feminist critics, public health experts, and academics with the personal testimonials of lay individuals who recount their experiences with virginity loss or abstinence culture. Distributed by Women Make Movies and funded by an online Kickstarter campaign, *How to Lose Your Virginity* has many of the qualities of activist cinema that connects larger political forces with the everyday life experiences of those who are affected by the contemporary cultural obsession with virginity.[27] Schechter's project extends beyond the text of the film to include a companion traveling interactive art exhibit (*The V-Card Diaries*) that includes over 200 stories of sexual experience and inexperience.[28] Like Jessica Valenti's companion documentary to her book *The Purity Myth* (2008), the film provides a deep engagement with contemporary abstinence culture that traces the historical transformations in definitions of virginity, the past and present of sex education, and the influence of abstinence culture on American popular culture and politics through the filmmaker's engagement with interview subjects.

As a unique genre of filmmaking, the documentary form employed in *How to Lose Your Virginity* provides the filmmaker a platform to directly refute, or even refuse, the discourses of abstinence-until-marriage advocates.[29] The film's argument is assembled from fragments of expert opinion and personal experience that coalesce in a collective voice that is both rational and emotive. The documentary's strength is derived from Schechter's ability to make meaningful connections between abstinence rhetoric in education and public policy and the sexual lives of everyday individuals. The film does more than chronicle the life cycle of the contemporary abstinence movement or expose the drawbacks of abstinence-only education; instead, it conducts a holistic and historically situated analysis of how virginity became a cultural obsession. Moreover, it connects abstinence-until-marriage discourse to the fetishization of virginity by the pornographic film industry, the wedding industry, and mainstream Hollywood. These connections are fortified not by voice-of-God narration but by Schechter's intimate involvement in the film. For example, she tries on wedding dresses to coax bridal consultants to discuss the role of virginity and purity in their sales and marketing discourse, she visits the set of a "barely legal" pornography film to converse with producers about how they openly capitalize on the virgin/whore binary, and she goes to college campuses to discuss the cultural shame associated with virginity loss outside marriage. Schechter's argument unfolds through discursive encounters that meet the documentary subjects where they live. Throughout the film, the distant connections between abstinence-only education and brothel-sponsored virginity auctions, between purity rings and the hypersexualization of young women become easier to imagine.

The film invests both everyday subjects and experts with unique kinds of expert knowledge. Whereas experts such as sex educator Bronwen Pardes, former surgeon general Joycelyn Elders, historian Hannah Blank, and prominent feminist critic Jessica Valenti provide audiences with academic expertise about the deleterious effects of abstinence culture, the testimonials of people such as Ellen Westberg, a former evangelical Christian, supply experiential knowledge that reflects the kind of epistemological advantage that arises from feminist standpoint. Some feminist scholars would suggest that as the subject of a vast majority of abstinence discourse, women experience the effects of abstinence culture differently than men. Therefore, their unique location might illuminate insights not seen in mainstream political discourse.[30] Testimonials reveal widespread confusion over the definition of virginity, the difficulties women face when confronted with the virgin/whore binary, and the challenges of women's enacted sexual agency in a culture of guilt and shame. The filmmaker's engagement with Westberg is particularly compelling because she gives her space to articulate the political nature of her personal experience with marriage, Christianity, and abstinence culture. Westberg reveals that she got married, in part, to feel authorized to have her first sexual experience. Speaking from her kitchen, Westberg unpacks her difficult experience with marriage and evangelicalism in ways that give intimate form to political problems.

The film gives the audience insights into the far-reaching effects of abstinence discourse. Testimonials and interviews are supplemented with the details about contemporary abstinence campaigns, the effects of abstinence education, and pop culture imagery of chaste sex icons such as Selena Gomez. The film also invites laughter by showing clips of outdated sex education videos and taped lectures of overzealous abstinence advocacy. As she did in her earlier film *I Was a Teenage Feminist* (2005), Schechter approaches the documentary as an extension of feminist politics and employs the voices of her subjects to make a coherent case against abstinence until marriage as a political ideal. The advantage of documentary film is that it gives the filmmaker space to build a persuasive case, aggregate evidence and testimonials, and refute dominant discourses with both expert opinion and direct experience. The filmmaker can be less concerned with verisimilitude and can be empowered by a variety of participatory, observational, and expository techniques of representation. The platform gives space to long-form arguments and detailed narratives that are connected by the interpretative agency of the filmmaker. *How to Lose Your Virginity* uses the documentary form to use feminist voices to rebut powerful abstinence campaigns.

Moving On: *Whip It!* (2009)

Perhaps the most difficult move for Hollywood will be to look past virginity for other significant touchstones of coming of age. As popular critics such as Jessica Valenti have noted, part of the problem with the culture's obsession with virginity is that it reduces the moral and social value of young women to whether or not they have had sex. Abstinence culture neglects other significant aspects of personal development and the challenges that build character. Abstinence advocates have less to say about young women's intellectual ambitions such as college and career than about their suitability for marriage and family.

Abstinence culture evaluates girls' personal character and predicts their future success on the basis of their sex acts alone. While sex-positive depictions are a necessary challenge to abstinence cinema, they must be accompanied by portrayals that bypass the subject altogether, that affirm the myriad ways young women (and men) can develop integrity and find empowerment.[31]

Although it may not appear this way, sex is not the only character-defining ritual filmmakers can use to capture the challenges of growing up.[32] *Whip It!* offers an interesting path forward in redefining the meaning of girlhood without reducing young women to their sexual status. This film focuses on other communal rituals that confer status on young woman. In *Whip It!*, Bliss Cavendar (Ellen Page) is a meek and shiftless teenager searching for a way out of her rural Texas hometown. Bliss's mother, a housewife and former beauty queen, tries to guide her into the town's cult of domesticity and pageantry despite her explicit disinterest in conventional femininity. Enamored with the physical prowess and spectacle of female roller derby, Bliss lies about her age to try out for the Hurl Scouts, a team of the Austin Roller Girls. The film chronicles her enculturation into the roller derby community, her struggles with her parents for independence and respect, and her discovery of physical and emotional strength. While one subplot features a romance between Bliss and a young musician named Oliver, the relationship's travails—marked by Oliver's indiscretions—emphasize the importance of independence and self-respect over love and romance.

Whip It! is a rare and moving depiction of girlhood that emphasizes physical strength, mental toughness, and female camaraderie over stereotypical feminine qualities. The filmmaker's choice to score Kings of Leon's single "Knocked Up" during the film's opening credits—a song ostensibly about teenage pregnancy— introduces an irreverent take on girlhood that looks past the predictable narrative of girls at risk.[33] The film refuses to reduce girlhood preoccupations to dating and relationships, choosing instead to focus on how young women can find voice and empowerment without men, parents, or other controlling influences. Page's portrayal of Bliss suggests that while they make mistakes, young girls are intelligent and capable of making their own choices. The film is an attempt to move on from virginity, to find a new vision of youth in which sex is but one important part of becoming an adult. *Whip It!* exemplifies how cinema can supplant the rhetoric of virginity with a new discourse that affirms that young women and men are not defined by who they have sex with or when they have sex. Moving on, then, is about locating youth where they are and depicting the various and fluid pathways to self-discovery that exist beyond sexuality. While abstinence is the prevailing ideology of everything from popular film and sex education, there is much space for telling different stories.

NOTES

INTRODUCTION   THE CINEMA OF ABSTINENCE

1. See Union of Concerned Scientists, "Abstinence-Only Sex Education Curriculum," September, 2005, http://www.ucsusa.org/center-for-science-anddemocracy/scientific_integrity/abuses_of_science/a-to-z/abstinence-only-curriculum.html#.VUUdkP2yNg0.

2. See Lauren Berlant, *The Queen of America Goes to Washington City: Essays on Sex and Citizenship* (Durham, NC: Duke University Press, 1997).

3. See Edward Ashbee, "The Bush Administration and the Politics of Sex Morality," in *Assessing the George W. Bush Presidency: A Tale of Two Terms*, edited by Andrew Roe and Jon Herbert (Edinburgh, UK: Edinburgh University Press, 2009), 199–215.

4. The screenplay for *Thirteen* was coauthored by the film's costar, Nikki Reed, who used a semi-autobiographical account of her own teenage experiences as inspiration for the narrative. See "Evan Rachel Wood and Nikki Read: Interview with Tom Johnson," TheCinemaSource, January 28, 2008, http://www.thecinemasource.com/blog/interviews/evan-rachel-wood-and-nikki-reed-interview-for-thirteen/.

5. Mas'ud Zavarzadeh, *Seeing Films Politically* (Albany: State University of New York Press, 1991), 40.

6. For more on the various sexual panics of the second Bush administration, see *The Moral Panic of Sexuality*, edited by Breanne Fahs, Mary L. Dudy, and Sarah Stage (New York: Palgrave Macmillan, 2013).

7. Timothy Shary, *Teen Movies: American Youth on Screen* (London: Wallflower, 2005).

8. See Gregory D. Black, *Hollywood Censored: Morality Codes, Catholics, and the Movies* (New York: Cambridge University Press, 1994); Jeremy Pascall and Clyde Jeavers, *A Pictorial History of Sex in the Movies* (London: Hamlyn, 1975); Jody W. Pennington, *The History of Sex in American Film* (Westport, CT: Praeger, 2007); Frank Walsh, *Sin and Censorship: The Catholic Church and the Motion Picture Industry* (New Haven, CT: Yale University Press, 1996).

9. See Kristy Maddux, *The Faithful Citizen: Popular Christian Media and Gendered Civic Identities* (Waco, TX: Baylor University Press, 2010), 24.

10. This passage comes from the King James Bible. Other biblical passages condemning premarital sex that abstinence organizations frequently refer to include Acts 15:20; 1 Corinthians 5:1, 6:13, 6:18, 10:8; 2 Corinthians 12:21; Galatians 5:19; Ephesians 5:3; Colossians 3:5; Jude 7; and Hebrews 13:4.

11. Focus on the Family, "Abstinence before Marriage," 2008, http://www.focusonthefamily.com/socialissues/social-issues/abstinence-before-marriage.aspx.

12. See Heather D. Boonstra, "Matter of Faith: Support for Comprehensive Sex Education among Faith-Based Organizations," *Guttmacher Policy Review* 11, no. 1 (2008): 17–22, http://www.guttmacher.org/pubs/gpr/11/1/gpr110117.html.

13. See Susan Friend Harding, *The Book of Jerry Falwell: Fundamentalist Language and Politics* (Princeton, NJ: Princeton University Press, 2001).

14. Janice M. Irvine, *Talk about Sex: The Battles over Sex Education in the United States* (Berkeley: University of California Press, 2004).

15. See Rebekah Saul, "Whatever Happened to the Adolescent Family Life Act?" *Guttmacher Report on Public Policy* 1, no. 2 (1998): 5–11, http://www.guttmacher.org/pubs/tgr/01/2/gr010205.html.

16. Ruth Rosen, *The World Split Open: How the Modern Women's Movement Changed America* (New York: Penguin Books, 2000), 333.

17. See Laura M. Carpenter, *Virginity Lost: An Intimate Portrait of First Sexual Experiences* (New York: New York University Press, 2005).

18. See Stephanie Coontz, *The Way We Never Were: American Families and the Nostalgia Trap* (New York: Basic Books, 2000).

19. See David J. Harding and Christopher Jencks, "Changing Attitudes toward Premarital Sex: Cohort, Period, and Aging Effects," *Public Opinion Quarterly* 67, no. 2 (2003): 211–226.

20. "A History of Federal Funding for Abstinence-Only-Until-Marriage Programs," Sexuality Information and Education Council of the United States, 2010, http://www.siecus.org/index.cfm?fuseaction=page.viewPage&pageID=1340&nodeID=1.

21. Ron Haskins and Carol Statuto Bevan, "Abstinence Education under Welfare Reform," *Children and Youth Services Review* 19, no. 5/6 (1997): 465–484; Melanie Heath, *One Marriage under God: The Campaign to Promote Marriage in America* (New York: New York University Press, 2012).

22. Shanta Pandey and Jeoung-hee Kim, "Path to Poverty Alleviation: Marriage or Postsecondary Education," *Journal of Family and Economic Issues* 29, no. 1 (2007): 166–184; David Shipler, *The Working Poor: Invisible in America* (New York: Knopf, 2008).

23. Joyce Purnick, "Welfare Bill: Legislating Morality?" *New York Times*, August 19, 1996, http://www.nytimes.com/1996/08/19/nyregion/welfare-bill-legislating-morality.html.

24. See John Santelli, Mary A. Ott, Maureen Lyon, Jennifer Rogers, Daniel Summers, and Rebecca Ann Schleifer, "Abstinence and Abstinence-Only Education: A Review of U.S. Policies and Programs," *Journal of Adolescent Health* 38, no. 1 (2006): 72–81.

25. See Melanie Heath, "Making Marriage Promotion into Public Policy: The Epistemic Culture of Statewide Initiatives," *Qualitative Sociology* 35, no. 4 (2012): 385–406.

26. Andy Kopsa, "Abstinence-Only: It's Baaaack," *Ms. Magazine*, December 22, 2011, http://msmagazine.com/blog/2011/12/22/abstinence-only-its-baaacck/.

27. Andy Kopsa, "Obama's Evangelical Gravy Train," *The Nation*, July 8, 2014, May 2, 2015, http://www.thenation.com/article/180435/obamas-evangelical-gravy-train.

28. See U.S. House of Representatives Committee on Government Reform—Minority Staff, *The Content of Federally Funded Abstinence-Only Education Programs*, prepared for Rep. Henry A. Waxman, December 1, 2004, http://www.democrats.reform.house.gov/Documents/20041201102153–50247.pdf.

29. Janet Elise Rosenbaum, "Patient Teenagers?: A Comparison of the Sexual Behavior of Virginity Pledgers and Matched Nonpledgers," *Pediatrics* 123, no. 1 (2009): 110–120; Janet Elise Rosenbaum, "Reborn a Virgin: Adolescents' Retracting of Virginity Pledges and Sexual Histories," *American Journal of Public Health* 96, no. 6 (2006): 1098–1103.

30. Hannah Bruckner and Peter Bearman, "After the Promise: The STD Consequences of Adolescent Virginity Pledges," *Journal of Adolescent Health* 36, no. 4 (2005): 271–278; Melina M. Bersamin, Samantha Walker, Elizabeth D. Waiters, Deborah A. Fisher, and Joel Grube, "Promising to Wait: Virginity Pledges and Adolescent Sexual Behavior," *Journal of Adolescent Health* 36, no. 5 (2004): 428–436.

31. For example, Republican presidential candidate Mitt Romney suggested during a televised debate in 2012 that abstinence and marriage are the solution to the epidemic of gun violence in America. See Mark Follman, "Romney Points Finger at Single Moms on Gun Violence," *Mother Jones*, October 17, 2012, http://www.motherjones.com/mojo/2012/10/romney-guns-single-moms.

32. David Bario, "Virginity Pledge Comes with a Ring—and Tarnish," *Chicago Tribune*, March 20, 2005, http://articles.chicagotribune.com/2005–03–20/features/0503200443_1_ring-purity-virginity.

33. Catherine Elsworth, "Virgin Territory," *The Telegraph* (UK), November 25, 2007, http://www.telegraph.co.uk/education/3355163/Virgin-territory.html.

34. Neil Cole, "How the Candie's Foundation and Bristol Palin Created a National Dialogue on Teen Pregnancy," *Huffington Post*, June 14, 2009, http://www.huffingtonpost.com/neil-cole/how-the-candies-foundatio_b_203701.html; Abstinence between Strong Teens International, Inc., "Shop," last modified May 2, 2015, http://www.abstinc.com/shop.html; Silver Ring Thing, "Apparel," last modified May 2, 2015, https://www.silverringthing.com/Dont_Drink_and_Park.asp?catID=17.

35. See Breanne Fahs, "Daddy's Little Girl: On the Perils of Chastity Clubs, Purity Balls, and Ritualized Abstinence," *Frontiers* 31, no. 3 (2010): 116–144; Jessica Valenti, *The Purity Myth* (New York: Seal, 2009).

36. For examples, see David Blankenhorn, *Fatherless America* (New York: Harper Perennial, 1996); Jim Burns, *The Purity Code: God's Plan for Sex and Your Body* (Bloomington, MN: Bethany House Publishers, 2008); Haylay DiMarco, *Technical Virgin: How Far Is Too Far?* (Grand Rapids, MI: Flemin H. Revell, 2006); Elizabeth Elliot, *Passion and Purity: Learning to Bring Your Life under Christ's Control* (Grand Rapids, MI: Baker Publishing, 2002); Dannah Gresh, *And the Bride Wore White: Seven Secrets to Sexual Purity* (Chicago: Moody Publishers, 2012); Joshua Harris, *Sex Is Not the Problem (Lust Is): Sexual Purity in a Lust-Saturated World* (Colorado Springs, CO: Multnomah Books, 1996); Jessica Psalidas, *Everlasting Purity* (Maitlin, FL: Xulon Press, 2008); Kris Vallotton, *Purity: The New Moral Revolution* (Shippensburg, PA: Destiny Image Publishers, 2011).

37. See "9 Celebrities Who've Worn Purity Rings," *Huffington Post*, July 2, 2013, http://www.huffingtonpost.com/2013/07/02/celebrities-purity-rings_n_3535439.html.

38. Tamar Jeffers McDonald, "Introduction," in *Virgin Territory: Representing Sexual Inexperience in Film*, edited by Tamar Jeffers McDonald (Detroit: Wayne State University Press, 2010), 1.

39. See Jody W. Pennington, *The History of Sex in American Film* (Westport, CT: Praeger, 2007).

40. See Hanne Blank, *Virgins: The Untouched History* (New York: Bloomsbury, 2007); Anke Bernau, *Virgins: A Cultural History* (London: Grant Books, 2007); Kathryn Schwarz, "The Wrong Questions: Thinking through Virginity," *differences: A Journal of Feminist Cultural Studies* 13, no. 2 (2002): 1–34.

41. Catherine Driscoll, *Teen Film: A Critical Introduction* (New York: Berg, 2011), 71.

42. Shelley Stamp Lindsey, "Is Any Girl Safe? Female Spectators at the White Slave Films," *Screen* 37, no. 1 (1996): 1–15; and Shelley Stamp Lindsey, "'Oil upon the Flames of Vice': The Battle over White Slave Films in New York City," *Film History* 9, no. 4 (1997): 351–364.

43. Chris Fujiwara, *The World and Its Double: The Life and Work of Otto Preminger* (New York: Macmillan Publishers, 2009), 143; see also Leonard J. Leff, and Jerold L. Simmons, *The Dame in the Kimono: Hollywood, Censorship, and the Production Code* (Lexington: University of Kentucky Press, 2001).

44. This includes films such as *Tea and Sympathy* (1956), *Blue Denim* (1959), *Splendor in the Grass* (1961), *Lolita* (1962), *Eighteen and Anxious* (1957), *Unwed Mother* (1958), *Diary of a High School Bride* (1959), and *Married Too Young* (1962). See Timothy Shary, "Virgin Springs: A Survey of Teen Films' Quest for Sexcess," in *Virgin Territory: Representing Sexual Inexperience in Film*, edited by Tamar Jeffers McDonald (Detroit: Wayne State University Press, 2010).

45. Shary, "Virgin Springs," 57.

46. Shary, *Teen Movies*, 63.

47. Lisa M. Dresner, "Love's Labor's Lost? Early 1980s Representations of Girls' Sexual Decision Making in *Fast Times at Ridgemont High* and *Little Darlings*," in *Virgin Territory: Representing Sexual Inexperience in Film*, edited by Tamar Jeffers McDonald (Detroit: Wayne State University Press, 2010), 174–200.

48. Bonnie Dow, *Prime-Time Feminism: Television, Media Culture, and the Women's Movement since 1970* (Philadelphia: University of Pennsylvania Press, 1996).

49. Marilyn Quayle, "Republican National Convention Address," August 19, 1992, http://www.c-span.org/video/?31358–1/republican-national-convention-address.

50. Christine J. Gardner, *Making Chastity Sexy: The Rhetoric of Evangelical Abstinence Campaigns* (Berkeley: University of California Press, 2011), 14.

51. Chuck Colson, "Nothing More Natural: Abstinence at Harvard," April 21, 2008, http://www.premaritalsex.info/nothing-more-natural/.

52. See Dow, *Prime-Time Feminism*.

53. Elspeth Probyn, "New Traditionalism and Post-Feminism: TV Does the Home," *Screen* 31, no. 2 (1990): 152.

54. Sarah Projansky, *Watching Rape: Film and Television in Postfeminist Culture* (New York: New York University Press, 2001), 2.

55. See also Ann Brooks, *Postfeminisms: Feminism, Theory, and Cultural Forms* (London: Routledge, 1997); Vicki Coppock, *The Illusion of Postfeminism: New Women, Old Myths* (London: Taylor & Francis, 1995); Bonnie J. Dow, "The Traffic in Men and the *Fatal Attraction* of Post-Feminist Masculinity," *Women's Studies in Communication* 29, no. 1 (2006): 113–131; Kristen Hoerl and Casey Ryan Kelly, "The Post-Nuclear Family and the Depoliticization of Unplanned Pregnancy in *Knocked Up*, *Juno*, and *Waitress*," *Communication and Critical/Cultural Studies* 7, no. 4 (2010): 360–380; Mary Douglas Vavrus, *Postfeminist News: Political Women in Media Culture* (Albany: State University of New York Press, 2002).

56. Angela McRobbie, "Postfeminism and Popular Culture: Bridget Jones and the New Gender Regime," in *Interrogating Postfeminism: Gender and the Politics of Popular Culture*, edited by Yvonne Tasker and Diane Negra (Durham, NC: Duke University Press, 2007), 28.

57. See Michelle Rodino-Colocino, "'Feminism as Ideology: Sarah Palin's Anti-Feminist Feminism and Ideology Critique," *Triple C: Cognition, Communication, Cooperation* 10, no. 2 (2012): 457–473.

58. See Mary Douglas Vavrus, "Opting Out Moms in the News: Selling New Traditionalism in the New Millennium," *Feminist Media Studies* 7, no. 1 (2007): 47–63.

59. See Jean Killborn, *Can't Buy My Love: How Advertising Changes the Way You Think and Feel* (New York: Touchstone, 2012).

60. Valenti, *The Purity Myth*, 65.

61. Yvonne Tasker and Diane Negra, "Introduction: Feminist Politics and Postfeminist Culture," in *Interrogating Postfeminism: Gender and the Politics of Popular Culture*, edited by Yvonne Tasker and Diane Negra (Durham, NC: Duke University Press, 2007), 11.

62. Frances Gateward and Murray Pomerance, "Introduction," in *Sugar, Spice, and Everything Nice: Cinemas of Girlhood*, edited by Frances Gateward and Murray Pomerance, 13–24 (Detroit: Wayne State University Press, 2002), 13.

63. See also Gayle Wald, "Clueless in the Neocolonial World Order," in *Sugar, Spice, and Everything Nice: Cinemas of Girlhood*, edited by Frances Gateward and Murray Pomerance, 5–70 (Detroit: Wayne State University Press, 2002).

64. Berlant, *The Queen of America Goes to Washington City*, 6.

65. Ibid.

66. See Kenneth Burke, *A Rhetoric of Motives* (Berkeley: University of California Press, 1959); David Blakesly, *Terministic Screens: Rhetorical Perspectives on Film* (Carbondale: Southern Illinois University Press, 2007).

67. Maddux, *Faithful Citizen*, 24.

68. See Blakesly, *Terministic Screens*; Barry Brummett, *Rhetorical Dimensions of Popular Culture* (Tuscaloosa: University of Alabama Press, 1990); Douglas Kellner, *Cinema Wars: Hollywood Film and Politics in the Bush-Cheney Era* (Malden, MA: Wiley-Blackwell, 2009); Michael Ryan and Douglas Kellner, *Camera Politica: The Politics and Ideology of Contemporary Hollywood* (Bloomington: Indiana University Press, 1988); Zavarzadeh, *Seeing Films Politically*.

69. In interdisciplinary studies of film, the meaning of "rhetoric" is protean and polysemous. If anything is consistent, it is that when rhetoric is invoked as either a methodology or object of inquiry it is often done so with disparagement and skepticism. See David Bordwell, *Meaning Making: Inference and Rhetoric in Interpretation of Cinema* (Cambridge, MA: Harvard University Press, 1991); and Zavarzadeh, *Seeing Films Politically*, 6.

70. Kenneth Burke, *Language as Symbolic Action: Essays on Life, Literature, and Method* (Berkeley: University of California Press, 1966).

71. Blakesly, *Terministic Screens*, 5.

72. Brummett, *Rhetorical Dimensions of Popular Culture*, 38.

73. Ryan and Kellner, *Camera Politica*, 13. See also Michael Ryan, "The Politics of Film: Discourse, Psychoanalysis, Ideology," in *Marxism and the Interpretation of Culture*, edited by Cary Nelson and Lawrence Grossberg, 477–486 (Urbana: University of Illinois Press, 1988).

74. Kellner, *Cinema Wars*; Ryan and Kellner, *Camera Politica*.

75. Kellner, *Cinema Wars*, 35.

76. Antonio Gramsci suggests that in democratic societies the ruling classes do not maintain power through force alone, but instead by eliciting popular adherence to their interests, ideals, and values, often in an attempt to infuse the social body with the belief that existing power structures are natural, innate, or otherwise taken-for-granted. See Antonio Gramsci, *Selections from the Prison Notebooks* (1936; rpt. New York: International Publishers, 1971). See also Stuart Hall, "The Whites of Their Eyes: Racist Ideologies in the Media," in *Gender, Race, and Class in Media: A Text-Reader*, 2nd ed., edited by Gail Dines and Jean Humez (Thousand Oaks, CA: Sage, 2002), 89–93.

77. Mary Ellen Brown, *Soap Opera and Women's Talk: The Pleasure of Resistance* (Thousand Oaks, CA: Sage, 1994), 5.

CHAPTER 1 MELODRAMA AND POSTFEMINIST ABSTINENCE

1. Nina Auerbach, *Our Vampires, Ourselves* (Chicago: University of Chicago Press, 1995), 145.

2. See Daryl Jones, *Horror: A Thematic History of Fiction and Film* (London: Arnold, 2002); Barbara Brodman and James E. Doan, *Images of the Modern Vampire: The Hip and Atavistic*

(Lanham, MD: Fairleigh Dickinson University Press, 2013); Nicola Nixon, "When Hollywood Sucks; or, Hungry Girls, Lost Boys, and Vampirism in the Age of Reagan," in *Blood Read: The Vampire as Metaphor in Contemporary Culture*, edited by Joan Gordon and Veronica Hollinger (Philadelphia: University of Pennsylvania Press, 1997).

3. Eugenia DeLamotte, *Perils of the Night: A Feminist Study of Nineteenth-Century Gothic* (Oxford: Oxford University Press, 1990), 21.

4. See Beverly LaHaye, *Raising Sexually Pure Kids: How to Prepare Your Children for the Act of Marriage* (Sisters, OR: Multnomah Publishers, 1998).

5. Ethan Sacks, "The 'Twilight Saga' Has Left a Mark on Hollywood As More Films Aimed at Teen Girls Start to Show Up," *New York Daily News*, February 3, 2013, http://www .nydailynews.com/entertainment/tv-movies/twilight-effect-movies-article-1.1252704; Rachel Abrams, "'Twilight's' Last Gleaning: Lionsgate Savors Big B.O. Opening, but Wall Street Revels in Franchise's Predictable Payoff," *Daily Variety*, November 11, 2012, 1.

6. See The Official Website of Stephenie Meyer, http://stepheniemeyer.com/bio.html.

7. See Giselle Liza Anatol, *Bringing Light to Twilight: Perspectives on a Pop Culture Phenomenon* (New York: Palgrave Macmillan, 2011).

8. Luchina Fisher, "Why Was 'Twilight' Director Axed from Sequel?" *ABC News*, December 10, 2008, http://abcnews.go.com/Entertainment/Movies/story?id=6420639&page=1.

9. Meyer also posted an unpublished version of the novel *Midnight Sun*, which narrates the *Twilight Saga* from the perspective of Edward. It is available at http://stepheniemeyer.com/midnightsun.html.

10. From the mid-1950s through the 1970s, Hammer Film Productions (United Kingdom) produced a series of formulaic and low-budget vampire films that enjoyed success in the United States thanks to distribution from Warner Bros.

11. For example, see Stacey Abbott, *Celluloid Vampires: Life after Death in the Modern World* (Austin: University of Texas Press, 2009); Ken Gelder, *Reading the Vampire* (London: Routledge, 2002); and Kendall Phillips, *Projected Fears: Horror Films and American Culture* (Westport, CT: Praeger, 2005).

12. Auerbach, *Our Vampires, Ourselves*, 6.

13. William Day, *Vampire Legends in Contemporary American Culture: What Becomes a Legend Most* (Lexington: University Press of Kentucky, 2002), 33.

14. See Maggie Parke and Natalie Wilson, *Theorizing Twilight: Critical Essays on What's at Stake in a Post-Vampire World* (Jefferson, NC: McFarland, 2011).

15. Bryan Alexander, "'Twilight' Leaves Bite Marks on Hollywood," *USA Today*, November 11, 2012, 5b.

16. "Toys 'R' Us Has Been Bitten, Transforming into THE Twilight Saga Destination," *PR Newswire*, November 3, 2009, http://www.prnewswire.com/news-releases/toysrus-has -been-bitten-transforming-into-the-twilight-saga-destination-68834177.html.

17. See https://twitter.com/TwilightMOMS.

18. Gloria Goodale, "Twilight Moms: Why Women Are Drawn to Teens' 'Eclipse,'" *Christian Science Monitor*, June 28, 2010, http://www.csmonitor.com/USA/2010/0628/Twilight -moms-Why-women-are-drawn-to-teens-Eclipse.

19. See Patrick Michels, "This Weekend, *Twilight* Superfans Make Downtown Dallas Their Playground," *Dallas Observer*, July 31, 2009, http://blogs.dallasobserver.com/ unfairpark/2009/07/this_weekend_twilight_superfan.php; "Vampire Fans Bitten by the Cruise Bug," *PR Newswire*, April 15, 2010, http://www.prnewswire.com/news -releases/vampire-fans-bitten-by-the-cruise-bug-90921624.html; Rachael Hendershot Parkin, "Breaking Faith: Disrupted Expectations and Ownership in Stephanie

Meyer's *Twilight* Saga," *Jeunesse: Young People, Texts, Cultures* 2, no. 2 (2010): 61–85; "'Twilight' Inspired Erotica to Be Published; Fan Fiction Based on the Series Becomes a Genre," *International Business Times*, November 8, 2012, http://www.ibtimes.com/twilight-inspired-erotica-be-published-fanfiction-based-series-becomes-genre-865476; "'Twilight' Fans Destination: Forks, Wash.," *NPR Morning Edition*, November 20, 2008, http://www.npr.org/templates/story/story.php?storyId=97241693. In addition to fan fiction, a number of other popular books attempt to make sense of the *Twilight* phenomenon, including Elaine Heath, *The Gospel According to Twilight: Women, Sex, and God* (Louisville, KY: Westminster John Knox Press, 2011); Maria Lindgren Leavenworth and Malin Isaksson, *Fanged Fan Fiction: Variations on Twilight, True Blood, and the Vampire Diaries* (Jefferson, NC: McFarland, 2013); Lois Gresh, *The Twilight Companion: The Unauthorized Guide to the Series* (New York: Macmillan, 2008); Nancy Reagin, *Twilight and History* (Hoboken, NJ: Wiley, 2010); Rebecca Housel and J. Jeremy Wisnewski, eds., *Twilight and Philosophy: Vampires, Vegetarians, and the Pursuit of Immortality* (Malden, MA: Blackwell, 2009).

20. Aaron Couch, "'Twilight' Wins 7 Razzie Awards Including Worst Picture," *Hollywood Reporter*, February 23, 2013, http://www.hollywoodreporter.com/news/twilight-wins-7-razzie-awards-423720.

21. For examples, see Christine Seifert, "Bite Me! (or Don't)," *Bitch Magazine*, 2008, http://bitchmagazine.org/article/bite-me-or-don't; and Terrance Rafferty, "Love and Pain and the Teenage Vampire Thing," *New York Times*, October 31, 2008, http://www.nytimes.com/2008/11/02/movies/moviesspecial/02raff.html?pagewanted=all&_r=0.

22. Stephenie Meyer, "Frequently Asked Questions: *Breaking Dawn*," http://stepheniemeyer.com/bd_faq.html.

23. For example, see Mariah Larsson and Ann Steiner, *Interdisciplinary Approaches to Twilight: Studies in Fiction, Media, and a Contemporary Cultural Experience* (Lund, Sweden: Nordic Academic Press, 2011); Chiho Nakagawa, "Safe Sex with Defanged Vampires: New Vampire Heroes in *Twilight* and the *Southern Vampire Mysteries*," *Journal of Popular Romance Studies* 2 (2011), http://jprstudies.org/2011/10/%E2%80%9Csafe-sex-with-defanged-vampires-new-vampire-heroes-in-twilight-and-the-southern-vampire-mysteries%E2%80%9D-by-chiho-nakagawa/; Anna Silver, "*Twilight* Is Not Good for Maidens: Gender, Sexuality, and the Family in Stephanie Meyer's *Twilight* Series," *Studies in the Novel* 42, no. 1/2 (2010): 121–138; Anatol, *Bringing Light to Twilight*.

24. See Natalie Wilson, *Seduced by Twilight: The Allure and Contradictory Messages of the Popular Saga* (Jefferson, NC: McFarland, 2011). It is important to note, however, that Wilson concludes that the narrative mandates that men must ultimately tame women.

25. Melissa A. Click, Jennifer Stevens Aubrey, and Elizabeth Behm-Morawitz, *Bitten by Twilight: Youth Culture, Media, and the Vampire Franchise* (New York: Peter Lang, 2010).

26. See Anne Morey, *Genre, Reception, and Adaptation in the "Twilight" Series* (Burlington, VT: Ashgate, 2013).

27. Ben Singer, *Melodrama and Modernity: Early Sensational Cinema in Contexts* (New York: Columbia University Press, 2013), 7.

28. Ibid., 295.

29. See Jan Campbell, *Film and Cinema Spectatorship: Melodrama and Mimesis* (Cambridge: Polity Press, 2005); Linda Williams, "Melodrama Revised," in *Refiguring American Film Genres: History and Theory*, edited by Nick Browne (Berkeley: University of California Press, 1998), 42–88; Linda Williams, "'Something Else Besides a Mother': *Stella Dallas* and the Maternal Melodrama," *Cinema Journal* 24, no. 1 (1984): 2–27; Laura Mulvey, "Notes on Sirk and Melodrama," *Movie* 25 (1977–78): 53–57.

30. Pam Cook, "Melodrama and the Women's Picture," in *Imitations of Life: A Reader on Film and Television Melodrama*, edited by Marcia Landy (Detroit: Wayne State University Press, 1991), 248–262; Barbara Creed, "The Position of Women in Hollywood Melodrama," *Australian Journal of Screen Theory* 4 (1978): 27–31.

31. Wilson, *Seduced by Twilight*, 13. See also Carrie Anne Platt, "Cullen Family Values: Gender and Sexual Politics in the Twilight Series," in *Bitten by Twilight: Youth Culture, Media, and the Vampire Franchise*, edited by Melissa A. Click, Jennifer Stevens Aubrey, and Elizabeth Behm-Morawitz (New York: Peter Lang, 2010), 76.

32. Randy Alcorn, "Guidelines for Sexual Purity," January 28, 2010, http://www.epm.org/resources/2010/Jan/28/guidelines-sexual-purity/.

33. Love Matters, "How to Start Over if You've Lost Your Virginity," last modified May 2, 2015, http://www.lovematters.com/startover.htm.

34. Alcorn, "Guidelines for Sexual Purity."

35. Kelly Coleen Mast, *Sex Respect: The Option of True Sexual Freedom* (Homer Glen, IL: Respect, Inc., 2001), 101.

36. Kris Frainie, *Why kNOw Abstinence Education Curriculum for Sixth Grade through High School: Teacher's Manual* (Chattanooga, TN: Abstinence Education Inc., 2002), 17.

37. Maureen Gallagher Duran, *Reasonable Reasons to Wait* (Chantilly, VA: A Choice in Education, 2003), 96.

38. Barbara Creed, *Phallic Panic: Film, Horror, and the Primal Uncanny* (Melbourne, Australia: Melbourne University Press, 2005).

39. Rose Fuller, Janet McLaughlin, and Andrew Asato, *FACTS—Family Accountability Communicating Teen Sexuality: Middle School and Senior High School Editions* (Portland, OR: Northwest Family Services, 2000), 12.

40. Mast, *Sex Respect*, 94.

41. Anne Badgley and Carrie Musselman, *Heritage Keepers Student Manual* (Charleston, SC: Heritage Community Services, 1999), 52.

42. The *Twilight* saga both removes the queer subtexts of vampire sexuality and does not include any characters who are apparently gay, lesbian, bisexual, or transgender.

43. Randall Patterson, "Students of Virginity," *New York Times*, March 30, 2008, http://www.nytimes.com/2008/03/30/magazine/30Chastity-t.html?pagewanted=all&_r=0.

44. See Mary Douglas Vavrus, "Opting Out Moms in the News: Selling the New Traditionalism in the New Millennium," *Feminist Media Studies* 7, no. 1 (2007): 52.

45. See Kristen Hoerl and Casey Ryan Kelly, "The Post-Nuclear Family and the Depoliticization of Unplanned Pregnancy in *Knocked Up*, *Juno*, and *Waitress*," *Communication and Critical/Cultural Studies* 7, no. 4 (2010): 337–359; Elspeth Probyn, "New Traditionalism and Post-Feminism: TV Does the Home," *Screen* 31, no. 2 (1990): 147–159; Judith Stacey, "The New Conservative Feminism," *Feminist Studies* 9, no. 3 (1983): 559–583.

46. Meyer, "Frequently Asked Questions."

47. See Stacy Gillis, Gilliam Howie, and Rebecca Munford, *Third Wave Feminism: A Critical Exploration* (London: Palgrave Macmillan, 2007); Leslie Heywood and Jennifer Drake, *Third Wave Agenda: Being Feminist, Doing Feminism* (Minneapolis: University of Minnesota Press, 1997).

48. Susan Faludi, *Backlash: The Undeclared War against American Women* (New York: Random House, 1991), 71.

49. For example, see Joshua Harris, *Why I Kissed Dating Goodbye* (Sisters, OR: Multnomah Press, 1997).

50. Helen Gurley Brown, *Sex and the Single Girl: The Unmarried Woman's Guide to Men* (New York: Bernard Geis Associates, 1962).

51. See Susan J. Douglas and Meredith W. Michaels, *The Mommy Myth* (New York: Simon and Schuster, 2005); Stephanie Coontz, *The Way We Never Were: American Families and the Nostalgia Trap* (New York: Basic Books, 1990).

52. The term "feminist killjoy" appears in chapter 2 of Sarah Ahmed, *The Promise of Happiness* (Durham, NC: Duke University Press, 2010).

53. See Mark Regnerus, "The Case for Early Marriage," *Christianity Today*, July 31, 2009, http://www.christianitytoday.com/ct/2009/august/16.22.html?start=7.

54. See Sarah Stephan and Grace Mally, *Before You Meet Prince Charming: A Guide to Radiant Purity* (Cedar Rapids, IA: Tomorrow's Forefathers, 2006); Stacy McDonald, *Raising Maidens of Virtue* (Cedar Rapids, IA: Tomorrow's Forefathers, 2006); Jamie Bishop, *The Princess and the Kiss: A Story of God's Gift of Purity* (Anderson, IN: Warner Press, 2000).

55. LaHaye, *Raising Sexually Pure Kids*, 161.

56. Badgley and Musselman, *Heritage Keepers Student Manual*, 52.

57. Ibid., 55.

58. See Lynn Arnaut, "Cruelty, Horror, and the Will to Redemption," *Hypatia* 18, no. 2 (2003): 155–188; Gail Bederman, *Manliness and Civilization* (Chicago: University of Chicago Press, 1995); Derek Buescher and Kent A. Ono, "Civilized Colonialism: Pocahontas as Neocolonial Rhetoric," *Women's Studies in Communication* 19, no. 2 (1996): 127–153; Dana Cloud, "'To Veil the Threat of Terror': Afghan Women and the 'Clash of Civilizations' in Imagery of the War on Terrorism," *Quarterly Journal of Speech* 90, no. 3 (2004): 285–306; Angela Davis, *Women, Race, and Class* (New York: Vintage, 1983); Caren J. Deming, "Miscegenation in Popular Western History and Fiction," in *Women and Western American Literature*, edited by Helen Winter Stauffer and Susan J. Rosowski (Troy, NY: Whiston, 1982), 90–99; Kent A. Ono, *Contemporary Media Culture and the Remnants of a Colonial Past* (New York: Peter Lang, 2009).

59. See Gayatri Chakravorty Spivak, "Can the Subaltern Speak?" in *Marxism and the Interpretation of Culture*, edited by Cary Nelson and Lawrence Grossberg (New York: Macmillan, 1988), 220–251.

60. See Richard Dyer, *White: Essays on Race and Culture* (New York: Routledge, 1997).

61. Wilson, *Seduced by Twilight*, 178.

62. See Patricia Hill Collins, *Black Feminist Thought: Knowledge, Consciousness, and the Politics of Empowerment* (London: Psychology Press, 2000).

63. This conception of private property as tied to a theory of individualism is derived from the political philosophy of John Locke. See John Locke, *Two Treatises on Government* (1689; reprint, New York: New American Library, 1965).

64. Mary Stuckey and John Murphy argue that these descriptions of North America as empty and awaiting subjugation prepared the land for colonization. See Mary Stuckey and John Murphy, "By Any Other Name: Rhetorical Colonialism in North America," *American Indian Culture and Research Journal* 25 (2001): 73–98.

65. The Cullens also summon vampires from South America, who embody the feminized archetype of Amazon, exuding an imposing but sexualized version of female physical prowess. Their powers include the ability to present illusory and deceptive realities to anyone they touch. Their tribal appearance once again codes nature as feminine and seductive.

66. Susan Rae Peterson argues that rape laws are an example of "male protection rackets" that offer women protection from violence and coercion in exchange for limitations on their freedom and autonomy. See Susan Rae Peterson, "Coercion and Rape: The State as a Male Protection Racket," in *Feminism and Philosophy*, edited by Mary Vetterling-Braggin (Totowa, NJ: Rowman and Allenheld, 1977), 360–371.

67. Mary Y. Hallab, *Vampire God: The Allure of the Undead in Western Culture* (Albany: State University of New York Press, 2009).

68. Ariel Levy, *Female Chauvinist Pigs: Women and the Rise of Raunch Culture* (New York: Free Press, 2006).

69. See Lauren Berlant and Michael Warner, "Sex in Public," *Critical Inquiry* 24, no. 2 (1998): 547–566.

70. See Christine J. Gardner, *Making Chastity Sexy: The Rhetoric of Evangelical Abstinence Campaigns* (Berkeley: University of California Press, 2011).

71. For a summary of the ongoing privatization of citizenship, see Wendy Brown, "American Nightmare: Neoliberalism, Neoconservativism, and De-Democratization," *Political Theory* 34, no. 6 (2006): 690–714; Wendy Brown, "Neoliberalism and the End of Liberal Democracy," *Theory & Event* 7, no. 1 (2003); Henry Giroux, *Public Spaces, Private Lives: Beyond the Culture of Cynicism* (Lanham, MD: Rowman & Littlefield, 2001); Henry Giroux, "The Terror of Neoliberalism: Rethinking the Significance of Cultural Politics," *College Literature* 32, no. 1 (2005): 1–19.

72. Ryalan Alleman, "6 Reasons (+2) to NOT Send Your Daughter to College," Fix the Family, http://www.fixthefamily.com/blog/6-reasons-to-not-send-your-daughter-to-college.

CHAPTER 2   MAN-BOYS AND BORN-AGAIN VIRGINS

1. John Blake, "Why Young Christians Aren't Waiting Anymore," *CNN*, September 27, 2001, http://religion.blogs.cnn.com/2011/09/27/why-young-christians-arent-waiting-anymore/.

2. See Morgan Lee, "LifeWay Relaunches Abstinence Program to Fight Culture Where 80% of Unmarried Christians Have Sex," *Christian Post*, January 10, 2014, http://www.christianpost.com/news/lifeway-relaunches-abstinence-program-to-fight-culture-where-80-of-unmarried-christians-have-sex-112395/.

3. Laura Carpenter, *Virginity Lost: An Intimate Portrait of First Sexual Experiences* (New York: New York University Press, 2005), 40.

4. See Brian Alexander, "Born-Again Virgins Claim to Rewrite the Past," *NBC News*, February 28, 2008, http://www.nbcnews.com/id/23254178/ns/health-sexual_health/t/born-again-virgins-claim-rewrite-past/#.VE5E4f2yNg0.

5. In addition to *The 40-Year-Old Virgin* (2005), such films include *Pineapple Express* (2008) and *Knocked Up* (2007).

6. For instance, *This Is 40* (2012), *Get Him to the Greek* (2010), *Funny People* (2009), and *Forgetting Sarah Marshall* (2008). Here I use the term "hegemonic masculinity" to denote prevailing modes of manliness that are defined by characteristics such as physical strength, self-reliance, independence, and competiveness. See Raewyn W. Connell, *Masculinities* (Berkeley: University of California Press, 2005); Robert Hanke, "Hegemonic Masculinity in *Thirtysomething*," *Critical Studies in Mass Communication* 7, no. 3 (1990): 231–248; Nick Trujillo, "Hegemonic Masculinity on the Mound: Media Representations of Nolan Ryan and American Sports Culture," *Critical Studies in Mass Communication* 8, no. 3 (1991): 290–308.

7. See *No Strings Attached* (2011), *He's Just Not That Into You* (2009), *27 Dresses* (2008), *Bridget Jones's Diary* (2001), *What Women Want* (2000), *You've Got Mail* (1998), *My Best Friend's Wedding* (1997), *As Good as It Gets* (1997), *Jerry McGuire* (1996), *Sleepless in Seattle* (1993), *Pretty Woman* (1990), and *When Harry Met Sally* (1989).

8. Here I include films such as *There's Something about Mary* (1998), *High Fidelity* (2000), *Meet the Parents* (2000), *About a Boy* (2002), *50 First Dates* (2004), *Along*

Came Polly (2004), *Zack and Miri Make a Porno* (2008), *She's Out of My League* (2010), *Hall Pass* (2011), *Safety Not Guaranteed* (2012), and *The Five-Year Engagement* (2012). See Tamar Jeffers McDonald, *Romantic Comedy: Boy Meets Girl Meets Genre* (London: Wallflower, 2007); Claire Mortimer, *Romantic Comedy* (London and New York: Routledge, 2010).

9. See John Albert, "'I Love You, Man': Bromances, the Construction of Masculinity, and the Continuing Evolution of the Romantic Comedy," *Quarterly Review of Film & Video* 30, no. 2 (2013): 159–172; and Kathleen Rowe, *The Unruly Woman: Gender and the Genres of Laughter* (Austin: University of Texas Press, 1995).

10. Tamar Jeffers McDonald, "Homme-Com: Engendering Change in Contemporary Romantic Comedy," in *Falling in Love Again: Romantic Comedy in Contemporary Cinema*, edited by Stacy Abbott and Debbie Jermyn (New York: I. B. Taurus, 2009), 146–159.

11. John Troyer and Chani Marchiselli, "Slack, Slackers, Slackest: Homosocial Bonding Practices in Contemporary Dude Cinema," in *Where the Boys Are: Cinemas of Masculinity and Youth*, edited by Murray Pomerance and Frances Gateward (Detroit, MI: Wayne State University Press, 2005), 264–278.

12. Aaron Taylor, "Adam Sandler, an Apologia: Anger, Arrested Adolescence, *Amour Fou*," in *Millennial Masculinity: Men in Contemporary American Cinema*, edited by Timothy Shary (Detroit, MI: Wayne State University Press, 2013), 19–51.

13. McDonald, *Romantic Comedy*, 17. To date, *The 40-Year-Old Virgin* has grossed $177,378,645 worldwide, which is impressive for its genre. See "The 40-Year-Old Virgin," Box Office Mojo, http://www.boxofficemojo.com/movies/?id=40yearoldvirgin.htm.

14. Manohla Dargis, "Film Review; Losing His Innocence, Not a Minute Too Soon," *New York Times*, August 19, 2005, http://query.nytimes.com/gst/fullpage.html?res =9C05EED8133EF93AA2575BC0A9639C8B63.

15. Michael O'Sullivan, "'Virgin': A Man on a Mission," *Washington Post*, August 19 2005, http://www.washingtonpost.com/wpdyn/content/article/2005/08/18/AR2005081800517.html.

16. David Denby, "Partners," *The New Yorker*, September 12, 2005, 102–103.

17. McDonald argues that traditional romantic comedies are implicitly concerned with the vicissitudes of sexual desire yet ultimately provide closure and fulfillment within the traditional fantasy structure of heterosexuality. Even in early screwball comedies such as *Bringing Up Baby* (1938), *His Girl Friday* (1940), *Pillow Talk* (1959), and *Send Me No Flowers* (1964), "the implication of sex" is sex that is "settled, secure," and takes place in the context of a relationship (14). The restrictiveness of the Production Code and later the MPAA rating system forced filmmakers to insert sexuality between the lines of the narrative or to imply, often with careful editing, that sex took place off screen.

18. For instance, *There's Something about Mary* features a comic depiction of male ejaculate accidentally used as hair-styling gel.

19. Claire Sisco King, "It Cuts Both Ways: *Fight Club*, Masculinity, and Abject Hegemony," *Communication and Critical/Cultural Studies* 6, no. 4 (2009): 366–385.

20. See Eric King Watts, "Border Patrolling and 'Passing' in Eminem's *8 Mile*," *Critical Studies in Media Communication* 22, no. 3 (2005): 187–206; Karen Lee Ashcraft and Lisa A. Flores, "'Slaves with White Collars': Persistent Performances of Masculinity in Crisis," *Text and Performance Quarterly* 23, no. 1 (2000): 1–29.

21. King, "It Cuts Both Ways," 367.

22. Albert, "'I Love You, Man,'" 162.

23. Michael Kimmel, *Manhood in America: A Cultural History* (New York: The Free Press, 1996).

24. James Gilbert, *Men in the Middle: Searching for Masculinity in the 1950s* (Chicago: University of Chicago Press, 2005).

25. See Steven Watts, *Mr. Playboy: Hugh Hefner and the American Dream* (Hoboken, NJ: Wiley, 2008).

26. See Barbara Ehrenreich, *The Hearts of Men: American Dreams and the Flight from Commitment* (New York: Random House, 1983); Shulamith Firestone, *The Dialectic of Sex: The Case for Feminist Revolution* (1970; reprint, New York: Macmillan, 2003); Jane Gerhard, *Desiring Revolution: Second-Wave Feminism and the Rewriting of the Twentieth-Century American Sexual Thought* (New York: Columbia University Press, 2013); Sheila Jeffreys, *Anticlimax: A Feminist Perspective on the Sexual Revolution* (Melbourne, Australia: Spinifex Press, 2012).

27. Leerom Medovoi, "A Yippie-Panther Pipe Dream: Rethinking Sex, Race, and the Sexual Revolution," in *Swinging Single: Representing Sexuality in the 1960s*, edited by Hilary Radner and Moya Luckett (Minneapolis: University of Minnesota Press, 1999), 133–180.

28. Over the question of whether *Playboy* was a positive step for women's liberation, Hefner drew fire from feminists such as Susan Brownmiller (who publicly admonished Hefner on *The Dick Cavett Show* in 1970) and Gloria Steinem, who published a feminist exposé of the Playboy Club after working as a bunny. See "A Bunny's Tale," *Show Magazine*, 1 June 1963, 66–68, 110.

29. Kimmel, *Manhood in America*, 274.

30. Carrie Pitzulo, *Bachelors and Bunnies: The Sexual Politics of Playboy* (Chicago: University of Chicago Press, 2011), 6.

31. Susan Faludi, *Stiffed: The Betrayal of the American Man* (New York: William Morrow and Company, 1999), 37.

32. This version of man-boy masculinity is exemplified by Paul Rudd's characters in *Knocked Up* (2008), *I Love You, Man* (2009), and, to a lesser extent *This Is 40* (2012), who are so alienated from themselves either by children or relationships with women that they can rediscover their manhood only through the infantile (and frequently grossout) pleasures of male camaraderie.

33. Another version of the man-boy is the bachelor or playboy intent on finding personal fulfillment through sexual conquest. In films such as *Old School* (2003), *Wedding Crashers* (2005), and *Crazy, Stupid Love* (2011) (and, of course, *The 40-Year-Old Virgin*), men reaffirm their heterosexual identities through fraternity-style sexual escapades and gross-out humor. In these films, the twenty- and thirty-something male's aversion to romantic coupling and obsession with casual sex accounts for his state of arrested emotional development. An altogether different kind of man-boy is the male character who retains his physical manhood but quite literally lives like a child. Adam Sandler typifies this overgrown petulant child in films such as *Billy Madison* (1995), *Happy Gilmore* (1996), *The Waterboy* (1998), and *Big Daddy* (1999), while Will Ferrell often explores the pleasures of men returning to childhood or expressing childlike wonderment in films such as *Elf* (2003), *Old School* (2003), and *Step Brothers* (2008).

34. Jody Pennington offers this assessment of *Annie Hall* in *The History of Sex in American Film* (Westport, CT: Praeger, 2007).

35. Set decorator K. C. Fox obtained most of the set decor for Andy's apartment from comic book conventions, eBay, and vintage toy stores. For the sake of authenticity, Fox even used a large spaceship poster from her adolescent son's bedroom as the centerpiece

of Andy's bedroom. Set and mise-en-scène choices are detailed in "The 40 Year Old Virgin Production Notes," *Entertainment Magazine Online*, August 17, 2005, accessed May 25, 2014, http://emol.org/film/archives/40yearoldvirgin/productionnotes.html.

36. See Barbara Creed, *The Monstrous-Feminine: Film, Feminism, Psychoanalysis* (London: Routledge, 1993).

37. This is a particularly important choice in light of the fact that the smitten but ultimately platonic male friend is a feature of many other romantic (and teen) comedies, e.g., *Pretty in Pink* (1986) and *There's Something about Mary* (1998). This character type is much more prevalent on television than in film.

38. Creed, *The Monstrous-Feminine*, 1.

39. Julia Kristeva, *Powers of Horror: An Essay on Abjection*, translated by Leon S. Roudiez (New York: Columbia University Press), 4.

40. Creed, *The Monstrous-Feminine*, 9.

41. Laura Mulvey, "Visual Pleasure of Narrative Cinema," *Screen* 6 (Autumn 1975): 6–18.

42. See also Barbara Creed, *Phallic Panic: Film, Horror, and the Primal Uncanny* (Melbourne, Australia: Melbourne University Press, 2005)

43. Andy is particularly horrified by the fact that the vomit smells like fish, which, read through a theory of abjection, might refer to the sight and smell of the vagina.

44. The concept of "terministic screens" is borrowed from Kenneth Burke, *Language as Symbolic Action: Essays on Life, Literature, and Method* (Berkeley: University of California Press, 1966).

45. See Sigmund Freud, "Medusa's Head," in *The Standard Edition of the Complete Psychological Works of Sigmund Freud*, vol. 18, *Beyond the Pleasure Principle, Group Psychology, and Other Works (1920–1922)*, trans. James Strachey (London: Hogarth, 1955), 273–274.

46. In his exploration of primitive rituals of defloration, Freud observed that male fears of vaginas is connected to castration anxiety. Hence, Freud describes a litany of vagina taboos throughout world cultures that address everything from menstruation to childbirth. But as Creed points out, Freud downplays the dread of woman as castrator (i.e., woman as powerful). Instead, Freud argues that male dread of the feminine is linked with the early childhood observation of mothers as castrated, a notion consistent with his theory of penis envy. See Freud, "The Taboo of Virginity (Contributions to the Psychology of Love, III)," in *The Standard Edition of the Complete Psychological Works of Sigmund Freud*, vol. 11, *Five Lectures on Psycho-Analysis, Leonardo Da Vinci, and Other Works (1910)*, translated by James Strachey (London: Hogarth, 1957), 191–208; and Creed, *The Monstrous-Feminine*, 119–121.

47. For example, Robert Loeb's *She-Manners: The Teen Girl's Book of Etiquette* (New York: Associated Press, 1959) advises young women: "To make him feel important, you have to forget your own desires for importance. Compliment him on his physical prowess, his mental acumen, his good looks, his virility. The worst mistake a girl can make is to make a man feel intellectually inferior or inadequate as a male. We men need a lot of reassurance. So lay it on thick but subtly. Stroke his ego. Let him think he's king much of the time. He will love you for it, and, you know, it will make you feel extremely feminine" (62).

48. The DVD's deleted scenes reveal that in this shot, actor Steve Carell actually had his chest waxed by a professional beautician.

49. For example, see "Real Life Stories," The Abstinence Resource Center, http://abstinenceresourcecenter.org/index.php/students/real_life_stories; Jon Fortenbury, "On 'Late'-In-Life Virginity Loss," *The Atlantic*, March 28, 2014, http://www.theatlantic.com/health/archive/2014/03/on-late-in-life-virginity-loss/284412/; Tim Stafford, "Can

You Become a Virgin Again?" *Christianity Today*, http://www.christianitytoday.com/iyf/hottopics/sexabstinence/can-you-become-virgin-again.html.

50. The film's homophobic subtexts, which include a lengthy exchange between Cal and David about "know how I know you're gay?" contribute to the film's overarching endorsement of heteronormative institutions and social rituals.

51. See Celestino Deleyto, "The New Road to Sexual Ecstasy: Virginity and Genre in *The 40-Year-Old Virgin*," in *Virgin Territory: Representing Sexual Inexperience in Film*, edited by Tamar Jeffers McDonald (Detroit, MI: Wayne State University Press, 2010), 255–268; McDonald, *Romantic Comedy*; Maria San Filippo, *The B Word: Bisexuality in Contemporary Film and Television* (Bloomington: Indiana University Press, 2013).

52. Deleyto, "The New Road to Sexual Ecstasy," 258.

53. Michel Foucault, *The History of Sexuality*, vol. 1, *An Introduction* (New York: Vintage, 1990).

54. See Herbert Marcuse, *One-Dimensional Man: Studies in the Ideology of Advanced Industrial Society* (Boston: Beacon Press, 1964).

55. Three good examples include Jim Burns, *The Purity Code: God's Plan for Sex and Your Body* (Ada, MI: Bethany House Publishers, 2008); Dannah K. Gresh, *And the Bride Wore White: Seven Secrets to Sexual Purity* (Chicago: Moody Publishers, 1999); and Lindsay Marsh Warren, *The Best Sex of My Life: Confessions of a Sexual Purity Revolution* (Bloomington, IN: Trafford Publishing, 2012).

56. "Take2 Renewed Virginity," PSC: A Pregnancy Resource Center for Northeast Ohio, http://www.pscstark.com/42; Vilma Conner, *Born-Again Virgin: How to Transform Your Life from Promiscuity Back into Purity* (Glendale, CA: Miracon Enterprises, 2009); Wendy Keller, *The Cult of the Born Again Virgin: How Single Women Can Reclaim Their Sexual Power* (Deerfield Beach, FL: Health Communication, Inc., 1999).

CHAPTER 3   MONSTROUS GIRLS AND ABSENTEE FATHERS

1. Randy Wilson quoted in James M. Dobson, *Bringing Up Girls* (Carol Stream, IL: Tyndale House Publishers, 2012), 108.

2. Ibid.

3. Robin Wood, *Hollywood: From Vietnam to Reagan and Beyond* (New York: Columbia University Press, 2003), 70.

4. Films include *Stigmata*, *The Exorcism of Emily Rose*, *Requiem*, *Exorcism: The Possession of Gail Bowers*, *Paranormal Activity*, *The Last Exorcism*, *Anneliese: The Exorcist Tapes*, *Exorcismus*, *The Devil Inside*, and *The Last Exorcism II*. Men can also become vulnerable to demons if they fail in spiritual combat. In *The Rite* and *The Devil Inside*, male priests are possessed after performing failed exorcisms. In rare cases, male possession reflects the general failure of men to live up to hegemonic notions of masculinity; an example is *The Possession of David O'Reilly*.

5. Carol Clover, *Men, Women, and Chain Saws: Gender in the Modern Horror Film* (Princeton, NJ: Princeton University Press, 1993), 72.

6. Examples include *Alien*, *The Texas Chainsaw Massacre*, *Carrie*, *Halloween*, *Jaws*, *The Last House on the Left*, *The Hills Have Eyes*, and *The Amityville Horror*.

7. See also Shohini Chaudhuri, *Feminist Film Theorists: Laura Mulvey, Kaja Silverman, Teresa de Lauretis, Barbara Creed* (London: Routledge, 2006).

8. Barbara Creed, "Horror and the Monstrous Feminine: An Imaginary Abjection," *Screen* 27, no. 1 (1986): 35; see also Barbara Creed, *The Monstrous-Feminine: Film, Feminism, and Psychoanalysis* (New York: Routledge, 1993).

9. Clover, *Men, Women, and Chain Saws*, 100.

10. Ibid., 82.

11. Ibid., 67.

12. Joshua Gunn, "The Rhetoric of Exorcism: George W. Bush and the Return of Political Demonology," *Western Journal of Communication* 68, no. 1 (2004): 8.

13. Bruce Wilson, "Most Americans 18–29 Years Old Believe in Demon Possession, Shows Survey," *Huffington Post*, October 12, 2013, http://www.huffingtonpost.com/bruce -wilson/most-americans-1829-years_b_4163588.html.

14. Jane Owens, *A Biblical View of Sexual Purity* (Bloomington, IN: Xlibris, 2010), 47.

15. Bryan Alexander, "Exorcism Movies Possess Big Success in Hollywood," *USA Today*, February 27, 2013, http://www.usatoday.com/story/life/movies/2013/02/27/last-exorcism -ashley-bell-eli-roth/1932993/.

16. Opening-weekend ticket sales: *The Exorcism of Emily Rose* ($75 million), *The Rite* ($96 million), and *The Devil Inside* ($34.5 million).

17. Creed, *The Monstrous-Feminine*, 34.

18. Tirdad Derakhshani, "Demonic-Possession Film—This Time with Hasidim," *Philadelphia Inquirer*, August 31, 2012, http://www.philly.com/philly/entertainment/movies/ 20120831_Demonic-possession_film_-_this_time_with_Hasidim.html.

19. Claudia Puig, "A Rabbi to the Rescue in Demonic 'Possession'; but That's the Film's Only Fresh Element," *USA Today*, August 30, 2012, 6D.

20. "The Possession (2012)," Internet Movie Database, accessed October 30, 2013, http:// www.imdb.com/title/tt0431021/?ref_=nv_sr_1.

21. David Blankenhorn, *Fatherless America* (New York: Harper Perennial, 1996).

22. See John P. Bartkowski, *The Promise Keepers: Servants, Soldiers, and Godly Men* (New Brunswick, NJ: Rutgers University Press, 2004).

23. Jim Burns, *The Purity Code: God's Plan for Sex and Your Body* (Wheaton, IL: Crossway, 2008), 17.

24. Rachel Lovingood, "True Love Waits: Living with Teens," August 17, 2011 http://www .ridgecrestcamps.com/parents-blog/true-love-waits-living-with-teens/.

25. Ibid.

26. Randy Alcorn, *The Purity Principle: God's Safeguards for Life's Dangerous Trails* (Colorado Springs, CO: Multnomah Books, 2003).

27. Yoram Bilu, "The Taming of Deviants and Beyond: An Analysis of *Dybbuk* Possession and Exorcism in Judaism," in *Spirit Possession in Judaism: Cases and Contexts from the Middle Ages to the Present*, edited by Matt Goldish (Detroit: Wayne State University Press, 2003), 46.

28. Joshua Harris, *Sex Is Not the Problem (Lust Is): Sexual Purity in a Lust-Saturated World* (Colorado Springs, CO: Multnomah Books, 1996), 39.

29. Dannah K. Gresh, *And the Bride Wore White: Seven Secrets to Sexual Purity* (Chicago: Moody Publishers, 1999).

30. True Love Waits, "Living with Teens."

31. Burns, *The Purity Code*, 17.

32. Clover, *Men, Women, and Chain Saws*, 65.

33. Tania Modleski, *Feminism without Women: Culture and Criticism in a "Postfeminist" Age* (New York: Routledge, 1991), 7; see also Susan Robinson, *Marked Men: White Masculinity in Crisis* (New York: Columbia University Press, 2000).

34. Jessica Psalidas, *Everlasting Purity* (Maitlin, FL: Xulon Press, 2008), 17.

35. Burns, *The Purity Code*, 14.

36. Christine J. Gardner, *Making Chastity Sexy: The Rhetoric of Evangelical Abstinence Campaigns* (Berkeley: University of California Press, 2011).

37. See Claire Sisco King, *Washed in Blood: Male Sacrifice, Trauma, and the Cinema* (New Brunswick, NJ: Rutgers University Press, 2011); Claire Sisco King, "Unqueering Horror: *Hellbent* and the Policing of the 'Gay Slasher,'" *Western Journal of Communication* 74, no. 3 (2010): 249–268; Claire Sisco King, "Acting Up and Sounding Off: Sacrifice and Performativity in *Alice, Sweet Alice*," *Text and Performance Quarterly* 27, no. 2 (2007): 124–142; Kendall Phillips, *Projected Fears: Horror Films and American Culture* (Westport, CT: Praeger, 2005); Kendall Phillips, *Dark Directions: Romero, Craven, Carpenter, and the Modern Horror Film* (Carbondale: Southern Illinois Press, 2012).

CHAPTER 4   ABSTINENCE, THE GLOBAL
SEX INDUSTRY, AND RACIAL VIOLENCE

1. "Taken (2008)," Internet Movie Database, http://www.imdb.com/title/tt0936501/?ref_=nv_sr_2.

2. "Taken 2 (2012)," Internet Movie Database, http://www.imdb.com/title/tt1397280/; "Taken 3 (2014)," Internet Movie Database, http://www.imdb.com/title/tt2446042/.

3. Christy Lemir, "Review: *Taken* on a Guilty-Pleasure Ride," *Associated Press*, January 28, 2009.

4. Mick Lasalle, "He's an Ex-CIA Agent—Of Course They Took His Kid," *San Francisco Chronicle*, January 30, 2009, E3.

5. See Jeremy Engels, and Greg Goodale, "'Our Battle Cry Will Be: Remember Jenny McCrea!' A Précis on the Rhetoric of Revenge," *American Quarterly* 61, no. 1 (2009): 93–112; Stuart Hall, "The Whites of Their Eyes: Racist Ideologies in the Media," in *Gender, Race, and Class in Media: A Text-Reader*, 2nd ed., edited by Gail Dines and Jean Humez (Thousand Oaks, CA: Sage, 2002), 89–93; Kent A. Ono, *Contemporary Media Culture and the Remnants of a Colonial Past* (New York: Peter Lang, 2009).

6. See Gail Bederman, *Manliness and Civilization* (Chicago: University of Chicago Press, 1995); Angela Davis, *Women, Race, and Class* (New York: Vintage Books, 1983).

7. Mark Thomas Connelly, *The Response to Prostitution in the Progressive Era* (Chapel Hill: University of North Carolina Press, 1980); Bryan Donovan, *White Slave Crusades: Race, Gender, and Anti-Vice Activism, 1887–1917* (Champaign: University of Illinois Press, 2006); Frederick Grittner, *White Slavery: Myth, Ideology, and American Law* (New York and London: Garland, 1990); Gretchen Soderlund, "Covering Urban Vice: The *New York Times*, 'White Slavery,' and the Construction of Journalistic Knowledge," *Critical Studies in Media Communication* 19, no. 4 (2002): 438–460.

8. Eric King Watts, "Border Patrolling and 'Passing' in Eminem's *8 Mile*," *Critical Studies in Media Communication* 22, no. 3 (2005): 187–206.

9. Ibid., 191.

10. Ono, *Contemporary Media Culture and the Remnants of a Colonial Past*.

11. See Pardis Mahdavi, *Trafficking and Terror: Constructing a Global Social Problem* (New York: Routledge, 2013).

12. Arina Grossu, "How Do We Eradicate Sex Trafficking?," *Christian Post*, February 6, 2014, http://www.christianpost.com/news/how-do-we-eradicate-sex-trafficking-114155/.

13. See Tony Nassif, "Human Trafficking Update," March 8, 2011, http://www.abstinence.net/our-blog/abstinence-posts/update-on-human-trafficking/.

14. Sold No More's staff requirements are listed in Melissa Gira Grant, "Fighting Sex Trafficking with Jesus: How the Religious Right's 'Healing' Hurts," *Salon.com*, April 27, 2014, http://www.salon.com/2014/04/27/fighting_sex_trafficking_with_jesus_how_the_religious_rights_healing_hurts/.

15. Judith Reisman, "'Taken' and Global Sex Traffic," *World Daily Net*, March 23, 2009, http://www.wnd.com/2009/03/92566/.

16. Ibid.

17. Gail Short, "Christine Caine: Hillsong Church, the A21 Campaign," *Outreach Magazine*, July 21, 2010, http://www.outreachmagazine.com/interviews/3728-christine-caine -hillsong-church-the-a21-campaign.html.

18. Tim Shipe, "'Taken' Some Life Lessons," *American Catholic*, July 18, 2009, http://the -american-catholic.com/2009/07/18/taken-some-life-lessons/.

19. U.S. Attorney's Office, District of Maryland, "Press Release: Millersville Man Sentenced for Posing as a Retired Army Special Forces Colonel," August 30, 2011, http://www .fbi.gov/baltimore/press-releases/2011/millersville-man-sentenced-for-posing-as-a -retired-army-special-forces-colonel.

20. See Emi Koyama, *War on Terror and War on Trafficking: A Sex Worker Activist Confronts the Anti-Trafficking Movement* (Portland, OR: Confluere Publications, 2011), http://eminism .org/store/pdf-zn/trafficking_web.pdf.

21. The notion that strong fathers are necessary to protect daughters from a sexually aggressive culture is explored in Meg Meeker and Margaret J. Meeker, *Strong Fathers, Strong Daughters: 10 Secrets Every Father Should Know* (New York: Random House, 2007).

22. Hernan Vera and Andrew Gordon, *Screen Saviors: Hollywood Fictions of Whiteness* (New York: Rowan & Littlefield, 2005).

23. Hall, "The Whites of Their Eyes," 89.

24. Richard Dyer, *White: Essays on Race and Culture* (New York: Routledge, 1997).

25. Thomas Nakayama and Robert Krizek, "Whiteness: A Strategic Rhetoric," *Quarterly Journal of Speech* 81, no. 3 (1999): 293.

26. Sec Karlyn Kohrs Campbell, *Man Cannot Speak for Her: A Critical Study of Early Feminist Rhetoric* (Westport, CT: Greenwood Press, 1989); Barbara Welter, "The Cult of True Womanhood," *American Quarterly* 18, no. 2 (1966): 151–174.

27. Derek Buescher and Kent Ono, "Civilized Colonialism: Pocahontas as Neocolonial Rhetoric," *Women's Studies in Communication* 19, no. 2 (1996): 127–153.

28. Iris Young, "Feminist Reactions to the Contemporary Security Regime," *Hypatia* 18, no. 1 (2003): 223–231.

29. See Susan Rae Peterson, "Coercion and Rape: The State as a Male Protection Racket," in *Feminism and Philosophy*, edited by Mary Vetterling-Braggin, 360–376 (Totowa, NJ: Rowman and Allenheld, 1977).

30. Jo Doezema, "Loose Women or Lost Women?: The Reemergence of the Myth of White Slavery in Contemporary Discourse of Trafficking in Women," *Gender Issues* 18, no. 1 (2000): 24.

31. See Jo Doezema, "Forced to Choose: Beyond the Voluntary v. Forced Prostitution Dichotomy," in *Global Sex Workers: Rights, Resistance, and Redefinition*, edited by Kamala Kempadoo and Jo Doezema (London: Routledge, 1998), 34–50; Nandita Sharma, "Anti-Trafficking Rhetoric and the Making of a Global Apartheid," *NWSA Journal* 17, no. 3 (2005): 88–111. See Ronald Weitzer, "The Social Construction of Sex Trafficking: Ideology and Institutionalization of a Moral Crusade," *Politics and Society* 35, no. 3 (2007): 447–475.

32. See ibid.

33. Anna Cornelia Fahey, "French and Feminine: Hegemonic Masculinity and the Emasculation of John Kerry in the 2004 Presidential Race," *Critical Studies in Media Communication* 2, no. 2 (2007): 132–150.

34. Pew Research Center, "U.S. Seen as Less Important, China as More Powerful: Section 4: U.S. Allies and Country Favorability," December 3, 2009, http://www.people-press.org/2009/12/03/section-4-u-s-allies-and-country-favorability/.

35. "Do You Want 'Freedom Fries' with That?," *CBS News*, March 11, 2003, http://www.cbsnews.com/2100-250_162-543555.html.

36. Buescher and Ono, "Civilized Colonialism," 132, Buescher and Ono's italics.

37. See Lynn Arnaut, "Cruelty, Horror, and the Will to Redemption," *Hypatia* 1, no. 2 (2003): 175.

38. Dana Cloud, "'To Veil the Threat of Terror': Afghan Women and the Clash of Civilizations in Imagery of the War on Terrorism," *Quarterly Journal of Speech* 90, no. 3 (2004): 285–306.

39. Edward Said, *Orientalism* (New York: Vintage Books, 1978), 3.

40. See Leila Ahmed, "Western Ethnocentrism and Perceptions of the Harem," *Feminist Studies* 8, no. 3 (1988): 521–534; Malek Alloula, *The Colonial Harem* (Minneapolis: University of Minnesota Press, 1986); Rachel Dubrofsky, "*The Bachelor*: Whiteness in the Harem," *Critical Studies in Media Communication* 23, no. 1 (2006): 39–56.

41. Jack Sheehan, *Reel Bad Arabs: How Hollywood Vilifies a People* (New York: Olive Branch Press, 2001).

42. See Alloula, *The Colonial Harem*; Dubrofsky, *The Surveillance of Women on Reality Television*, 38.

CHAPTER 5   SEXPLOITATION IN ABSTINENCE SATIRES

1. See Timothy Shary, *Generation Multiplex: The Image of Youth in Contemporary American Cinema* (Austin: University of Texas Press, 2002); Sarah Ward, "*Ferris Bueller's Day Off* and the History of Teen Film," *Screen Education* 76 (Summer 2015): 116–121.

2. See Richard Van Heertum, ed., *Hollywood Exploited: Public Pedagogy, Corporate Movies, and Cultural Crisis* (London: Palgrave Macmillan, 2010); and Henry Giroux, *Breaking into the Movies: Film and the Culture of Politics* (Hoboken, NJ: Wiley, 2001).

3. Timothy Shary, "Virgin Springs: A Survey of Teen Films' Quest for Sexcess," in *Virgin Territory: Representing Sexual Inexperience in Film*, edited by Tamar Jeffers McDonald (Detroit, MI: Wayne State University Press, 2010), 66–67.

4. See Tanya Krzywinska, *Sex and the Cinema* (London: Wallflower, 2006).

5. Mainstream Hollywood has also cashed in on exploitation aesthetics, high-budget remakes, and topics once considered taboo. Exploitation has become a Hollywood cinematic style. See Ernest Mathijs and James Sexton, *Cult Cinema* (Hoboken, NJ: Wiley, 2012); and Paul Watson, "There's No Accounting for Taste: Exploitation Cinema and the Limits of Film Theory," in *Trash Aesthetics: Popular Culture and Its Audience*, edited by Deborah Cartmell, I. Q. Hunter, Heidi Kay, and Imelda Wheleyan (London: Pluto Press, 1997), 66–83.

6. Paul Booth, "Slash and Porn: Media Subversion, Hyper-Articulation, and Parody," *Continuum: Journal of Media & Cultural Studies* 28, no. 3 (2014): 396–409.

7. Pam Cook, "'Exploitation' Films and Feminism," *Screen* 17, no. 2 (1976): 122–127.

8. For an overview of the politics of John Hughes's films, see Rebekah Brammer, "Left of Centre: Teen Life, Love, and Pain in the Films of John Hughes," *Screen Education* 56 (2009): 22–28.

9. It is important to distinguish between exploitation films and B movies. Colloquially, the term B movie is shorthand for a "bad" movie or camp film, but as an industry term, B movies refer to the second half of a double feature, the film that followed a

higher-quality blockbuster. While they were typically of lower quality, they became popular during the Great Depression as studios struggled to maintain robust movie attendance. The classical B movie declined with the rise of broadcast television in the 1950s. In addition, while B movies were aimed at general audiences, exploitation films target niche audiences such as teenagers and include explicitly inappropriate material such as sex, violence, drug use, and gore. For a history of the B movie and its relationship to the exploitation genre, see Randall Clark, *At a Theatre or Drive-In near You: The History, Culture, and Politics of the American Exploitation Film* (New York: Routledge, 1995); Mike Quarles, *Down and Dirty: Hollywood's Exploitation Film-makers and Their Movies* (Jefferson, NC: McFarland, 2001); and Eric Schaefer, "Resisting Refinement: The Exploitation Film and Self-Censorship," *Film History* 6, no. 3 (1994): 293–313.

10. There are several epochs in the history of exploitation films. The so-called golden age of exploitation films lasted through 1959, at which point the breakup of the Hollywood studio monopoly opened up new distribution channels for low-budget features with explicit content. Previously, many of these early films could be publicly screened only if their content was deemed educational. The "grindhouse films" of the 1960s and 1970s were exhibited in former burlesque theaters. These theaters made fitting venues in terms of content and in their ability to turn a quick profit. Finally, the contemporary exploitation film is often a straight-to-DVD or straight-to-Internet release. Yet Ric Meyers, a famous evangelist for the exploitation film (particularly low-budget Kung Fu features), argues that once major studios began producing slasher films such as *Friday the 13th*, the exploitation industry had been successfully assimilated into the structure of Hollywood. As a consequence of critical attention from some Hollywood directors, including Eli Roth, Quentin Tarantino, and Rob Zombie, the postmodern or neoexploitation film remains a highly stylized, sometimes ironic, art-house homage to the genre. For a brief insider history and comprehensive catalogue, see Ric Meyers, *For One Week Only: The World of Exploitation Films* (1983; reprint, Guilford, CT: Eirini Press, 2011).

11. Clark, *At a Theatre or Drive-In near You.*

12. Amassing a comprehensive list of subgenres is difficult because many exploitation films cannot be found in guides or catalogues. In fact, many films were never registered with the National Film Registry and were only sporadically covered in trade journals. See Eric Schaefer, *"Bold! Daring! Shocking! True!": A History of Exploitation Films, 1919–1959* (Durham, NC: Duke University Press, 1999).

13. See Robert Rector and Kirk A. Johnson, "Teenage Sexual Abstinence and Academic Achievement," *Heritage Foundation Reports*, October 27, 2005, http://www.heritage.org/research/reports/2005/10/teenage-sexual-abstinence-and-academic-achievement.

14. One of the most iconic examples of the virgin/whore dichotomy was the Abstinence Clearinghouse's 2007 annual convention theme: "Abstinence Is a Black & White Issue: Purity vs. Promiscuity." See Jessica Valenti, *The Purity Myth* (New York: Seal, 2009), 143.

15. In 2011, Dead Sea Productions also released the low-budget (approximately $50,000) soft-core pornography film *20-Year-Old Virgins*, which explicitly spoofs films such as *Fast Times at Ridgemont High*, *American Pie*, *Superbad*, *The 40-Year-Old Virgin*, and *Boogie Nights*.

16. Co-founded by David Latt and David Rimawi in 1997, Asylum Pictures is renowned for "mockbusters" such as *Almighty Thor* (2011), *Age of the Hobbits* (2012), and *Atlantic Rim* (2013). The average budget for Asylum Pictures films is under half a million dollars, and not a single production has failed to make a profit. Despite the poor acting

and low production values, Asylum Pictures has a cult following of quasi-ironic fans who purchase the films for both private viewing and Asylum-themed parties. The company's impact on the film industry and Hollywood fandom is chronicled by David Katz in "From Asylum, the People Who Brought You (a Movie Kinda Sorta Like) *Pacific Rim*," *GQ*, August 1, 2013, http://www.gq.com/entertainment/movies-and-tv/201308/sharknado-atlantic-rim-pacific-rim-asylum-movie-spoof?currentPage=1.

17. *I Am Virgin* was produced by Cheezy Flicks Entertainment, a film production and distribution company that specializes in re-releasing cult B movies on DVD. In its original productions, Cheezy Flicks has primarily capitalized on the zombie trend in contemporary horror. *I Am Virgin*, a transparent spoof of *I Am Legend*, was produced for approximately $100,000.

18. See Timothy Shary, *Teen Movies: American Youth on Screen* (London: Wallflower, 2005).

19. See Carmine Sarracino and Kevin M. Scott, *The Porning of America: The Rise of Porn Culture, What It Means, and Where It's Going* (Boston: Beacon Press, 2008); and Tristan Taormino, Constance Penley, Celine Shimizu, and Mireille Miller-Young, eds., *The Feminist Porn Book: The Politics of Producing Pleasure* (New York: Feminist Press at CUNY, 2013).

20. Lisa Nesselson, "Live Virgin," *Daily Variety*, July 31, 2000, 25.

21. Amanda Hess, "Mississippi Sex Ed Class Compares Women to Dirty Peppermint Patties," *Slate Magazine*, April 3, 2014, http://www.slate.com/blogs/xx_factor/2014/04/03/mississippi_sex_ed_class_compares_women_to_dirty_peppermint_patties.html.

22. Ibid.

23. "American Virgin (2009)," Internet Movie Database, http://www.imdb.com/title/tt1318044/.

24. See Schaefer's description of how abject depictions were expunged from early Hollywood only to be displaced into the exploitation industry. See Schaefer, *"Bold! Daring! Shocking! True!,"* 8.

25. See Laura M. Carpenter, "Virginity Loss in Reel/Real Time: Using Popular Movies to Navigate Sexual Initiation," *Sociological Forum* 24, no. 4 (2009): 804–827.

CONCLUSION: COUNTERNARRATIVES

1. Aliyah Frumin, "Elizabeth Smart: Abstinence-Only Can Make Rape Survivors Feel 'Dirty,' 'Filthy,'" *MSNBC News*, May 5, 2013, http://www.msnbc.com/hardball/elizabeth-smart-abstinence-only-education-ca.

2. See Trip Gabriel and Denise Grady, "In Republican Race, a Heated Battle over the HPV Vaccine," *New York Times*, September 13, 2011, http://www.nytimes.com/2011/09/14/us/politics/republican-candidates-battle-over-hpv-vaccine.html?_r=0; Laura Sessions Stepp, "Anti-Science and Anti-Contraception," *CNN*, May 22, 2012, http://www.cnn.com/2012/05/21/opinion/stepp-conservatives-contraception/.

3. See Laura Bassett, "Potential GOP Presidential Contenders: Defund Planned Parenthood," *Huffington Post*, April 4, 2011, http://www.huffingtonpost.com/2011/04/04/gop-presidential-defund-planned-parenthood_n_844614.html.

4. Maggie Fazeli Fard, "Sandra Fluke, Georgetown Student Called a 'Slut' by Rush Limbaugh," *Washington Post*, March 3, 2012, http://www.washingtonpost.com/blogs/the-buzz/post/rush-limbaugh-calls-georgetown-student-sandra-fluke-a-slut-for-advocating-contraception/2012/03/02/gIQAvjfSmR_blog.html.

5. See Jessica Valenti, "Hobby Lobby Ruling Proves Men of the Law Still Can't Get Over 'Immoral' Women Having Sex," *The Guardian*, June 30, 2014, http://www.theguardian.com/commentisfree/2014/jun/30/hobby-lobby-ruling-law-immoral-women-sex.

6. Beverly LaHaye Institute and Janice Shaw Crouse, "Brief of Beverly LaHaye Institute and Janice Shaw Crouse, Ph.D. as Amici Curiae in Support of Hobby Lobby Stores Inc. and Conestoga Wood Specialties Corp., Et Al.," http://www.americanbar.org/content/dam/aba/publications/supreme_court_preview/briefs-v3/13–354–13–356_amcu_bli-etal.authcheckdam.pdf.

7. A 2014 social scientific study found a correlation between women's growing financial independence and men's impulse to moralize about women's promiscuity. See Michael E. Price, Nicholas Pound, and Isabel M. Scott, "Female Economic Dependence and the Morality of Promiscuity," *Archives of Sex Behavior*, June 25, 2014, accessed July 17, 2014, http://link.springer.com/article/10.1007%2Fs10508–014–0320–4.

8. Patricia Hill Collins, *Black Feminist Thought: Knowledge, Consciousness, and the Politics of Empowerment* (New York: Routledge, 2000).

9. *Another Gay Movie* (2006) is one film, however, brings attention to the erasure of queer identity in teen sexquest and virginity-pact films by satirizing *American Pie* with an all-gay cast.

10. See Pat Macpherson, "The Revolution of Little Girls," in *Offwhite: Readings of Power, Privilege, and Resistance*, edited by Michelle Fine, Lois Weis, Linda Power Pruitt, and April Burns (London: Routledge, 2004), 175–185.

11. Terry Eagleton, *Ideology: An Introduction* (New York: Verso, 1991), 115.

12. George Lipsitz, *Time Passages: Collective Memory and American Popular Culture* (Minneapolis: University of Minnesota Press, 1990), 16–17. As similar claim is made about the potential of popular culture in Fredric Jameson, "Reification and Utopia in Mass Culture," *Social Text* 1 (Winter 1979): 130–148.

13. One example is the way women's countercinema encounters patriarchy with experimental Brechtian film techniques that make ideology transparent by denaturalizing the discourse and image of women. See bell hooks, "The Oppositional Gaze: Black Female Spectators," in *The Feminism and Visual Culture Reader*, edited by Amelia Jones (London: Routledge, 2003), 94–105; Claire Johnston, "'Women's Cinema as Counter-Cinema," in *Movies and Methods*, edited by Bill Nichols (Berkeley: University of California Press, 1976), 208–217; Annette Kuhn, "Women's Cinema and Feminist Film Criticism," *Screen* 16, no. 3 (1975): 107–112; and R. Patrick Kinsman, "She's Come Undone: *Chantal Akerman's Jeanne Dielman, 23 Quai du Commerce, 1080 Bruxelles* (1975) and Countercinema," *Quarterly Review of Film and Video* 24 (2007): 217–224.

14. Tara Culp-Ressler, "Katelyn Campbell Receives Outpouring of Support after Protesting High School Abstinence Assembly," *Think Progress*, April 19, 2013, at http://thinkprogress.org/health/2013/04/19/1893611/katelyn-campbell-support/.

15. Kimberly A. Johnson and Ann Werner, *The Virgin Diaries* (CreateSpace Independent Publishing Platform, 2010).

16. Jess Weixler won the Sundance Film Festival Special Jury Prize for Acting for her role as Dawn in *Teeth*. The film also received critical praise for its emphasis on female empowerment. See Gabriella Burnham, "2007 Film Festival Focus Centers on Female Screenwriters," *Inquirer and Mirror*, November 17, 2007, http://www.ack.net/femalescreen060707.html; and "2007 Sundance Film Festival Award Winners," *Salt Lake Tribune*, January 28, 2007, http://www.sltrib.com/ci_5105046. See also Martin Fradely, "'Hell Is a Teenage Girl'?: Postfeminism and Contemporary Teen Horror," in *Postfeminism and Contemporary Hollywood Cinema*, edited by Joel Gwynne and Nadine Muller (London: Palgrave Macmillan, 2013), 205–221.

17. In the past several years, some women have published insider accounts of growing up in abstinence culture. These women typically report everything from sexual abuse to

feelings of worthlessness and impurity. See Anne Almasy, "The Vulgar Face of Purity Culture," *Huffington Post*, September 9, 2013, http://www.huffingtonpost.com/anne-almasy/the-vulgar-face-of-purity_b_3882864.html; Lynn Beisner, "How Christian Purity Culture Enabled My Stepfather to Sexually Abuse Me," April 24, 2014, http://www.alternet.org/how-christian-purity-culture-enabled-my-step-dad-sexually-abuse-me; and Diane E. Anderson, "Purity Culture as Rape Culture: Why the Theological Is Political," October 22, 2013, http://rhrealitycheck.org/article/2013/10/22/purity-culture-as-rape-culture-why-the-theological-is-political/. The daughters of former Alaska governor Sarah Palin and Louisiana congressperson Bill Cassidy, both of whom are prominent abstinence proponents, became pregnant as teenagers. See "Louisiana's Bill Cassidy Says Teen Daughter Pregnant, Report Says," *CNN*, July 3, 2014, http://politicalticker.blogs.cnn.com/2014/07/03/louisianas-bill-cassidy-says-teen-daughter-pregnant-report-says/. For a summary of the domestic and international failures of abstinence advocacy, see Andy Kopsa, "Obama's Evangelical Gravy Train," *The Nation*, July 8, 2014, http://www.thenation.com/article/180435/obamas-evangelical-gravy-train; Tara Culp-Ressler, "Federal Funds Awarded to Abstinence-Only Education Programs," *Think Progress*, October 10, 2010. http://thinkprogress.org/health/2012/10/10/987411/federal-funds-abstinence-only-programs/; and Jessica Valenti, "Abstinence Sex Education Doesn't Work. It Teaches Lies to Ill-Informed Virgins," *The Guardian*, July 15, 2015, http://www.theguardian.com/commentisfree/2014/jul/15/abstinence-sex-education-teaches-virgins-teens.

18. Carol Clover's discussion of the slasher film's "final girl" is exemplary in this regard. She argues that in *Halloween*, *Friday the 13th*, and *The Texas Chainsaw Massacre*, the murder of promiscuous teens symbolizes punishment for their transgressions against conventional morality. The purity and innocence of the last surviving girl in the film (the one left to tell the story) enables her to escape punishment and confront the evil the killer embodies. See Carol Clover, *Men, Women, and Chainsaws: Gender in the Modern Horror* (Princeton, NJ: Princeton University Press, 1993), 35–41.

19. For a discussion of the "public screen," see Kevin Deluca and Jennifer Peeples, "From Public Sphere to Public Screen: Democracy, Activism, and the 'Violence' of Seattle," *Critical Studies in Media Communication* 19, no. 2 (2002): 125–151.

20. See Emanuel Levy, *Cinema of Outsiders: The Rise of American Independent Film* (New York: NYU Press, 1999); Geoff King, Claire Molloy, and Yannis Tzioumakis, *American Independent Cinema: Indie, Indiewood and Beyond* (London: Routledge, 2013); Michael Z. Newman, *Indie: An American Film Culture* (New York: Columbia University Press, 2013); and Sherry B. Ortner, *Not Hollywood: Independent Film at the Twilight of the American Dream* (Durham, NC: Duke University Press, 2013).

21. See Wendy Brown, *Regulating Aversions: Tolerance in an Age of Identity and Empire* (Princeton, NJ: Princeton University Press, 2006).

22. This is trope is typical of rape-revenge films that feature female protagonists such as *Hard Candy* (2005), *I Spit on Your Grave* (1979; 2010), *Sleeping with the Enemy* (1991), and *The Girl with the Dragon Tattoo* (2009; 2010). See Jacinda Reed, *The New Avengers: Feminism, Femininity, and the Rape-Revenge Cycle* (Manchester, UK: Manchester University Press, 2000); and Alexandra Heller-Nicholas, *Rape-Revenge Films: A Critical Study* (Jefferson, NC: MacFarland, 2011).

23. This refrain appears frequently in purity literature, but a fitting example can be found at Abortion Facts, "How to Say No to Sex," last modified May 2, 2015, http://www.abortionfacts.com/literature/how-to-say-no-to-sex.

24. A similarly sex-positive discourse has emerged in films about disease and disability. For instance, in *The Fault in Our Stars* (2014), Hazel is a teenage cancer patient who

meets Gus in a support group. She loses her virginity in the process of maximizing the time she has left. While this film does not dwell on the subject, it suggests a very modest but important point that sex is a fundamental aspect of the human condition. The precariousness of a life overshadowed by terminal disease illustrates the significance of taken-for-granted rituals. Another example is *The Sessions* (2012). Mark is a polio survivor who, through the help of a professional sexual surrogate, loses his virginity and learns to develop his sexuality. His exploration of physical intimacy empowers him to find love and fulfillment despite the challenges of his disability. This film invites the audience to consider the privilege of being able-bodied and challenges the presumed asexuality of disabled bodies. The most important relationship in the film is between Mark and his priest, Father Brendan. Even though he is reluctant to discuss sex out of wedlock, Father Brendan's very close friendship with Mark forces him to recognize the importance of sexual agency in Mark's journey of self-discovery. The use of precarious and disabled bodies in each of the films communicates that sexuality is a fundamental but overlooked aspect of emotional health and development.

25. Rafer Guzman, "'The To Do List' Review: High Ick Factor," *Newsday*, July 23, 2013, http://www.newsday.com/entertainment/movies/the-to-do-list-review-high-ick-factor-1.5761277. A composite of Internet and newspaper reviews reveal that only 47 percent of critics evaluated the film favorably. See "The To-Do List (2013)," Rotten Tomatoes, http://www.rottentomatoes.com/m/the_to_do_list/. One of the most positive reviews of the film came from the *New York Times*; see Neil Genzlinger, "Movie Review: Some Things You Can't Learn from a Book: Aubrey Plaza Stars in 'The To-Do List," *New York Times*, July 25, 2013, http://www.nytimes.com/2013/07/26/movies/aubrey-plaza-stars-in-the-to-do-list.html?_r=0.

26. Bill Nichols, *Engaging Cinema: An Introduction to Film Studies* (New York: W. W. Norton Company, 2010), 99.

27. See the Kickstarter page for the "How to Lose Your Virginity" project at https://www.kickstarter.com/projects/1313570620/how-to-lose-your-virginity.

28. See "Submit Your Story to the V-Card Diaries," http://www.virginitymovie.com/tell-your-story/.

29. This contrasts strongly with documentary-style news programming, which is constrained by the norms of journalistic objectivity. For instance, *ABC News* framed a story about purity balls as an apolitical investigation into a relatively unknown subculture. See "Purity Balls: Lifting the Veil on Special Ceremony," *ABC News*, March 3, 2014, http://abcnews.go.com/Nightline/video/purity-balls-lifting-veil-special-ceremony-23061335.

30. See Collins, *Black Feminist Thought*; Sandra Harding, "Introduction: Standpoint Theory as a Site of Political, Philosophic, and Scientific Debate," in *The Feminist Standpoint Theory Reader: Intellectual and Political Controversies*, edited by Sandra Harding (New York: Routledge, 2004), 1–16.

31. For boys, a film such as *Boyhood* (2014) begins to look past sexual status as an important marker of manhood. It is a film about growing up that was shot with the same child actor (Ellar Coltrane) over twelve years. Director Richard Linklater said that he avoided virginity loss because it was too obvious for a coming-of-age story. See Scott Raab, "ESQ&A: Richard Linklater and Ethan Hawke," *Esquire Magazine*, July 8, 2014, http://www.esquire.com/entertainment/movies/interviews/a23730/richard-linklater-ethan-hawke-interview-0814/.

32. The recent release of *Very Good Girls* (2014) and *Premature* (2014) sustains the message that sexual status is the exclusive metric of coming of age.

33. The song is also a nod to Ellen Page's role in *Juno* (2007), in which she played a teenager who becomes pregnant and gives her child up for adoption. I decided not to include *Juno* in this chapter because the film focuses much more on teenage pregnancy than on the subject of virginity and abstinence. Moreover, as I have argued with Kristen E. Hoerl, *Juno*'s progressive irreverence toward teenage sexuality is muted by its postfeminist representations of reproductive choice. See Kristen Hoerl and Casey Ryan Kelly, "The Post-Nuclear Family and the Depoliticization of Unplanned Pregnancy in *Knocked Up*, *Juno*, and *Waitress*," *Communication and Critical/Cultural Studies* 7, no. 4 (2010): 360–380.

FILMOGRAPHY

About a Boy. Directed by Chris Weitz and Paul Weitz. DVD, Universal City, CA: Universal Pictures Home Entertainment, 2002.

Abraham Lincoln: Vampire Hunter. Directed by Timur Bekmambetov. DVD, Los Angeles: 20th Century Fox Home Entertainment, 2012.

Along Came Polly. Directed by John Hamburg. DVD, Universal City, CA: Universal Pictures Home Entertainment, 2004.

American Beauty. Directed by Sam Mendes. DVD, Universal City, CA: DreamWorks Pictures, 1999.

American Gangster. Directed by Ridley Scott. DVD, Universal City, CA: Universal Pictures Home Entertainment, 2007.

American Gigolo. Directed by Paul Schrader. Motion picture, 1980. DVD, Hollywood, CA: Paramount Home Entertainment, 2000.

American Girl. Directed by Jordan Brady. DVD, Beverley Hills, CA: Metro Goldwyn Mayer, 2002.

American Graffiti. Directed by George Lucas. Motion picture, 1973. DVD, Universal City, CA: Universal Pictures Home Entertainment, 1998.

American History X. Directed by Tony Kaye. DVD, Burbank, CA: Warner Home Video, 1998.

American Hustle. Directed by David O. Russell. DVD, Culver City, CA: Columbia Pictures, 2013.

American Pie. Directed by Paul Weitz and Chris Weitz. DVD, Universal City, CA: University Pictures Home Entertainment, 1999.

American Psycho. Directed by Mary Harron. DVD, Santa Monica, CA: Lionsgate Entertainment, 2000.

American Violet. Directed by Tim Disney. Motion picture, 2008. DVD, New York: Samuel Goldwyn Entertainment, 2009.

American Virgin. Directed by Jean-Pierre Marois. Motion picture, 1999. DVD, Santa Monica: CA: Lionsgate Entertainment, 2000.

American Virgin. Directed by Clare Kilner. DVD, LaCrosse, WI: Echo Bridge Entertainment, 2009.

Annie Hall. Directed by Woody Allen. Motion picture, 1977. DVD, Los Angeles: 20th Century Fox Home Entertainment, 2000.

Apartment 143. Directed by Carles Torrens. DVD, New York: Magnolia Home Entertainment, 2012.

As Good As It Gets. Directed by James L. Brooks. DVD, Culver City, CA: Sony Pictures Home Entertainment, 1998.

Attack of the Virgin Mummies. Directed by Daryl Carstensen. DVD, North Hollywood, CA: Plutonium Films, 2004.

The Ballad of Jack and Rose. Directed by Rebecca Miller. DVD, Los Angeles: MGM, 2005.

The Birth of a Nation. Directed by D. W. Griffith. Motion picture, 1913. DVD, Wellton, FL: Inspired Studio, 2001.

Blackhawk Down. Directed by Ridley Scott. Motion picture, 2001. DVD, Culver City, CA: Sony Pictures Home Entertainment, 2002.

Blade. Directed by Stephen Norrington. DVD, Los Angeles: New Line Home Video, 1998.

Blue Denim. Directed by Philip Dunne. Motion picture, 1959. DVD, Los Angeles: 20th Century Fox,

Boyz n the Hood. Directed by John Singleton. DVD, Culver City, CA: Sony Pictures Home Entertainment, 1991.

Beauty and the Beast. Directed by Gary Trousdale and Kirk Wise. Motion picture, 1991. DVD, Los Angeles: Walt Disney Video, 2002.

Big Daddy. Directed by Dennis Dugan. DVD, Culver City, CA: Sony Pictures Home Entertainment, 1999.

Big Trouble in Little China. Directed by John Carpenter. Motion picture, 1986. DVD, Los Angeles: 20th Century Fox Home Entertainment, 2002.

Billy Madison. Directed by Tamra Davis. Motion picture, 1995. DVD, Universal City, CA: Universal Pictures Home Entertainment, 2005.

Bram Stoker's Dracula. Directed by Francis Ford Coppola and Kim Aubry. Motion picture, 1992. DVD, Culver City, CA: Sony Pictures Home Entertainment, 2007.

The Breakfast Club. Directed by John Hughes. Motion picture, 1985. DVD, Universal City, CA: Universal Home Entertainment, 2008.

Bridget Jones's Diary. Directed by Sharon Maguire. Motion picture, 2001. DVD, Santa Monica: CA: Lionsgate Entertainment, 2011.

Bringing Up Baby. Directed by Howard Hawks. Motion picture, 1938. DVD, Atlanta, GA: Turner Home Entertainment, 2011.

Brides of Blood. Directed by Gerardo De Leon and Eddie Romero. Motion picture, 1971. DVD, West Conshohocken, PA: Alpha New Cinema, 2010.

Breaking Dawn. Directed by Bill Condon. Motion picture, 2012. DVD, Universal City, CA: Summit Entertainment, 2013.

Breaking Dawn 2. Directed by Bill Condon. DVD, Universal City: CA: Summit Entertainment, 2013.

Breaking Wind. Directed by Craig Moss. Motion picture, 2011. DVD, Santa Monica: CA: Lionsgate Entertainment, 2012.

Can't Buy Me Love. Directed by Michael Swerdlick. Motion picture, 1987. DVD, Burbank, CA: Buena Vista Home Entertainment, 2002.

Case 39. Directed by Christian Alvart. Motion picture, 2009. DVD, Hollywood, CA: Paramount Home Entertainment, 2010.

The Cheerleaders. Directed by Paul Glickler. Motion picture, 1973. DVD, Troy, MI: Anchor Bay. 2011.

Cherry Falls. Directed by Geoffrey Wright. DVD, Universal City, CA: Polygram/USA Home Entertainment, 2000.

Cooley High. Directed by Michael Schultz. Motion picture, 1975. DVD, Los Angeles: American International Pictures.

Commando. Directed by Mark L. Lester. Motion picture, 1985. DVD, Los Angeles: 20th Century Fox Home Entertainment, 1999.

Conan the Barbarian. Directed by John Milius. Motion picture, 1982. DVD, Universal City, CA: Universal Pictures Home Entertainment, 2011.

Crazy, Stupid Love. Directed by Glenn Ficarra and John Requa. DVD, Burbank, CA: Warner Home Video, 2011.

Cruel Intentions. Directed by Roger Kumble. DVD, Culver City, CA: Sony Pictures Home Entertainment, 1999.

Damaged Goods. Directed by H. Haile Chace. Motion picture, 1970. DVD, Seattle, WA: Something Weird Video, 2012.

Dark Water. Directed by Walter Salles. DVD, Burbank, CA: Buena Vista Home Entertainment, 2005.

Death Wish. Directed by Michael Winner. Motion picture, 1974. DVD, Burbank, CA: Warner Home Video, 2006.

The Defiant Ones. Directed by Stanley Kramer. Motion picture, 1958. DVD, Los Angeles: MGM, 2001.

Diary of a High School Bride. Directed by Burt Topper. Motion picture, 1959. DVD, Los Angeles: American International Pictures.

Die Hard. Directed by John McTiernan. Motion picture, 1988. DVD, Los Angeles: 20th Century Fox Home Entertainment, 2007.

Dirty Dancing. Directed by Emile Ardolino. Motion picture, 1987. DVD, Santa Monica: CA: Lionsgate Entertainment, 2003.

Dirty Harry. Directed by Don Siegel. Motion picture, 1971. DVD, Burbank, CA: Warner Home Video, 2010.

Dracula. Directed by Tod Browning. Motion picture, 1931. DVD, Universal City, CA: Universal Pictures Home Entertainment, 1999.

Dune. Directed by David Lynch. Motion picture, 1984. DVD, Universal City, CA: Universal Pictures Home Entertainment, 1998.

Easy A. Directed by Will Gluck. DVD, Culver City, CA: Sony Pictures Home Entertainment, 2010.

Eclipse. Directed by David Slade. DVD, Universal City, CA: Summit Entertainment, 2010.

Eighteen and Anxious. Directed by Joe Parker. Motion picture, 1957. DVD, Los Angeles: Republic Pictures.

The 18-Year-Old Virgin. Directed by Tamara Olson. DVD, Burbank, CA: The Asylum, 2010.

Elf. Directed by Jon Favreau. DVD, Los Angeles: New Line Home Entertainment, 2004.

Entrails of a Virgin. Directed by Kazuo "Giara" Komizu. Motion picture, 1986. DVD, Romulus, MI: Synapse Films, 2004.

EuroTrip. Directed by Jeff Schaffer. DVD, Burbank, CA: Warner Home Video, 2004.

The Exorcist. Directed by William Friedkin. Motion picture, 1973. DVD, Burbank, CA: Warner Home Video, 2010.

The Exorcism of Emily Rose. Directed by Scott Derrickson. DVD, Culver City, CA: Sony Pictures Home Entertainment, 2005.

The Expendables. Directed by Sylvester Stallone. DVD, Santa Monica, CA: Lionsgate Entertainment, 2010.

Falling Down. Directed by Joel Schumacher. Motion picture, 1993. DVD, Burbank, CA: Warner Home Video, 2012.

The Fault in Our Stars. Directed by Josh Boone. DVD, Los Angeles: 20th Century Fox Home Entertainment, 2014.

Fast Times at Ridgemont High. Directed by Amy Heckerling. Motion picture, 1982. DVD, Universal City, CA: Universal Pictures Home Entertainment, 2004.

Ferris Bueller's Day Off. Directed by John Hughes. Motion picture, 1986. DVD, Burbank, CA: Warner Home Video, 2006.

50 First Dates. Directed by Peter Segal. DVD, Culver City, CA: Sony Pictures Home Entertainment, 2004.

The Five-Year Engagement. Directed by Nicholas Stoller. DVD, Universal City, CA: Universal Home Entertainment, 2012.

Flash Gordon. Directed by Mike Hodges. Motion picture, 1980. DVD, Universal City, CA: Universal Pictures Home Entertainment, 1998.

Forget Paris. Directed by Billy Crystal. Motion picture, 1995. DVD, Atlanta, GA: Turner Home Entertainment, 2000.

Forgetting Sarah Marshall. Directed by Nicholas Stoller. DVD, Universal City, CA: Universal Pictures Home Entertainment, 2008.

The 40-Year-Old Virgin. Directed by Judd Apatow. DVD, Universal City, CA: Universal Home Entertainment, 2005.

Frankenstein. Directed by James Whale. Motion picture, 1931. DVD, Universal City, CA: Universal Pictures Home Entertainment, 1999.

French Kiss. Directed by Lawrence Kasdan. Motion picture, 1995. DVD, Los Angeles: 20th Century Fox Home Entertainment, 2003.

Friday the 13th. Directed by Sean S. Cunningham. Motion picture, 1980. DVD, Hollywood, CA: Paramount Home Entertainment, 2013.

Fright Night. Directed by Tom Holland. Motion picture, 1985. DVD, Culver City, CA: Sony Pictures Home Entertainment, 1999.

Funny People. Directed by Judd Apatow. DVD, Universal City, CA: Universal Pictures Home Entertainment, 2009.

Get Him to the Greek. Directed by Nicholas Stoller. DVD, Universal City, CA: Universal Pictures Home Entertainment, 2010.

The Girl with the Dragon Tattoo. Directed by David Fincher. Motion picture, 2011. DVD, Culver City, CA: Sony Pictures Home Entertainment, 2012.

Goin' All the Way! VHS. Directed by Richard Freeman. DVD, Thousand Oaks, CA: Monterey Home Video, 2002.

The Graduate. Directed by Mike Nichols. Motion picture, 1967. DVD, Embassy Pictures Corporation. 2007.

The Grapes of Wrath. Directed by John Ford. Motion picture, 1940. DVD, Los Angeles, CA: 20th Century Fox Home Entertainment, 2004.

Guess Who's Coming to Dinner. Directed by William Rose. Motion picture, 1967. DVD, Culver City, CA: Sony Pictures Home Entertainment, 1999.

Halloween. Directed by John Carpenter. Motion picture, 1978. DVD, Troy, MI: Anchor Bay. 2007.

Hall Pass. Directed by Bobby Farrelly and Peter Farrelly. DVD, Burbank, CA: Warner Home Video, 2011.

Happy Gilmore. Directed by Dennis Dugan. Motion picture, 1996. DVD, Universal City, CA: Universal Pictures Home Entertainment, 2005.

Hard Candy. Directed by David Slade. DVD, Santa Monica, CA: Lionsgate. 2006.

Harry Potter and the Sorcerer's Stone. Directed by Chris Columbus. Motion picture, 2001. DVD, Burbank, CA: Warner Home Video, 2002.

Harum Scarum. Directed by Gene Nelson. Motion picture, 1965. DVD, Burbank, CA: Warner Home Video, 2004.

He's Just Not That Into You. Directed by Ken Kwapis. Motion picture, 2008. DVD, Los Angeles: New Line Home Video, 2009.

High Fidelity. Directed by Stephen Frears. DVD, Burbank, CA: Touchstone Home Entertainment, 2000.

His Girl Friday. Directed by Howard Hawks. Motion picture, 1940. DVD, London: Reel Enterprises. 2006.

The Horror of Dracula. Directed by Terence Fisher. Motion picture, 1958. DVD, Burbank, CA: Warner Home Video, 2010.

How to Lose Your Virginity. Directed by Therese Shechter. DVD, Washington, DC: Trixie Films. 2013.

The Hunger Games. Directed by Gary Ross. Motion picture, 2012. DVD, Santa Monica, CA: Lionsgate Entertainment, 2012.

I Am Legend. Directed by Francis Lawrence. DVD, Burbank, CA: Warner Home Video, 2008.

I Am Virgin. Directed by Sean Skelding. DVD, Portland, OR: IMDFilms, 2010.

I Love You, Man. Directed by John Hamburg. DVD, Burbank, CA: Warner Home Video, 2013.

Indiana Jones and the Raiders of the Lost Ark. Directed by Steven Spielberg. 1981. DVD, Hollywood, CA: Paramount Home Entertainment, 2008.

Indiana Jones and the Temple of Doom. Directed by Steven Spielberg. Motion picture, 1984. DVD, Hollywood, CA: Paramount Home Entertainment, 2008.

Interview with a Vampire. Directed by Neil Jordan. DVD, Burbank, CA: Warner Home Video, 2000.

Is Any Girl Safe? Directed by Jacques Jaccard. Motion picture, 1916. DVD, New York: States Rights, Anti-Vice Motion Picture Company.

I Spit on Your Grave. Directed by Meir Zarchi. Motion picture, 1978. DVD, Troy, MI: Anchor Bay. 2007.

Jerry McGuire. Directed by Cameron Crowe. DVD, Culver City, CA: Sony Pictures Home Entertainment, 1996.

The Jewel of the Nile. Directed by Lewis Teague. Motion picture, 1985. DVD, Los Angeles: 20th Century Fox Home Entertainment, 2006.

Juno. Directed by Jason Reitman. Motion picture, 2007. DVD, Los Angeles: 20th Century Fox Home Entertainment, 2008.

Kids. Directed by Larry Clark. Motion picture, 1996. DVD, Santa Monica, CA: Trimark. 1997.

Knocked Up. Directed by Judd Apatow. Motion picture, 2007. DVD, Universal City, CA: Universal Pictures Home Entertainment, 2007.

The Last American Virgin. Directed by Boaz Davidson. Motion picture, 1982. DVD, Los Angeles: MGM (Video & DVD), 2003.

The Last Exorcism. Directed by Daniel Stamm. Motion picture, 2010. DVD, Santa Monica, CA: Lionsgate Entertainment, 2011.

Leon, the Professional. Directed by Luc Besson. Motion picture, 1994. DVD, Culver City, CA: Sony Pictures Home Entertainment, 1998.

Lethal Weapon. Directed by Richard Donner. Motion picture, 1987. DVD, Burbank, CA: Warner Home Video, 1997.

Let the Right One In. Directed by Tomas Alfredson. DVD, New York: Magnolia Home Entertainment, 2009.

The Limey. Directed by Steven Soderbergh. Motion picture, 1999. DVD, Santa Monica, CA: Lionsgate Entertainment, 2001.

Little Darlings. Directed by Ronald F. Maxwell. Motion picture, 1980. DVD, Hollywood, CA: Paramount Home Entertainment, 1998.

Lolita. Directed by Stanley Kubrick. Motion picture, 1962. DVD, Burbank, CA: Warner Home Video, 1999.

The Lord of the Rings: The Return of the King. Directed by Peter Jackson. DVD, Los Angeles: New Line Home Video, 2004.

Losin' It. Directed by Curtis Hanson. Motion picture, 1983. DVD, Los Angeles: MGM (Video & DVD), 2001.

The Lost Boys. Directed by Joel Schumacher. Motion picture, 1987. DVD, Burbank, CA: Warner Home Video, 2010.

Mark of the Vampire. Directed by Tod Browning. Motion picture, 1935. DVD, Los Angeles: Metro-Goldwyn-Mayer, 2006.

Married Too Young. Directed by George Moskov. Motion picture, 1962. DVD, Los Angeles: Headline Productions.

Martin. Directed by George Romero. Motion picture, 1977. DVD, New York: Libra Films International.

Matewan. Directed by John Sayles. Motion picture, 1987. DVD, Portland, OR: PDX, 1999.

Meatballs. Directed by Ivan Reitman. Motion picture, 1979. DVD, Santa Monica, CA: Lionsgate Entertainment, 2012.

Meet the Parents. Directed by Jay Roach. DVD, Universal City, CA: Universal Pictures Home Entertainment, 2001.

Mom and Dad. Directed by William Beaudine. 1945. DVD, New York: Video Dimensions, 2012.

The Moon Is Blue. Directed by Otto Preminger. 1953. DVD, Burbank, CA: Warner Home Video, 2009.

My Best Friend's Wedding. Directed by P. J. Hogan. Motion picture, 1997. DVD, Culver City, CA: Sony Pictures Home Entertainment, 1998.

National Lampoon's European Vacation. Directed by Amy Heckerling. 1985. DVD, Burbank, CA: Warner Home Video, 2002.

Near Dark. Directed by Kathryn Bigelow. Motion picture, 1987. DVD, Troy, MI: Anchor Bay, 2002.

Never Say Never Again. Directed by Irvin Kershner. Motion picture, 1983. DVD, Los Angeles: MGM (Video & DVD), 2000.

New Moon. Directed by Chris Weitz. DVD, Universal City, CA: Summit Entertainment, 2010.

Norma Rae. Directed by Martin Ritt. Motion picture, 1979. DVD, Los Angeles: 20th Century Fox Home Entertainment, 2002.

North Country. Directed by Niki Caro. DVD, Burbank, CA: Warner Home Video, 2006.

Nosferatu. Directed by F. W. Murnau. Motion picture, 1922. DVD, New York: Kino Lorber Films, 2007.

Nosferatu the Vampyre. Directed by Werner Herzog. Motion picture, 1979. DVD, Troy, MI: Anchor Bay, 2002.

No Strings Attached. Directed by Ivan Reitman. DVD, Burbank, CA: Warner Home Video, 2011.

Old School. Directed by Todd Phillips. DVD, Burbank, CA: Warner Home Video, 2003.

Once Bitten. Directed by Howard Storm. Motion picture, 1985. DVD, Los Angeles: 20th Century Fox Home Entertainment, 2013.

Pillow Talk. Directed by Michael Gordon. Motion picture, 1959. DVD, Universal City, CA: Universal Pictures Home Entertainment, 2009.

Pineapple Express. Directed by David Gordon Green. DVD, Culver City, CA: Sony Pictures Home Entertainment, 2009.

The Pink Panther. Directed by Blake Edwards. Motion picture, 1964. DVD, Los Angeles: MGM (Video & DVD), 2006.

Porky's. Directed by Bob Clark. Motion picture, 1982. DVD, Los Angeles: 20th Century Fox Home Entertainment, 2006.

The Possession. Directed by Ole Bornedal. Motion picture, 2012. DVD, Santa Monica, CA: Lionsgate Entertainment, 2013.

Predator. Directed by John McTiernan. Motion picture, 1987. DVD, Los Angeles: 20th Century Fox Home Entertainment, 2004.

Premature. Directed by Dan Beers. DVD, Orland Park, IL: MPI Home Video, 2014.

Pretty Woman. Directed by Garry Marshall. Motion picture, 1990. DVD, Burbank, CA: Buena Vista Home Entertainment, 2005.

Protect Your Daughter. Directed by Klaytan W. Kirby. Motion picture, 1932. DVD, Philadelphia: Alpha Video, 2006.

The Purity Myth: The Virginity Movement's War against Women. Directed by Jeremy Earp. DVD, Northampton, MA: Media Education Foundation, 2009.

Queen of the Damned. Directed by Michael Rymer. Motion picture, 2002. DVD, Burbank, CA: Warner Home Video, 2010.

Rambo: First Blood. Directed by Ted Kotcheff. Motion picture, 1982. DVD, Santa Monica, CA: Lionsgate Entertainment, 2004.

Rambo: First Blood Part II. Directed by George P. Cosmatos. Motion picture, 1985. DVD, Santa Monica, CA: Lionsgate Entertainment, 2004.

Reefer Madness. Directed by Louis J. Gasnier. Motion picture, 1936. DVD, Los Angeles: 20th Century Fox Home Entertainment, 2002.

Revenge of the Virgins. Directed by Peter Perry Jr. Motion picture, 1959. DVD, Seattle, WA: Something Weird Video, 2003.

Risky Business. Directed by Paul Brickman. 1983. DVD, Burbank, CA: Warner Home Video, 2008.

Robocop. Directed by Paul Verhoeven. Motion picture, 1987. DVD, Los Angeles: Orion Pictures Corporation, 2001.

Romancing the Stone. Directed by Robert Zemeckis. Motion picture, 1984. DVD, Los Angeles: 20th Century Fox Home Entertainment, 2006.

Safety Not Guaranteed. Directed by Colin Trevorrow. DVD, Culver City, CA: Sony Pictures Home Entertainment, 2012.

Sahara. Directed by Breck Eisner. DVD, Burbank, CA: Warner Home Video, 2005.

Saved! Directed by Brian Dannelly. DVD, Los Angeles: MGM (Video & DVD), 2004.

Say Anything. Directed by Cameron Crowe. Motion picture, 1989. DVD, Los Angeles: 20th Century Fox Home Entertainment, 2009.

Scream. Directed by Wes Craven. Motion picture, 1996. DVD, Los Angeles: Walt Disney Video, 2001.

The Searchers. Directed by John Ford. Motion picture, 1956. DVD, Burbank, CA: Warner Home Video, 1997.

Send Me No Flowers. Directed by Norman Jewison. Motion picture, 1964. DVD, Universal City, CA: Universal Pictures Home Entertainment, 2003.

The Sessions. Directed by Ben Lewin. DVD, Los Angeles: Fox Searchlight. 2013.

Sex Madness. Directed by Dwain Esper. Motion picture, 1938. DVD, Philadelphia: Alpha Video, 2005.

Shadow of the Vampire. Directed by E. Elias Merhige. Motion picture, 2001. DVD, Santa Monica, CA: Lionsgate Entertainment, 2003.

She Shoulda Said No! Directed by Sam Newfield. Motion picture, 1949. DVD, Philadelphia: Alpha Video, 2006.

She's Out of My League. Directed by Jim Field Smith. DVD, Burbank, CA: Warner Home Video, 2010.

Sleeping with the Enemy. Directed by Joseph Ruben. Motion picture, 1991. DVD, Los Angeles: 20th Century Fox Home Entertainment, 2003.

Sleepless in Seattle. Directed by Nora Ephron. Motion picture, 1993. DVD, Culver City, CA: Sony Pictures Home Entertainment, 2003.

Silent Hill. Directed by Chris Sikorowski and Christopher Gans. DVD, Culver City, CA: Sony Pictures Home Entertainment, 2006.

Sixteen Candles. Directed by John Hughes. Motion picture, 1984. DVD, Universal City, CA: Universal Pictures Home Entertainment, 2008.

Splendor in the Grass. Directed by Elia Kazan. Motion picture, 1961. DVD, Burbank, CA: Warner Home Video, 2009.

Stagecoach. Directed by John Ford. Motion picture, 1939. DVD, New York: Criterion Collection. 2010.

Stargate. Directed by Roland Emmerich. Motion picture, 1994. DVD, Santa Monica, CA: Lionsgate Entertainment, 2003.

Star Wars, Episode IV: A New Hope. Directed by George Lucas. Motion picture, 1977. DVD, Los Angeles: 20th Century Fox Home Entertainment, 2006.

Step Brothers. Directed by Adam McKay. DVD, Culver City, CA: Sony Pictures Home Entertainment, 2008.

Superbad. Directed by Greg Mottola. DVD, Culver City, CA: Sony Pictures Home Entertainment, 2007.

The Sure Thing. Directed by Rob Reiner. Motion picture, 1985. DVD, Los Angeles: 20th Century Fox Home Entertainment, 2003.

Taken. Directed by Pierre Moral. Motion picture, 2008. DVD, Los Angeles: 20th Century Fox Home Entertainment, 2009.

Talladega Nights: The Ballad of Ricky Bobby. Directed by Adam McKay. DVD, Los Angeles: 20th Century Fox Home Entertainment, 2006.

Tea and Sympathy. Directed by Vincente Minnelli. Motion picture, 1956. DVD, Los Angeles: MGM, 2011.

Teeth. Directed by Mitchell Lichtenstein. Motion picture, 2007. DVD, New York: Dimension Extreme, 2008.

The Texas Chainsaw Massacre. Directed by Tobe Hooper. Motion picture, 1974. DVD, Orland Park, IL: Dark Sky Films, 2006.

There's Something about Mary. Directed by Bobby Farrelly and Peter Farrelly. Motion picture, 1998. DVD, Los Angeles: 20th Century Fox Home Entertainment, 2005.

The Thief of Baghdad. Directed by Alexander Korda and Michael Powell. Motion picture, 1940. DVD, New York: Criterion Collection. 2010.

Thirteen. Directed by Catherine Hardwicke. Motion picture, 2000. DVD, Los Angeles: Fox Searchlight, 2004.

This Is 40. Directed by Judd Apatow. Motion picture, 2012. DVD, Universal City, CA: Universal Home Entertainment, 2013.

Titanic. Directed by James Cameron. Motion picture, 1997. DVD, Hollywood, CA: Paramount Home Entertainment, 2012.

The To-Do List. Directed by Maggie Carey. DVD, Los Angeles: CBS Films. 2013.

Traffic in Souls. Directed by George Loane Tucker. Motion picture, 1913. DVD, Philadelphia: Alpha Video, 2014.

True Lies. Directed by James Cameron. Motion picture, 1994. DVD, Los Angeles: 20th Century Fox Home Entertainment, 1999.

27 Dresses. Directed by Anne Fletcher. DVD, Los Angeles: 20th Century Fox Home Entertainment, 2008.

Twilight. Directed by Catherine Hardwicke. Motion picture, 2008. DVD, Universal City, CA: Summit Entertainment, 2013.

Unwed Mother. Directed by Walter Doniger. Motion picture, 1958. DVD, Tulsa, OK: VCI Video, 2006.

Vamp. Directed by Richard Wenk. Motion picture, 1986. DVD, Chatsworth, CA: Image Entertainment, 2011.

Vampires Suck. Directed by Jason Friedberg and Aaron Seltzer. DVD, Los Angeles: 20th Century Fox Home Entertainment, 2010.

Vampyr. Directed by Carl Theodor Dreyer. Motion picture, 1932. DVD, New York: Criterion Collection, 2008.

Very Good Girls. Directed by Naomi Foner. DVD, Plano, TX: Well Go USA, 2014.

A Virgin among the Living Dead. Directed by Jess Franco. Motion picture, 1973. DVD, New York: Redemption, 2013.

Virgin in Hollywood. Directed by Klaytan W. Kirby. Motion picture, 1932. DVD, Philadelphia: Alpha Video, 2006.

The Virginity Hit. Directed by Andrew Gurlund and Huck Botko. Motion picture, 2010. DVD, Culver City, CA: Columbia Pictures, 2011.

Virgin Sacrifice. Directed by Fernando Wagner. Motion picture, 1959. DVD, Philadelphia: Alpha Video, 2011.

Virgins from Hell. Directed by Ackyl Anwari. Motion picture, 1987. DVD, New York: Mondo Macabro, 2006.

The Virgins of Sherwood Forests. Directed by Cybil Richards. DVD, New York: Wizard Entertainment, 2000.

The Virgin Suicides. Directed by Sofia Coppola. Hollywood, CA: DVD, Paramount Home Entertainment, 2000.

Virgin Witch. Directed by Ray Austin. Motion picture, 1972. DVD, New York: Kino Lorber Films. 2007.

The Waterboy. Directed by Frank Coraci. Motion picture, 1998. DVD, Burbank, CA: Touchstone Home Entertainment, 1999.

What Women Want. Directed by Nancy Meyer. Motion picture, 2000. DVD, Burbank, CA: Warner Home Video, 2001.

Wedding Crashers. Directed by David Dobkin. Motion picture, 2005. DVD, Los Angeles: New Line Home Video, 2006.

Weird Science. Directed by John Hughes. Motion picture, 1985. DVD, Universal City, CA: Universal Home Entertainment, 2008.

When Harry Met Sally. Directed by Rob Reiner. Motion picture, 1989. DVD, Los Angeles: 20th Century Fox Home Entertainment, 2008.

Whip It! Directed by Drew Barrymore. Motion picture, 2009. DVD, Los Angeles: Fox Searchlight, 2010.

You've Got Mail. Directed by Nora Ephron. Motion picture, 1998. DVD, Burbank, CA: Warner Home Video, 1999.

Zack and Miri Make a Porno. Directed by Scott Mosier. DVD, Los Angeles: MGM, 2008.

BIBLIOGRAPHY

Abbot, Stacey. *Celluloid Vampires: Life after Death in the Modern World.* Austin: University of Texas Press, 2009.

Abrams, Rachel. "'Twilight's' Last Gleaning: Lionsgate Savors Big B. O. Opening, but Wall Street Revels in Franchise's Predictable Payoff." *Daily Variety,* November 11, 2012, 1.

Ahmed, Leila. "Western Ethnocentrism and Perceptions of the Harem." *Feminist Studies* 8, no. 3 (1988): 521–534.

Ahmed, Sarah. *The Promise of Happiness.* Durham, NC: Duke University Press, 2010.

Albert, John. "'I Love You, Man': Bromances, the Construction of Masculinity, and the Continuing Evolution of the Romantic Comedy." *Quarterly Review of Film & Video* 30, no. 2 (2013): 159–172.

Alcorn, Randy. "Guidelines for Sexual Purity." Eternal Perspectives Ministry, January 28, 2010. http://www.epm.org/resources/2010/Jan/28/guidelines-sexual-purity/.

———. *The Purity Principle: God's Safeguards for Life's Dangerous Trails* (Colorado Springs, CO: Multnomah Books, 2003).

Alexander, Bryan. "Born-Again Virgins Claim to Rewrite the Past." *NBC News,* February 28, 2008. http://www.nbcnews.com/id/23254178/ns/health-sexual_health/t/born-again -virgins-claim-rewrite-past/.

———. "Exorcism Movies Possess Big Success in Hollywood." *USA Today,* February, 27 2013. http://www.usatoday.com/story/life/movies/2013/02/27/last-exorcism-ashley-bell-eli -roth/1932993/.

———. "'Twilight' Leaves Bite Marks on Hollywood." *USA Today,* November 11, 2012, 5b.

Alleman, Ryalan. "6 Reasons (+2) to NOT Send Your Daughter to College." Fix the Family, September 8, 2013. http://www.fixthefamily.com/blog/6-reasons-to-not-send-your -daughter-to-college.

Alloula, Malek. *The Colonial Harem.* Minneapolis: University of Minnesota Press, 1986.

Almasy, Anne. "The Vulgar Face of Purity Culture." *Huffington Post,* September 9, 2013. http://www.huffingtonpost.com/anne-almasy/the-vulgar-face-of-purity_b_3882864.html.

Anatol, Giselle Liza. *Bringing Light to Twilight: Perspectives on a Pop Culture Phenomenon.* New York: Palgrave Macmillan, 2011.

Anderson, Diane E. "Purity Culture as Rape Culture: Why the Theological Is Political." RH Reality Check, October 22, 2013. http://rhrealitycheck.org/article/2013/10/22/purity -culture-as-rape-culture-why-the-theological-is-political/.

Arnaut, Lynn. "Cruelty, Horror, and the Will to Redemption." *Hypatia* 18, no. 2 (2003): 155–188.

Ashbee, Edward. "The Bush Administration and the Politics of Sex Morality." In *Assessing the George W. Bush Presidency: A Tale of Two Terms,* edited by Andrew Roe and Jon Herbert, 199–215. Edinburgh, UK: Edinburgh University Press, 2009.

Ashcraft, Karen Lee, and Lisa A. Flores. "'Slaves with White Collars': Persistent Performances of Masculinity in Crisis," *Text and Performance Quarterly* 23, no. 1 (2000): 1–29.

Auerbach, Nina. *Our Vampires, Ourselves*. Chicago: University of Chicago Press.

Badgley, Anne, and Carrie Musselman. *Heritage Keepers Student Manual*. Charleston, SC: Heritage Community Services, 1999.

Bario, David. "Virginity Pledge Comes with a Ring—and Tarnish." *Chicago Tribune*, March 20, 2005. http://articles.chicagotribune.com/2005–03–20/features/0503200443_1_ring -purity-virginity.

Bartkowski, John P. *The Promise Keepers: Servants, Soldiers, and Godly Men*. New Brunswick, NJ: Rutgers University Press, 2004.

Bassett, Laura. "Potential GOP Presidential Contenders: Defund Planned Parenthood." *Huffington Post*, April 4, 2011. http://www.huffingtonpost.com/2011/04/04/gop-presidential -defund-planned-parenthood_n_844614.html.

Bederman, Gail. *Manliness and Civilization*. Chicago: University of Chicago Press, 1995.

Beisner, Lynn. "How Christian Purity Culture Enabled My Stepfather to Sexually Abuse Me." Alternet, April 24, 2014. http://www.alternet.org/how-christian-purity-culture -enabled-my-step-dad-sexually-abuse-me.

Berlant, Lauren. *The Queen of America Goes to Washington City: Essays on Sex and Citizenship*. Durham, NC: Duke University Press, 1997.

Berlant, Lauren, and Michael Warner. "Sex in Public." *Critical Inquiry* 24, no. 2 (1998): 547–566.

Bernau, Anke. *Virgins: A Cultural History*. London: Grant Books, 2007.

Bersamin, Melina M., Samantha Walker, Elizabeth D. Waiters, Deborah A. Fisher, and Joel Grube. "Promising to Wait: Virginity Pledges and Adolescent Sexual Behavior." *Journal of Adolescent Health* 36, no. 5 (2005): 428–436.

Beverly LaHaye Institute and Janice Shaw Crouse. "Brief of Beverly LaHaye Institute and Janice Shaw Crouse, Ph.D. as Amici Curiae in Support of Hobby Lobby Stores Inc. and Conestoga Wood Specialties Corp., et Al." 134 S. Ct. 2751 (2014). http://www.americanbar .org/content/dam/aba/publications/supreme_court_preview/briefs-v3/13–354–13–356 _amcu_bli-etal.authcheckdam.pdf.

Bilu, Yoram. "The Taming of Deviants and Beyond: An Analysis of *Dybbuk* Possession and Exorcism in Judaism." In *Spirit Possession in Judaism: Cases and Contexts from the Middle Ages to the Present*, edited by Matt Goldish, 1–32. Detroit, MI: Wayne State University Press, 2003.

Bishop, Jamie. *The Princess and the Kiss: A Story of God's Gift of Purity*. Anderson, IN: Warner Press, 2000.

Black, Gregory D. *Hollywood Censored: Morality Codes, Catholics, and the Movies*. New York: Cambridge University Press, 1994.

Blake, John. "Why Young Christians Aren't Waiting Anymore." *CNN*, September 27, 2001. http://religion.blogs.cnn.com/2011/09/27/why-young-christians-arent-waiting -anymore/.

Blakesly, David. *Terministic Screens: Rhetorical Perspectives on Film*. Carbondale: Southern Illinois University Press, 2007.

Blank, Hannah. *Virgins: The Untouched History*. New York: Bloomsbury, 2007.

Blankenhorn, David. *Fatherless America*. New York: Harper Perennial, 1996.

Boonstra, Heather D. "Matter of Faith: Support for Comprehensive Sex Education among Faith-Based Organizations." *Guttmacher Policy Review* 11, no. 1 (2008): 17–22. http://www .guttmacher.org/pubs/gpr/11/1/gpr110117.html.

Booth, Paul. "Slash and Porn: Media Subversion, Hyper-Articulation, and Parody." *Continuum: Journal of Media & Cultural Studies* 28, no. 3 (2014): 396–409.

Bordwell, David. *Meaning Making: Inference and Rhetoric in Interpretation of Cinema.* Cambridge, MA: Harvard University Press, 1991.

Brammer, Rebekah. "Left of Centre: Teen Life, Love, and Pain in the Films of John Hughes." *Screen Education* 56 (2009): 22–28.

Brodman, Barbara, and James E. Doan. *Images of the Modern Vampire: The Hip and Atavistic.* Lanham, MD: Fairleigh Dickinson University Press, 2013.

Brooks, Ann. *Postfeminisms: Feminism, Theory, and Cultural Forms.* London: Routledge, 1997.

Brown, Helen Gurley. *Sex and the Single Girl: The Unmarried Woman's Guide to Men.* New York: Bernard Geis Associates, 1962.

Brown, Mary Ellen. *Soap Opera and Women's Talk: The Pleasure of Resistance.* Thousand Oaks, CA: Sage, 1994.

Brown, Wendy. "American Nightmare: Neoliberalism, Neoconservativism, and De-Democratization." *Political Theory* 34, no. 6 (2006): 690–714.

———. "Neo-Liberalism and the End of Liberal Democracy." *Theory & Event 7, no. 1 (2003):* 1–21.

———. *Regulating Aversions: Tolerance in an Age of Identity and Empire.* Princeton, NJ: Princeton University Press, 2006.

Bruckner, Hannah, and Peter Bearman. "After the Promise: The STD Consequences of Adolescent Virginity Pledges." *Journal of Adolescent Health* 36, no. 4 (2005): 271–278.

Brummett, Barry. *Rhetorical Dimensions of Popular Culture.* Tuscaloosa: University of Alabama Press, 1990.

Buescher, Derek, and Kent A. Ono. "Civilized Colonialism: Pocahontas as Neocolonial Rhetoric." *Women's Studies in Communication* 19, no. 2 (1996): 127–153.

Burke, Kenneth. *Language as Symbolic Action: Essays on Life, Literature, and Method.* Berkeley: University of California Press, 1966.

———. *A Rhetoric of Motives.* Berkeley: University of California Press, 1959.

Burnham, Gabriella. "2007 Film Festival Focus Centers on Female Screenwriters." *Inquirer and Mirror*, November 17, 2007. http://www.ack.net/femalescreen060707.html.

Burns, Jim. *The Purity Code: God's Plan for Sex and Your Body.* Bloomington, MN: Bethany House Publishers, 2008.

Campbell, Jane. *Film and Cinema Spectatorship: Melodrama and Mimesis.* Cambridge: Polity Press.

Campbell, Karlyn Kohrs. *Man Cannot Speak for Her: A Critical Study of Early Feminist Rhetoric.* Westport, CT: Greenwood Press, 1989.

Carpenter, Laura M. "Virginity Loss in Reel/Real Time: Using Popular Movies to Navigate Sexual Initiation." *Sociological Forum* 24, no. 4 (2009): 804–827.

———. *Virginity Lost: An Intimate Portrait of First Sexual Experiences.* New York: New York University Press, 2005.

Chaudhuri, Shohini. *Feminist Film Theorists: Laura Mulvey, Kaja Silverman, Teresa de Lauretis, Barbara Creed.* New York: Routledge, 2006.

Clark, Randall. *At a Theatre or Drive-In near You: The History, Culture, and Politics of the American Exploitation Film.* New York: Routledge, 1995.

Click, Melissa A., Jennifer Stevens Aubrey, and Elizabeth Behm-Morawitz. *Bitten by Twilight: Youth Culture, Media, and the Vampire Franchise.* New York: Peter Lang, 2010.

Cloud, Dana. "'To Veil the Threat of Terror': Afghan Women and the Clash of Civilizations in Imagery of the War on Terrorism." *Quarterly Journal of Speech* 90, no. 3 (2004): 285–306.

Clover, Carol. *Men, Women, and Chainsaws: Gender in the Modern Horror.* Princeton, NJ: Princeton University Press, 1993.

Cole, Nei. "How the Candie's Foundation and Bristol Palin Create a National Dialogue on Teen Pregnancy." *Huffington Post,* June 14, 2009. http://www.huffingtonpost.com/neil-cole/how-the-candies-foundatio_b_203701.html.

Collins, Patricia Hill. *Black Feminist Thought: Knowledge, Consciousness, and the Politics of Empowerment.* London: Psychology Press, 2000.

Colson, Chuck. "Nothing More Natural: Abstinence at Harvard." Sexual Purity: Premarital Sex and Abstinence, April 21, 2008. http://www.premaritalsex.info/nothing-more-natural/.

Connell, Raewyn W. *Masculinities.* Berkeley: University of California Press, 2005.

Connelly, Mark Thomas. *The Response to Prostitution in the Progressive Era.* Chapel Hill: University of North Carolina Press, 1980.

Conner, Vilma. *Born-Again Virgin: How to Transform Your Life from Promiscuity Back into Purity.* Glendale, CA: Miracon Enterprises, 2009.

Cook, Pam. "'Exploitation' Films and Feminism." *Screen* 17, no. 2 (1976): 122–127.

——. "Melodrama and the Women's Picture." In *Imitations of Life: A Reader on Film and Television Melodrama,* edited by Marcia Landy, 248–262. Detroit, MI: Wayne State University Press, 1991.

Coontz, Stephanie. *The Way We Never Were: American Families and the Nostalgia Trap.* New York: Basic Books, 2000.

Coppock, Vicki. *The Illusion of Postfeminism: New Women, Old Myths.* London: Taylor & Francis, 1995.

Couch, Aaron. "'Twilight' Wins 7 Razzie Awards Including Worst Picture." *Hollywood Reporter,* February 23, 2013. http://www.hollywoodreporter.com/news/twilight-wins-7-razzie-awards-423720.

Creed, Barbara. "Horror and the Monstrous Feminine: An Imaginary Abjection." *Screen* 27, no. 1 (1986): 44–71.

——. *The Monstrous-Feminine: Film, Feminism, Psychoanalysis.* London: Routledge, 1993.

——. *Phallic Panic: Film, Horror, and the Primal Uncanny.* Melbourne, Australia: Melbourne University Press, 2005.

——. "The Position of Women in Hollywood Melodrama." *Australian Journal of Screen Theory* 4 (1978): 27–31.

Culp-Ressler, Tara. "Katelyn Campbell Receives Outpouring of Support after Protesting High School Abstinence Assembly." Think Progress, April 19, 2013. http://thinkprogress.org/health/2013/04/19/1893611/katelyn-campbell-support/.

Dargis, Manohla. "Film Review; Losing His Innocence, Not a Minute Too Soon." *New York Times,* August 19, 2005. http://query.nytimes.com/gst/fullpage.html?res=9C05EED8133EF93AA2575BC0A9639C8B63.

Davis, Angela. *Women, Race, and Class.* New York: Vintage, 1983.

Day, William. *Vampire Legends in Contemporary American Culture: What Becomes a Legend Most. Lexington: University Press of Kentucky, 2002.

DeLamotte, Eugenia. *Perils of the Night: A Feminist Study of NineteenthCentury Gothic.* Oxford: Oxford University Press, 1990.

Deleyto, Celestino. "The New Road to Sexual Ecstasy: Virginity and Genre in *The 40-Year-Old Virgin.*" In *Virgin Territory: Representing Sexual Inexperience in Film,* edited by Tamar Jeffers McDonald, 255–268. Detroit, MI: Wayne State University Press, 2010.

Deluca, Kevin, and Jennifer Peeples. "From Public Sphere to Public Screen: Democracy, Activism, and the 'Violence' of Seattle." *Critical Studies in Media Communication* 19, no. 2 (2002): 125–151.

Deming, Caren J. "Miscegenation in Popular Western History and Fiction." In *Women and Western American Literature*, edited by Helen Winter Stauffer and Susan J. Rosowski, 90–99. Troy, NY: Whiston, 1982.

Denby, David. "Partners." *The New Yorker*, September 12, 2005, 102–103.

Derakhshani, Tirdad. "Demonic-Possession Film—This Time with Hasidim." *Philadelphia Inquirer*, August 31, 2012. http://www.philly.com/philly/entertainment/movies/20120831_Demonic-possession_film_-_this_time_with_Hasidim.html.

DiMarco, Haylay. *Technical Virgin: How Far Is Too Far?* Grand Rapids, MI: Flemin H. Revell, 2006.

Dobson, James M. *Bringing Up Girls*. Carol Stream, IL: Tyndale House Publishers, 2012.

Doezema, Jo. "Forced to Choose: Beyond the Voluntary v. Forced Prostitution Dichotomy." In *Global Sex Workers: Rights, Resistance, and Redefinition*, edited by Kamala Kempadoo and Jo Doezema, 34–50. New York: Routledge, 1998.

———. "Loose Women or Lost Women?: The Reemergence of the Myth of White Slavery in Contemporary Discourse of Trafficking in Women." *Gender Issues* 18, no. 1 (2000): 23–50.

Donovan, Bryan. *White Slave Crusades: Race, Gender, and Anti-Vice Activism, 1887–1917*. Champaign-Urbana: University of Illinois Press, 2006.

Douglas, Susan J., and Meredith W. Michaels. *The Mommy Myth*. New York: Simon and Schuster, 2005.

Dow, Bonnie. *Prime-Time Feminism: Television, Media Culture, and the Women's Movement since 1970*. Philadelphia: University of Pennsylvania Press, 1996.

———. "The Traffic in Men and the *Fatal Attraction* of Post-Feminist Masculinity." *Women's Studies in Communication* 29, no. 1 (2006): 113–131.

"Do You Want 'Freedom Fries' with That?" *CBS News*, March 11, 2003. http://www.cbsnews.com/news/do-you-want-freedom-fries-with-that/.

Driscoll, Catherine. *Teen Film: A Critical Introduction*. New York: Berg, 2011.

Dubrofsky, Rachel. "*The Bachelor*: Whiteness in the Harem." *Critical Studies in Media Communication* 23, no. 1 (2006): 39–56.

———. *The Surveillance of Women on Reality Television: Watching The Bachelor and The Bachelorette*. Lanham, MD: Lexington Books, 2011.

Duran, Maureen Gallagher. *Reasonable Reasons to Wait*. Chantilly, VA: A Choice in Education, 2003.

Dyer, Richard. *White: Essays on Race and Culture*. New York: Routledge, 1997.

Eagleton, Terry. *Ideology: An Introduction*. New York: Verso, 1991.

Ehrenreich, Barbara. *The Hearts of Men: American Dreams and the Flight from Commitment*. New York: Random House, 1983.

Elliot, Elizabeth. *Passion and Purity: Learning to Bring Your Life under Christ's Control*. Grand Rapids, MI: Baker Publishing, 2002.

Elsworth, Catherine. "Virgin Territory." *The Telegraph*, November 25, 2007. http://www.telegraph.co.uk/education/3355163/Virgin-territory.html.

Engels, Jeremy, and Greg Goodale. "'Our Battle Cry Will Be: Remember Jenny McCrea!' A Précis on the Rhetoric of Revenge." *American Quarterly* 61, no. 1 (2009): 93–112.

"Evan Rachel Wood and Nikki Read: Interview with Tom Johnson." TheCinemaSource, January 28, 2008. http://www.thecinemasource.com/blog/interviews/evan-rachel-wood-and-nikki-reed-interview-for-thirteen/.

Fahey, Anna Cornelia. "French and Feminine: Hegemonic Masculinity and the Emasculation of John Kerry in the 2004 Presidential Race." *Critical Studies in Media Communication* 24, no. 2 (2007): 132–150.

Fahs, Breanne. "Daddy's Little Girls: On the Perils of Chastity Clubs, Purity Balls, and Ritualized Abstinence." *Frontiers* 31, no. 3 (2010): 116–144.

Fahs, Breanne, Mary L. Dudy, and Sarah Stage. *The Moral Panic of Sexuality.* New York: Palgrave Macmillan, 2013.

Faludi, Susan. *Backlash: The Undeclared War against American Women.* New York: Random House, 1991.

Fard, Maggie Fazeli. "Sandra Fluke, Georgetown Student Called a 'Slut' by Rush Limbaugh." *Washington Post*, March 3, 2012. http://www.washingtonpost.com/blogs/the-buzz/ post/rush-limbaugh-calls-georgetown-student-sandra-fluke-a-slut-for-advocating -contraception/2012/03/02/gIQAvjfSmR_blog.html.

Firestone, Shulamith. *The Dialectic of Sex: The Case for Feminist Revolution.* 1970. Reprint, New York: Macmillan, 2003.

Fisher, Luchina. "Why Was 'Twilight' Director Axed from Sequel?" *ABC News*, December 10, 2008. http://abcnews.go.com/Entertainment/Movies/story?id=6420639.

Focus on the Family. "Abstinence before Marriage: The Issue." https://www.focusonthefamily .com/socialissues/family/abstinence-before-marriage/abstinence-before-marriage -issue.

Follman, Mark. "Romney Points Finger at Single Moms on Gun Violence." *Mother Jones*, October 17, 2012. http://www.motherjones.com/mojo/2012/10/romney-guns-single-moms.

Fortenbury, Jon. "On 'Late'-in-Life Virginity Loss." *The Atlantic*, March 28, 2014. http://www .theatlantic.com/health/archive/2014/03/on-late-in-life-virginity-loss/284412/.

Foucault, Michel. *The History of Sexuality.* Volume 1, *An Introduction.* New York: Vintage, 1990.

Fradely, Martin. "'Hell Is a Teenage Girl'?: Postfeminism and Contemporary Teen Horror." In *Postfeminism and Contemporary Hollywood Cinema*, edited by Joel Gwynne and Nadine Muller, 205–221. London: Palgrave Macmillan, 2013.

Frainie, Kris. *Why kNOw Abstinence Education Curriculum for Sixth Grade through High School: Teacher's Manual.* Chattanooga, TN: Abstinence Education Inc., 2002.

Freud, Sigmund. "Medusa's Head." In *The Standard Edition of the Complete Psychological Works of Sigmund Freud.* Vol. 18, *Beyond the Pleasure Principle, Group Psychology, and Other Works (1920–1922)*, translated by James Strachey, 273–274. London: Hogarth, 1955.

———. "The Taboo of Virginity (Contributions to the Psychology of Love, III)." In *The Standard Edition of the Complete Psychological Works of Sigmund Freud.* Vol. 11, *Five Lectures on Psycho-Analysis, Leonardo Da Vinci, and Other Works (1910)*, translated by James Strachey, 191–208. London: Hogarth, 1957.

Frumin, Aliyah. "Elizabeth Smart: Abstinence-Only Can Make Rape Survivors Feel 'Dirty,' 'Filthy.'" *MSNBC News*, May 5, 2013. http://www.msnbc.com/hardball/elizabeth-smart -abstinence-only-education-ca.

Fujiwara, Chris. *The World and Its Double: The Life and Work of Otto Preminger.* New York: Macmillan Publishers, 2009.

Fuller, Rose, Janet McLaughlin, and Andrew Asato. *FACTS—Family Accountability Communicating Teen Sexuality: Middle School and Senior High School Editions.* Portland, OR: Northwest Family Services, 2000.

Gabriel, Trip, and Denise Grady. "In Republican Race, a Heated Battle over the HPV Vaccine." *New York Times*, September 13, 2011. http://www.nytimes.com/2011/09/14/us/ politics/republican-candidates-battle-over-hpv-vaccine.html?_r=0.

Gardner, Christine J. *Making Chastity Sexy: The Rhetoric of Evangelical Abstinence Campaigns.* Berkeley: University of California Press, 2011.

Gateward, Frances, and Murray Pomerance, eds. *Sugar, Spice, and Everything Nice: Cinemas of Girlhood.* Detroit, MI: Wayne State University Press, 2002.

Gelder, Ken, *Reading the Vampire.* London: Routledge, 2002.

Genzlinger, Neil. "Movie Review: Some Things You Can't Learn from a Book: Aubrey Plaza Stars in 'The To-Do List." *New York Times*, July 25, 2013. http://www.nytimes.com/2013/07/26/movies/aubrey-plaza-stars-in-the-to-do-list.html?r=0.

Gerhard, Jane. *Desiring Revolution: Second-Wave Feminism and the Rewriting of the Twentieth-Century American Sexual Thought.* New York: Columbia University Press, 2013.

Gilbert, James. *Men in the Middle: Searching for Masculinity in the 1950s.* Chicago: University of Chicago Press, 2005.

Gillis, Stacy, Gilliam Howie, and Rebecca Munford. *Third Wave Feminism: A Critical Exploration.* London: Palgrave Macmillan, 2007.

Giroux, Henry. *Breaking into the Movies: Film and the Culture of Politics.* Hoboken, NJ: Wiley, 2001.

———. *Public Spaces, Private Lives: Beyond the Culture of Cynicism.* Lanham, MD: Rowman & Littlefield, 2001.

———. "The Terror of Neoliberalism: Rethinking the Significance of Cultural Politics." *College Literature 3, no. 1 (2005): 1–19.*

Goodale, Gloria. "Twilight Moms: Why Women Are Drawn to Teens' 'Eclipse.'" *Christian Science Monitor*, June 28, 2010. http://www.csmonitor.com/USA/2010/0628/Twilight-moms-Why-women-are-drawn-to-teens-Eclipse.

Gramsci, Antonio. *Selections from the Prison Notebooks.* 1936. Reprint, New York: International Publishers, 1971.

Grant, Melissa Gira. "Fighting Sex Trafficking with Jesus: How the Religious Right's 'Healing' Hurts." *Salon.com*, April 27, 2014. http://www.salon.com/2014/04/27/fighting_sex_trafficking_with_jesus_how_the_religious_rights_healing_hurts/.

Gresh, Dannah. *And the Bride Wore White: Seven Secrets to Sexual Purity.* Chicago: Moody Publishers, 2012.

Gresh, Lois. *The Twilight Companion: The Unauthorized Guide to the Series.* New York: Macmillan, 2008.

Grittner, Frederick. *White Slavery: Myth, Ideology, and American Law.* New York: Garland, 1990.

Grossu, Arina. "How Do We Eradicate Sex Trafficking?" *Christian Post*, February 6, 2014. http://www.christianpost.com/news/how-do-we-eradicate-sex-trafficking-114155/.

Gunn, Joshua. "The Rhetoric of Exorcism: George W. Bush and the Return of Political Demonology." *Western Journal of Communication* 68, no. 1 (2004): 1–23.

Guzman, Rafer. "'The To Do List' Review: High Ick Factor." *Newsday*, July 23, 2013. http://www.newsday.com/entertainment/movies/the-to-do-list-review-high-ick-factor-1.5761277.

Hall, Stuart. "The Whites of Their Eyes: Racist Ideologies in the Media." In *Gender, Race, and Class in Media: A Text-Reader*, 2nd ed., edited by Gail Dines and Jean Humez Sage, 89–93. Thousand Oaks, CA: Sage, 2002.

Hallab, Mary Y. *Vampire God: The Allure of the Undead in Western Culture.* Albany: State University of New York Press, 2009.

Hanke, Robert. "Hegemonic Masculinity in *Thirtysomething*." *Critical Studies in Mass Communication* 7, no. 3 (1990): 231–248.

Harding, David J., and Christopher Jencks. "Changing Attitudes toward Premarital Sex: Cohort, Period, and Aging Effects." *Public Opinion Quarterly* 67, no. 2 (2003): 211–226.

Harding, Sandra. "Introduction: Standpoint Theory as a Site of Political, Philosophic and Scientific Debate." In *The Feminist Standpoint Theory Reader: Intellectual and Political Controversies*, edited by Sandra Harding, 1–16. New York: Routledge, 2004.

Harding, Susan Friend. *The Book of Jerry Falwell: Fundamentalist Language and Politics.* Princeton, NJ: Princeton University Press, 2001.

Harris, Joshua. *Sex Is Not the Problem (Lust Is): Sexual Purity in a Lust-Saturated World.* Colorado Springs: Multnomah Books, 1996.

———. *Why I Kissed Dating Goodbye.* Sisters, OR: Multnomah Press, 1997.

Haskins, Ron, and Carol Statuto Bevan. "Abstinence Education under Welfare Reform." *Children and Youth Services Review* 19, no. 5/6 (1997): 465–484.

Heath, Elaine. *The Gospel According to Twilight: Women, Sex, and God.* Louisville, KY: Westminster John Knox Press, 2011.

Heath, Melanie. "Making Marriage Promotion into Public Policy: The Epistemic Culture of Statewide Initiatives." *Qualitative Sociology* 35, no. 4 (2012): 385–406.

———. *One Marriage under God: The Campaign to Promote Marriage in America.* New York: New York University Press, 2012.

Heller-Nicholas, Alexandra. *Rape-Revenge Films: A Critical Study.* Jefferson, NC: MacFarlane Press, 2011.

Hess, Amanda. "Mississippi Sex Ed Class Compares Women to Dirty Peppermint Patties." *Slate Magazine,* April 3, 2014. http://www.slate.com/blogs/xx_factor/2014/04/03/mississippi_sex_ed_class_compares_women_to_dirty_peppermint_patties.html.

"A History of Federal Funding for Abstinence-Only-Until-Marriage Programs." Sexuality Information and Education Council of the United States, 2010. http://www.siecus.org/index.cfm?fuseaction=page.viewpage&pageid=1340&nodeid=1.

Heywood, Leslie, and Jennifer Drake. *Third Wave Agenda: Being Feminist, Doing Feminism.* Minneapolis: University of Minnesota Press, 1997.

Hoerl, Kristen, and Casey Ryan Kelly. "The Post-Nuclear Family and the Depoliticization of Unplanned Pregnancy in *Knocked Up, Juno,* and *Waitress.*" *Communication and Critical/Cultural Studies* 7, no. 4 (2010): 360–380.

hooks, bell. "The Oppositional Gaze: Black Female Spectators." In *The Feminism and Visual Culture Reader,* edited by Amelia Jones, 94–105. London: Routledge, 2003.

Housel, Rebecca, and J. Jeremy Wisnewski, eds. *Twilight and Philosophy: Vampires, Vegetarians, and the Pursuit of Immortality.* Malden, MA: Blackwell, 2009.

"How to Say No to Sex." AbortionFacts.com. http://www.abortionfacts.com/literature/how-to-say-no-to-sex.

"How to Start over If You've Lost Your Virginity." Love Matters.com. http://www.lovematters.com/startover.htm.

Irvine, Janice M. *Talk about Sex: The Battles over Sex Education in the United States.* Berkeley: University of California Press, 2004.

Jameson, Fredric. "Reification and Utopia in Mass Culture." *Social Text* 1 (Winter 1979): 130–148.

Jeffreys, Sheila. *Anticlimax: A Feminist Perspective on the Sexual Revolution.* Melbourne, Australia: Spinifex Press, 2012.

Johnson, Kimberly A., and Ann Werner. *The Virgin Diaries.* North Charleston, SC: CreateSpace Independent Publishing Platform, 2010.

Johnston, Claire. "'Women's Cinema as Counter-Cinema." In *Movies and Methods,* edited by Bill Nichols, 208–217. Berkeley: University of California Press, 1976.

Jones, Daryl. *Horror: A Thematic History of Fiction and Film.* London: Arnold, 2002.

Katz, David. "From Asylum, the People Who Brought You (a Movie Kinda Sorta Like) *Pacific Rim.*" *GQ,* August 1, 2013. http://www.gq.com/entertainment/movies-and-tv/201308/sharknado-atlantic-rim-pacific-rim-asylum-movie-spoof?currentPage=1.

Keller, Wendy. *The Cult of the Born Again Virgin: How Single Women Can Reclaim Their Sexual Power.* Deerfield Beach, FL: Health Communication, Inc., 1999.

Kellner, Douglas. *Cinema Wars: Hollywood Film and Politics in the Bush-Cheney Era.* Malden, MA: Wiley-Blackwell, 2009.

Killborn, Jean. *Can't Buy My Love: How Advertising Changes the Way You Think and Feel.* New York: Touchstone, 2012.

Kimmel, Michael. *Manhood in America: A Cultural History.* New York: The Free Press, 1996.

King, Claire Sisco. "Acting Up and Sounding Off: Sacrifice and Performativity in *Alice, Sweet Alice.*" *Text and Performance Quarterly* 27, no. 2 (2007): 124–142.

———. "It Cuts Both Ways: *Fight Club*, Masculinity, and Abject Hegemony." *Communication and Critical/Cultural Studies* 6, no. 4 (2009): 366–385.

———. "Unqueering Horror: *Hellbent* and the Policing of the 'Gay Slasher.'" *Western Journal of Communication* 74, no. 3 (2010): 249–268.

———. *Washed in Blood: Male Sacrifice, Trauma, and the Cinema.* New Brunswick, NJ: Rutgers University Press, 2011.

King, Geoff, Claire Molloy, and Yannis Tzioumakis. *American Independent Cinema: Indie, Indiewood, and Beyond.* London: Routledge, 2013.

Kinsman, R. Patrick. "She's Come Undone: *Chantal Akerman's Jeanne Dielman, 23 Quai du Commerce, 1080 Bruxelles* (1975) and Countercinema." *Quarterly Review of Film and Video* 24 (2007): 217–224.

Kopsa, Andy. "Abstinence-Only: It's Baaaack." *Ms. Magazine*, December 22, 2011. http://msmagazine.com/blog/2011/12/22/abstinence-only-its-baaack/.

———. "Obama's Evangelical Gravy Train." *The Nation*, July 8, 2014. http://www.thenation.com/article/180435/obamas-evangelical-gravy-train.

Koyama, Emi. *War on Terror and War on Trafficking: A Sex Worker Activist Confronts the Anti-Trafficking Movement.* Portland, OR: Confluere Publications, 2011.

Kristeva, Julia. *Powers of Horror: An Essay on Abjection.* Translated by Leon S. Roudiez. New York: Columbia University Press.

Krzywinska, Tanya. *Sex and the Cinema.* London: Wallflower, 2006.

Kuhn, Annette. "Women's Cinema and Feminist Film Criticism." *Screen* 16, no. 3 (1975): 107–112.

LaHaye, Beverly. *Raising Sexually Pure Kids: How to Prepare Your Children for the Act of Marriage.* Sisters, OR: Multnomah Publishers, 1998.

Larsson, Mariah, and Ann Steiner. *Interdisciplinary Approaches to Twilight: Studies in Fiction, Media, and a Contemporary Cultural Experience.* Lund, Sweden: Nordic Academic Press, 2011.

Lasalle, Mick. "He's an Ex-CIA Agent—Of Course They Took His Kid." *San Francisco Chronicle*, January 30, 2009, E3.

Leavenworth, Maria Lindgren, and Malin Isaksson. *Fanged Fan Fiction: Variations on Twilight, True Blood, and the Vampire Diaries.* Jefferson, NC: McFarlane, 2013.

Lee, Morgan. "LifeWay Relaunches Abstinence Program to Fight Culture Where 80% of Unmarried Christians Have Sex." *Christian Post*, January 10, 2014. http://www.christianpost.com/news/lifeway-relaunches-abstinence-program-to-fight-culture-where-80-of-unmarried-christians-have-sex-112395/.

Lemir, Christy. "Review: *Taken* on a Guilty-Pleasure Ride." *Associated Press*, January 28, 2009.

Levy, Ariel. *Female Chauvinist Pigs: Women and the Rise of Raunch Culture.* New York: Free Press, 2006.

Levy, Emanuel. *Cinema of Outsiders: The Rise of American Independent Film.* New York: New York University Press, 1999.

Lindsey, Shelley Stamp. "Is Any Girl Safe? Female Spectators at the White Slave Films." *Screen* 37, no. 1 (1996): 1–15.

———. "'Oil upon the Flames of Vice': The Battle over White Slave Films in New York City." *Film History* 9, no. 4 (1997): 351–364.

Lipsitz, George. *Time Passages: Collective Memory and American Popular Culture.* Minneapolis: University of Minnesota Press, 1990.

Locke, John. *Two Treatises on Government.* 1689. Reprint, New York: New American Library, 1965.

Loeb, Robert. *She-Manners: The Teen Girl's Book of Etiquette.* New York: Associated Press, 1959.

"Lousiana's Bill Cassidy Says Teen Daughter Pregnant, Report Says." *CNN*, July 3, 2014, http:// politicalticker.blogs.cnn.com/2014/07/03/louisianas-bill-cassidy-says-teen-daughter -pregnant-report-says/.

Macpherson, Pat. "The Revolution of Little Girls." In *Offwhite: Readings of Power, Privilege, and Resistance,* edited by Michelle Fine, Lois Weis, Linda Power Pruitt, and April Burns, 175–185. London: Routledge, 2004.

Maddux, Kristy. *The Faithful Citizen: Popular Christian Media and Gendered Civic Identities.* Waco, TX: Baylor University Press, 2010.

Mahdavi, Pardis. *Trafficking and Terror: Construction a Global Social Problem.* New York: Routledge, 2013.

Marcuse, Herbert. *One-Dimensional Man: Studies in the Ideology of Advanced Industrial Society.* Boston: Beacon Press, 1964.

Mast, Kelly Coleen. *Sex Respect: The Option of True Sexual Freedom.* Homer Glen, IL: Respect, Inc., 2001.

Mathijs, Ernest, and James Sexton. *Cult Cinema.* Hoboken, NJ: Wiley, 2012.

McDonald, Stacy, *Raising Maidens of Virtue.* Cedar Rapids, IA: Tomorrow's Forefathers, 2006.

McDonald, Tamar Jeffers. "Homme-Com: Engendering Change in Contemporary Romantic Comedy." In *Falling in Love Again: Romantic Comedy in Contemporary Cinema,* edited by Stacy Abbott and Debbie Jermyn, 146–159. New York: I. B. Taurus, 2009.

———. *Romantic Comedy: Boy Meets Girl Meet Genre.* London: Wallflower, 2007.

———. *Virgin Territory: Representing Sexual Inexperience in Film.* Detroit, MI: Wayne State University Press, 2010.

McRobbie, Angela. "Postfeminism and Popular Culture: Bridget Jones and the New Gender Regime." In *Interrogating Postfeminism: Gender and the Politics of Popular Culture,* edited by Yvonne Tasker and Diane Negra, 27–39. Durham, NC: Duke University Press, 2007.

Medovoi, Leerom. "A Yippie-Panther Pipe Dream: Rethinking Sex, Race, and the Sexual Revolution." In *Swinging Single: Representing Sexuality in the 1960s,* edited by Hilary Radner and Moya Luckett, 133–180. Minneapolis: University of Minnesota Press, 1999.

Meeker, Meg, and Margaret J. Meeker. *Strong Fathers, Strong Daughters: 10 Secrets Every Father Should Know.* New York: Random House, 2007.

Meyers, Ric. *For One Week Only: The World of Exploitation Films.* Guilford, CT: Eirini Press, 2011.

Michels, Patrick. "This Weekend, *Twilight* Superfans Make Downtown Dallas Their Playground." *Dallas Observer,* July 31, 2009. http://www.dallasobserver.com/news/this -weekend-twilight-superfans-make-downtown-dallas-their-playground-7117634.

Modleski, Tania. *Feminism without Women: Culture and Criticism in a "Postfeminist" Age.* New York: Routledge, 1991.

Morey, Anne. *Genre, Reception, and Adaptation in the "Twilight" Series.* Burlington, VT: Ashgate, 2013.

Mortimer, Claire. *Romantic Comedy.* London: Routledge, 2010.

Mulvey, Laura. "Notes on Sirk and Melodrama." *Movie* 25 (1977–78): 53–57.

———. "Visual Pleasure of Narrative Cinema." *Screen* 6 (Autumn 1975): 6–18.

Nakagawa, Chiho. "Safe Sex with Defanged Vampires: New Vampire Heroes in *Twilight* and the *Southern Vampire Mysteries.*" *Journal of Popular Romance Studies* 2 (2011). http://jprstudies.org/2011/10/%E2%80%9Csafe-sex-with-defanged-vampires-new-vampire-heroes-in-twilight-and-the-southern-vampire-mysteries%E2%80%9D-by-chiho-nakagawa/.

Nakayama, Thomas, and Robert Krizek. "Whiteness: A Strategic Rhetoric." *Quarterly Journal of Speech* 81, no. 3 (1999): 291–309.

Nassif, Tony. "Human Trafficking Update." Abstinence Clearinghouse, March 8, 2011. http://www.abstinence.net/our-blog/abstinence-posts/update-on-human-trafficking/.

Nesselson, Lisa. "Live Virgin." *Daily Variety*, July 31, 2000, 25.

Newman, Michael Z. *Indie: An American Film Culture.* New York: Columbia University Press, 2013.

Nichols, Bill. *Engaging Cinema: An Introduction to Film Studies.* New York: W. W. Norton Company, 2010.

"9 Celebrities Who've Worn Purity Rings." *Huffington Post*, July 2, 2013. http://www.huffingtonpost.com/2013/07/02/celebrities-purity-rings_n_3535439.html.

Nixon, Nicola. "When Hollywood Sucks, or Hungry Girls, Lost Boys, and Vampirism in the Age of Reagan." In *Blood Read: The Vampire as Metaphor in Contemporary Culture,* edited by Joan Gordon and Veronica Hollinger, 115–128. Philadelphia: University of Pennsylvania Press, 1997.

Ono, Kent A. *Contemporary Media Culture and the Remnants of a Colonial Past.* New York: Peter Lang, 2009.

Ortner, Sherry B. *Not Hollywood: Independent Film at the Twilight of the American Dream.* Durham, NC: Duke University Press, 2013.

O'Sullivan, Michael. "'Virgin': A Man on a Mission." *Washington Post,* August 19, 2005. http://www.washingtonpost.com/wp-dyn/content/article/2005/08/18/AR2005081800517.html.

Owens, Jane. *A Biblical View of Sexual Purity.* Bloomington, IN: Xlibris, 2010.

Pandey, Shanta, and Jeoung-hee Kim. "Path to Poverty Alleviation: Marriage or Postsecondary Education?" *Journal of Family and Economic Issues* 29, no. 1 (2007): 166–184

Parke, Maggie, and Natalie Wilson. *Theorizing Twilight: Critical Essays on What's at Stake in a Post-Vampire World.* Jefferson, NC: McFarland, 2011.

Parkin, Rachael Hendershot. "Breaking Faith: Disrupted Expectations and Ownership in Stephenie Meyer's Twilight Saga." *Jeunesse: Young People, Texts, Cultures* 2, no. 2 (2010): 61–85.

Pascall, Jeremy, and Clyde Jeavers. *A Pictorial History of Sex in the Movies.* London: Hamlyn, 1975.

Patterson, Randall. "Students of Virginity." *New York Times,* March 30, 2008. http://www.nytimes.com/2008/03/30/magazine/30Chastity-t.html?pagewanted=all.

Pennington, Jody W. *The History of Sex in American Film.* Westport, CT: Praeger, 2007.

Peterson, Susan Rae. "Coercion and Rape: The State as a Male Protection Racket." In *Feminism and Philosophy,* edited by Mary Vetterling-Braggin, 360–371. Totowa, NJ: Rowman and Allenheld, 1977.

Pew Research Center. "U.S. Seen as Less Important, China as More Powerful: Section 4: U.S. Allies and Country Favorability." Pew Research Center: U.S. Politics and Policy, December 3, 2009. http://www.people-press.org/2009/12/03/section-4-u-s-allies-and-country-favorability/.

Phillips, Kendall. *Dark Directions: Romero, Craven, Carpenter, and the Modern Horror Film.* Carbondale: Southern Illinois Press, 2012.

———. *Projected Fears: Horror Films and American Culture*. Westport, CT: Praeger, 2005.

Pitzulo, Carrie. *Bachelors and Bunnies: The Sexual Politics of Playboy*. Chicago: University of Chicago Press, 2011.

Platt, Carrie Anne. "Cullen Family Values: Gender and Sexual Politics in the Twilight Series." In *Bitten by Twilight: Youth Culture, Media, and the Vampire Franchise*, edited by Melissa A. Click, Jennifer Stevens Aubrey, and Elizabeth Behm-Morawitz, 71–86. New York: Peter Lang, 2010.

Price, Michael E., Nicholas Pound, and Isabel M. Scott. "Female Economic Dependence and the Morality of Promiscuity." *Archives of Sex Behavior*, June 25, 2014. Accessed July 17, 2014. http://link.springer.com/article/10.1007%2Fs10508-014-0320-4.

Probyn, Elspeth. "New Traditionalism and Post-Feminism: TV Does the Home." *Screen* 31, no. 2 (1990): 147–159.

Projansky, Sarah. *Watching Rape: Film and Television in Postfeminist Culture*. New York: New York University Press, 2001.

Psaladis, Jessica. *Everlasting Purity*. Maitlin, FL: Xulon Press, 2008.

Puig, Claudia. "A Rabbi to the Rescue in Demonic 'Possession'; but That's the Film's Only Fresh Element." *USA Today*, August 30, 2012, 6D. http://usatoday30.usatoday.com/LIFE/usaedition/2012-08-31-Review-of-The-Possession_ST_U.htm.

"Purity Balls: Lifting the Veil on Special Ceremony." *ABC News*, March 3, 2014. http://abcnews.go.com/Nightline/video/purity-balls-lifting-veil-special-ceremony-23061335.

Purnick, Joyce. "Welfare Bill: Legislating Morality?" *New York Times*, August 19, 1996. http://www.nytimes.com/1996/08/19/nyregion/welfare-bill-legislating-morality.html.

Quarles, Mike. *Down and Dirty: Hollywood's Exploitation Filmmakers and Their Movies*. Jefferson, NC: McFarlane, 2001.

Quayle, Marilyn "Republican National Convention Address." August 19, 1992. http://www.c-span.org/video/?31358-1/republican-national-convention-address.

Raab, Scott. "ESQ&A: Richard Linklater and Ethan Hawke." *Esquire Magazine*, July 8, 2014, http://www.esquire.com/entertainment/movies/interviews/a23730/richard-linklater-ethan-hawke-interview-0814/.

Rafferty, Terrance. "Love and Pain and the Teenage Vampire Thing." *New York Times*, October 31, 2008. http://www.nytimes.com/2008/11/02/movies/moviesspecial/02raff.html?pagewanted=all&_r=0.

Reagin, Nancy. *Twilight and History*. Hoboken, NJ: Wiley, 2010.

"Real Life Stories." The Abstinence Resource Center. http://www.abstinenceresourcecenter.org/real-life-stories/.

Rector, Robert, and Kirk A. Johnson. "Teenage Sexual Abstinence and Academic Achievement." *Heritage Foundation Reports*, October 27, 2005. http://www.heritage.org/research/reports/2005/10/teenage-sexual-abstinence-and-academic-achievement.

Reed, Jacinda. *The New Avengers: Feminism, Femininity, and the Rape-Revenge Cycle*. Manchester, UK: Manchester University Press, 2000.

Regnerus, Mark. "The Case for Early Marriage." *Christianity Today*, July 31, 2009. http://www.christianitytoday.com/ct/2009/august/16.22.html?start=7.

Reisman, Judith. "'Taken' and Global Sex Traffic." *World Daily Net*, March 23, 2009. http://www.wnd.com/2009/03/92566/.

Robinson, Susan. *Marked Men: White Masculinity in Crisis*. New York: Columbia University Press, 2000.

Rodino-Colocino, Michelle. "'Feminism' as Ideology: Sarah Palin's Anti-Feminist Feminism and Ideology Critique." *Triple C: Cognition, Communication, Cooperation* 10, no. 2 (2012): 457–473.

Rosen, Ruth. *The World Split Open: How the Modern Women's Movement Changed America*. New York: Penguin Books, 2000.

Rosenbaum, Janet Elise. "Patient Teenagers?: A Comparison of the Sexual Behavior of Virginity Pledgers and Matched Nonpledgers." *Pediatrics* 123, no. 1 (2009): 110–120.

———. "Reborn a Virgin: Adolescents' Retracting of Virginity Pledges and Sexual Histories." *American Journal of Public Health* 96, no. 6 (2006): 1098–1103.

Rowe, Kathleen. *The Unruly Woman: Gender and the Genres of Laughter*. Austin: University of Texas Press, 1995.

Ryan, Michael. "The Politics of Film: Discourse, Psychoanalysis, Ideology." In *Marxism and the Interpretation of Culture*, edited by Cary Nelson and Lawrence Grossberg, 477–486. Urbana: University of Illinois Press, 1988.

Ryan, Michael, and Douglas Kellner. *Camera Politica: The Politics and Ideology of Contemporary Hollywood*. Bloomington: Indiana University Press, 1988.

Sacks, Ethan. "The 'Twilight Saga' Has Left a Mark on Hollywood As More Films Aimed at Teen Girls Start to Show Up." *New York Daily News*, February 3, 2013. http://www.nydailynews.com/entertainment/tv-movies/twilight-effect-movies-article-1.1252704.

Said, Edward. *Orientalism*. New York: Vintage Books, 1978.

San Filippo, Maria. *The B Word: Bisexuality in Contemporary Film and Television*. Bloomington: Indiana University Press, 2013.

Santelli, John, Mary A. Ott, Maureen Lyon, Jennifer Rogers, Daniel Summers, and Rebecca Ann Schleifer. "Abstinence and Abstinence-Only Education: A Review of U.S. Policies and Programs." *Journal of Adolescent Health* 38, no. 1 (2006): 72–81.

Sarracino, Carmine, and Kevin M. Scott. *The Porning of America: The Rise of Porn Culture, What It Means, and Where It's Going*. Boston: Beacon Press, 2008.

Saul, Rebekah. "Whatever Happened to the Adolescent Family Life Act?" *Guttmacher Report on Public Policy* 1, no. 2 (1998): 5–11. http://www.guttmacher.org/pubs/tgr/01/2/gr010205.html.

Schaefer, Eric. *"Bold! Daring! Shocking! True!": A History of Exploitation Films, 1919–1959*. Durham, NC: Duke University Press, 1999.

———. "Resisting Refinement: The Exploitation Film and Self-Censorship." *Film History* 6, no. 3 (1994): 293–313.

Schwarz, Kathryn. "The Wrong Question: Thinking through Virginity." *differences: A Journal of Feminist Cultural Studies* 13, no. 2 (2002): 1–34.

Seifert, Christine. "Bite Me! (or Don't)." *Bitch Magazine*, 2008, http://bitchmagazine.org/article/bite-me-or-dont.

Sharma, Nandita. "Anti-Trafficking Rhetoric and the Making of a Global Apartheid." *NWSA Journal* 17, no. 3 (2005): 88–111.

Shary, Timothy. *Generation Multiplex: The Image of Youth in Contemporary American Cinema*. Austin: University of Texas Press, 2002.

———. *Teen Movies: American Youth on Screen*. London: Wallflower, 2005.

———. "Virgin Springs: A Survey of Teen Films' Quest for Sexcess." In *Virgin Territory: Representing Sexual Inexperience in Film*, edited by Tamar Jeffers McDonald, 54–67. Detroit, MI: Wayne State University Press, 2010.

Sheehan, Jack. *Reel Bad Arabs: How Hollywood Vilifies a People*. New York: Olive Branch Press, 2001.

Shipe, Tim. "'Taken' Some Life Lessons." *American Catholic*, July 18, 2009. http://the-american-catholic.com/2009/07/18/taken-some-life-lessons/.

Shipler, David. *The Working Poor: Invisible in America*. New York: Knopf, 2008.

Short, Gail. "Christine Caine: Hillsong Church, the A21 Campaign." *Outreach Magazine*, July 21, 2010. http://www.outreachmagazine.com/interviews/3728-christine-caine -hillsong-church-the-a21-campaign.html.

Silver, Anna. "Twilight Is Not Good for Maidens: Gender, Sexuality, and the Family in Stephenie Meyer's *Twilight* Series." *Studies in the Novel* 42, no. 1/2 (2010): 121–138.

Singer, Ben. *Melodrama and Modernity: Early Sensational Cinema in Contexts*. New York: Columbia University Press, 2013.

Soderlund, Gretchen. "Covering Urban Vice: The *New York Times*, 'White Slavery,' and the Construction of Journalistic Knowledge." *Critical Studies in Media Communication* 19, no. 4 (2002): 438–460.

Stacey, Judith. "The New Conservative Feminism." *Feminist Studies* 9, no. 3 (1983): 559–583.

Stafford, Tim. "Can You Become a Virgin Again?" Christianity Today: Hot Topics. N.d. http:// www.christianitytoday.com/iyf/hottopics/sexabstinence/can-you-become-virgin -again.html.

Stanley, Alessandra. "Television Review: 'The Secret of the American Teenager': A Teenage Pregnancy, Packaged as a Prime-Time Cautionary Tale." *New York Times*, July 1, 2008. http://www.nytimes.com/2008/07/01/arts/television/01stan.html?_r=0.

Steinem, Gloria. "A Bunny's Tale." *Show Magazine*, June 1, 1963, 90, 92, 94, 118.

Stephan, Sarah, and Grace Mally. *Before You Meet Prince Charming: A Guide to Radiant Purity*. Cedar Rapids, IA: Tomorrow's Forefathers, 2006.

Stepp, Laura Sessions. "Anti-Science and Anti-Contraception." *CNN*, May 22, 2012. http:// www.cnn.com/2012/05/21/opinion/stepp-conservatives-contraception/.

Stuckey, Mary, and John Murphy. "By Any Other Name: Rhetorical Colonialism in North America." *American Indian Culture and Research Journal* 25 (2001): 73–98.

"Take2 Renewed Virginity." PSC: A Pregnancy Resource Center for Northeast Ohio. http:// www.pscstark.com/42.

Taormino, Tristan, Constance Penley, Celine Shinizu, and Mireille Miller-Young. *The Feminist Porn Book: The Politics of Producing Pleasure*. New York: The Feminist Press at the City University of New York, 2013.

Tasker, Yvonne, and Diane Negra, eds. *Interrogating Postfeminism: Gender and the Politics of Popular Culture*. Durham, NC: Duke University Press, 2007.

Taylor, Aaron. "Adam Sandler, an Apologia: Anger, Arrested Adolescence, *Amour Fou*." In *Millennial Masculinity: Men in Contemporary American Cinema*, edited by Timothy Shary, 19–51. Detroit, MI: Wayne State University Press, 2013.

"Toys 'R' Us Has Been Bitten, Transforming into THE Twilight Saga Destination." *PR Newswire*, November 3, 2009. http://www.prnewswire.com/news-releases/toysrus-has-been -bitten-transforming-into-the-twilight-saga-destination-68834177.html.

Troyer, John, and Chani Marchiselli. "Slack, Slackers, Slackest: Homosocial Bonding Practices in Contemporary Dude Cinema." In *Where the Boys Are: Cinemas of Masculinity and Youth*, edited by Murray Pomerance and Frances Gateward, 264–278. Detroit, MI: Wayne State University Press, 2005.

Trujillo, Nick. "Hegemonic Masculinity on the Mound: Media Representations of Nolan Ryan and American Sports Culture." *Critical Studies in Mass Communication* 8, no. 3 (1991): 290–308.

"'Twilight' Fans Destination: Forks, Wash." *NPR Morning Edition*, November 20, 2008. http:// www.npr.org/templates/story/story.php?storyId=97241693.

"'Twilight'-Inspired Erotica to Be Published; Fan Fiction Based on the Series Becomes a Genre." *International Business Times*, November 8, 2012. http://www.ibtimes.com/twilight -inspired-erotica-be-published-fanfiction-based-series-becomes-genre-865476.

Union of Concerned Scientists. "Abstinence-Only Education." September 2005. http://www
.ucsusa.org/our-work/center-science-and-democracy/promoting-scientific-integrity/
abstinence-only-education.html#.VYlIZvlViko.

U.S. Attorney's Office, District of Maryland. "Press Release: Millersville Man Sentenced for
Posing as a Retired Army Special Forces Colonel." August 30, 2011. http://www.fbi.gov/
baltimore/press-releases/2011/millersville-man-sentenced-for-posing-as-a-retired
-army-special-forces-colonel.

U.S. House of Representatives Committee on Government Reform—Minority Staff. *The Content of Federally Funded Abstinence-Only Education Programs.* Prepared for Rep. Henry A.
Waxman. Washington, DC: U.S. House of Representatives, 2004.

Valenti, Jessica. "Abstinence Sex Education Doesn't Work. It Teaches Lies to Ill-Informed
Virgins." *The Guardian,* July 15, 2015. http://www.theguardian.com/commentisfree/
2014/jul/15/abstinence-sex-education-teaches-virgins-teens.

———. "Hobby Lobby Ruling Proves Men of the Law Still Can't Get Over 'Immoral'
Women Having Sex." *The Guardian,* June 30, 2014. http://www.theguardian.com/
commentisfree/2014/jun/30/hobby-lobby-ruling-law-immoral-women-sex.

———. *The Purity Myth.* New York: Seal, 2009.

Vallotton, Kris. *Purity: The New Moral Revolution.* Shippensburg, PA: Destiny Image Publishers, 2011.

"Vampire Fans Bitten by the Cruise Bug." *PR Newswire,* April 15, 2010. http://www.prnewswire
.com/news-releases/vampire-fans-bitten-by-the-cruise-bug-90921624.html.

Van Heertum, Richard, ed. *Hollywood Exploited: Public Pedagogy, Corporate Movies, and Cultural
Crisis.* London: Palgrave Macmillan, 2010.

Vavrus, Mary Douglas. "Opting Out Moms in the News: Selling New Traditionalism in the
New Millennium." *Feminist Media Studies* 7, no. 1 (2007): 47–63.

———. *Postfeminist News: Political Women in Media Culture.* Albany: State University of New
York Press, 2002.

Vera, Hernan, and Andrew Gordon. *Screen Saviors: Hollywood Fictions of Whiteness.* New York:
Rowman & Littlefield, 2005.

Walsh, Frank. *Sin and Censorship: The Catholic Church and the Motion Picture Industry.* New
Haven, CT: Yale University Press, 1996.

Ward, Sarah. "*Ferris Bueller's Day Off* and the History of Teen Film." *Screen Education* 76
(Summer 2015): 116–121.

Warren, Lindsay Marsh. *The Best Sex of My Life: Confessions of a Sexual Purity Revolution.*
Bloomington, IN: Trafford Publishing, 2012.

Watson, Paul. "There's No Accounting for Taste: Exploitation Cinema and the Limits of Film
Theory." In *Trash Aesthetics: Popular Culture and Its Audience,* edited by Deborah Cartmell, I. Q. Hunter, Heidi Kay, and Imelda Wheleyan, 66–83. London: Pluto Press, 1997.

Watts, Eric King. "Border Patrolling and 'Passing' in Eminem's *8 Mile.*" *Critical Studies in
Media Communication* 22, no. 3 (2005): 187–206.

Watts, Steven. *Mr. Playboy: Hugh Hefner and the American Dream.* Hoboken, NJ: Wiley, 2008.

Weitzer, Ronald. "The Social Construction of Sex Trafficking: Ideology and Institutionalization of a Moral Crusade." *Politics and Society* 35, no. 3 (2007): 447–475.

Welter, Barbara. "The Cult of True Womanhood: 1820–1860." *American Quarterly* 18, no. 2
(1966): 151–174.

Williams, Linda. "Melodrama Revised." In *Refiguring American Film Genres: History and Theory,* edited by Nick Browne, 42–88. Berkeley: University of California Press, 1998.

———. "'Something Else Besides a Mother': *Stella Dallas* and the Maternal Melodrama."
Cinema Journal 24, no. 1 (1984): 2–27.

Wilson, Bruce. "Most Americans 18–29 Years Old Believe in Demon Possession, Shows Survey." *Huffington Post*, October 12, 2013. http://www.huffingtonpost.com/bruce-wilson/most-americans-1829-years_b_4163588.html.

Wilson, Natalie. *Seduced by Twilight: The Allure and Contradictory Messages of the Popular Saga.* Jefferson, NC: McFarlane, 2011.

Wood, Robin. *Hollywood: From Vietnam to Reagan and Beyond.* New York: Columbia University Press, 2003.

Young, Iris. "Feminist Reactions to the Contemporary Security Regime." *Hypatia* 18, no. 1 (2003): 223–231.

Zavarzadeh, Mas'ud. *Seeing Films Politically.* Albany: State University of New York Press, 1991.

INDEX

ABOUT THE AUTHOR

CASEY RYAN KELLY (PhD, University of Minnesota, Twin Cities) is an associate professor of critical communication and media studies at Butler University. His research has appeared in *Journal of Communication Inquiry*, *Rhetoric Society Quarterly*, *Critical Studies in Media Communication*, *Feminist Media Studies*, *Communication and Critical/Cultural Studies*, *Western Journal of Communication*, *Communication Quarterly*, *Women's Studies in Communication*, *Argumentation and Advocacy*, and *Advances in the History of Rhetoric*.

CPSIA information can be obtained
at www.ICGtesting.com
Printed in the USA
LVOW04s1044030216

PP10538000001BA/1/P